Income
Inequality
IN
America

ISSUES IN WORK AND HUMAN RESOURCES

Daniel J.B. Mitchell, Series Editor

WORKING IN THE TWENTY-FIRST CENTURY
Policies for Economic Growth Through Training,
Opportunity, and Education
David I. Levine

INCOME INEQUALITY IN AMERICA
An Analysis of Trends
Paul Ryscavage

HARD LABOR
Poor Women and Work in the Post-Welfare Era
Joel F. Handler and Lucie White

Income *Inequality* IN America

AN ANALYSIS OF TRENDS

Paul Ryscavage

M.E. Sharpe
Armonk, New York
London, England

Library of Congress Cataloging-in-Publication Data

Ryscavage, Paul.
Income inequality in America : an analysis of trends / Paul Ryscavage.
p.   cm.—(Issues in work and human resources)
Includes bibliographical references and index.
ISBN 0-7656-0233-4 (hardcover : alk. paper).
ISBN 0-7656-0234-2 (pbk. : alk. paper)
1. Income distribution—United States.   I. Title.
HC110.I5R95   1998
339.2′2′0973—dc21
98-23186
CIP

Printed in the United States of America

The paper used in this publication meets the minimum requirements of
American National Standard for Information Sciences—
Permanence of Paper for Printed Library Materials,
ANSI Z 39.48-1984.

BM (c)   10   9   8   7   6   5   4   3   2   1
BM (p)   10   9   8   7   6   5   4   3   2   1

For my wife
Karen
whose encouragement and understanding
are never-ending

Contents

List of Tables and Figures

Tables

Figures

Foreword

Income inequality has become a major policy concern. The rise in inequality, by various measures, invokes an image of a society divided between "haves" and "have-nots." In turn, that image suggests the possibility of eventual political repercussions and, perhaps, social unrest. Will events such as the Los Angeles riots of 1992 become a feature of the American scene? At a less dramatic level, the rise in inequality suggests revisiting such long-standing policies as welfare programs, minimum wage laws, and laws that regulate collective bargaining. And it leads to examination of new programs, such as "living wage ordinances," applicable to contractors of municipal governments.

In this volume, Paul Ryscavage reviews the various indexes of income inequality. Unfortunately, there is no one theoretically correct measure of the concept of inequality. Thus, it is best to look at several measurement tools and approaches. Even the definition of "income" must be examined. Apart from money income, individuals may receive various in-kind subsidies from government programs. And they may receive non-wage benefits—such as health insurance—from employers. The fact that all approaches to measurement suggest widening inequality is important, since it allows discussion to proceed to factors associated with this trend.

Finding an explanation for the widening of inequality after the early 1970s has challenged economists and other researchers. International trade competition, especially in products that displace low-skilled/low-wage workers is a commonly cited candidate for causing widened inequality. The trade argument has been echoed across the political spectrum by presidential candidates as varied as Pat Buchanan, Ross Perot, Richard Gebhardt, and Jerry Brown. But many scholars believe changing technology, which moves demand away from those at the bottom of the wage scale, is a more significant factor. This debate has yet to be resolved.

What is known, Ryscavage points out, is that there have been fluctuations in income inequality before the post–World War II period. It appears the Great Depression and World War II were periods in which inequality diminished after peaking in the 1920s. The rise of unions and the inauguration of various social programs in that era seemed to coincide with a compression of the income distribution. Indeed at the time, many in the New Deal administration believed that income inequality had contributed to insufficient consumption by wage earners and thus sparked or aggravated the Depression.

Since there has been no Great Depression associated with current inequality, trade remains a popular villain, even if academics often downplay its significance. Given the popularity of trade-as-a-villain in income inequality, it is useful to examine cross-country trends. If there is an international influence, its impact should be visible in developed countries outside the United States. Inequality did increase in many (but not all) countries beginning in the 1970s. But the degree to which inequality rose varied by country. And the United States seemed to be taking the lead in the pace of the rise. Institutional arrangements may well play a role. Some observers have noted that the United States also led in job creation during this period, suggesting that countries may resist widening inequality but at a social and economic cost in unemployment.

If there is a bright spot in this review of inequality, it is Ryscavage's evidence that the American trend toward rising inequality diminished in the 1990s. Thus, the social tensions that might follow from a further widening of the income gap may be at least arrested. Unfortunately, at this point it is impossible to predict that a turnaround point, or even a stopping point, has been reached. But what can be done is to provide accurate and comprehensive documentation of what has occurred and that is something this volume surely does with finesse.

Daniel J. B. Mitchell

Preface

This book is about the incomes of persons, families, and households and the relationship of their incomes to one another. The way this relationship is observed in this book is through an income distribution in which incomes are ranked from the lowest to the highest. As is commonly known today, the United States' income distribution has become more dispersed in recent years, that is, the distance between the lower and upper parts of the distribution has grown.

The growth in income inequality has attracted much attention from various segments of our society. The media have reported on the issue extensively, often from the standpoint of "fairness," or how the nation's economic prosperity of recent decades has not been shared by everyone. Politicians, sensing the unease over growing income inequality from members of their constituencies, have debated the significance of this economic development.

Economists, and other social researchers, have also focused on the growth in income differences in the United States over the past years. While the vast majority of them today agree that income inequality (and earnings inequality) has grown, there is still disagreement over the cause or causes. Countless studies have explored various explanations and many important insights have been gained. Unfortunately, for persons not that familiar with income and earnings data and the methodologies used by researchers in investigating inequality, their studies and research are oftentimes difficult to understand. For persons such as beginning economics students and others with a serious interest in the topic, it is obvious that there is a need for a "primer" on income inequality.

This book represents such a primer. It too is a technical book, but one that can be very useful to those who want to learn more about income inequality than what is found in the popular print and electronic media. The subject of income inequality is complicated and has many facets—from those relating to the sources of income data to those involving the many ways inequality can be measured. In a book of this kind, not all of these can be addressed in great detail and some, such as the ethics of income distribution, are not discussed. However, it is possible to touch upon important facets that provide the reader with the necessary "stepping stones" to further and deeper study of income inequality.

The organizing theme of this book is the trend in income inequality in America over the twentieth century, with particular emphasis on the last few decades. By examining the trend, many of the questions relating to income inequality analysis will be answered. As was mentioned, this topic has been studied extensively by economists and other researchers over the years and this book would not be possible without their work. Many of them are referenced in the text, but all deserve a special thanks. In addition, recognition must also be given to the dedicated economists, statisticians, and demographers of the federal government responsible for the development of the income, earnings, and labor force statistics that have been the subject of such intense study.

Last, several individuals were very important in the preparation of this book and they should be acknowledged. Helpful advice, comments, and suggestions to an earlier version were provided by Peter Henle, a former Deputy Assistant Secretary of Labor in President Carter's administration; Marvin H. Kosters, Resident scholar and director, Economic Policy Studies, American Enterprise Institute; Frank Levy, Daniel Rose Professor of Urban Economics, Massachusetts Institute of Technology; and Daniel H. Weinberg, chief, and Charles T. Nelson, assistant division chief, both from the Housing and Household Economics Statistics Division, U.S. Bureau of the Census.

Income *Inequality* IN America

1

The Income Distribution:
Incomes as Outcomes

Our nation stands on the threshold of the twenty-first century. Our economy, the largest and strongest in the world, spearheads the march into the next century proudly displaying the virtues of a free-market, capitalistic system. A soaring stock market, rising incomes, and low inflation and unemployment have been the hallmarks of the mid-1990s. Yet, beneath the fanfare there lies a small but nagging economic worry in the minds of many—a worry that has existed for many years now, and it ebbs and flows with the health of the economy.

It is a worry about whether our society is slowly splitting into two groups, "the haves and the have nots," or what economists refer to as growing income inequality. Today, this worry is not the kind people lose sleep over or the kind that consumes one's every waking moment. But it is the kind of worry that can provoke discussion and debate anywhere—from Main Street to the halls of Congress.

Economists who study the income distribution nearly all agree that it has grown more unequal in recent years. They have traced the origins of growing income disparities to the changes that have taken place in the economy and society. Both, to differing degrees, have altered the shape of the income distribution. But agreement over the "specific" causes of growing inequality has yet to be reached. Is it the result of technological changes in the economy that favor the highly skilled and best-educated workers? Is it the nation's trading policies that result in the erosion of low-skilled, high-paid jobs? Is it the breakdown of the family as a viable economic unit in today's economy? Or is it a combination of all these, as well as other factors?

Because of the uncertainty over the causes of growing income inequality, there is much debate over what to do about it—or, for that matter, whether the worry that has been associated with it is justified. Those to the left in the political spectrum have suggested certain governmental interventions.[1] Those to the right are less inclined to intervene and suggest that rising inequality is simply the result of the operation of the free market.[2] It can be a contentious issue.

In many respects, growing income inequality has served as a backdrop for much of the political debate in Washington in recent years, whether it was over balancing the federal budget, cutting taxes, reforming welfare, or settling labor disputes. Cries of "class warfare" have often been heard from the political parties. Indeed, President Clinton used the issue of growing income inequality when he said, in reference to one of the Republicans' budget proposals, "We have enough income inequality in America as it is."[3] And it could be argued that the passage of the Balanced Budget Act of 1997 and the Taxpayers Reduction Act of 1997 was, in part, our political parties' response to voters' concerns over growing income inequality and its many manifestations.

For the average American, whenever some economic development becomes the subject of popular debate, like deficit reduction or NAFTA, confusion soon emerges over what is being discussed. Such is the case with growing income inequality. Without doubt, the concept is more elusive than other economic phenomena, such as unemployment, inflation, or poverty.[4] It probably means different things to different people. For some it may mean the rich are getting richer while the poor are getting poorer; for others, it may have something to do with what the media once called the "declining middle class"; and for still yet others it may mean the contrast between the astronomical salaries of some of our corporations' chief executive officers (CEOs) and the desperate lives of the homeless.

In addition, as Americans hear more and more about growing income inequality, certain questions may come to mind that have been answered in the media only partially or incorrectly, or answered not at all. For example, how is income inequality measured? How long has it been rising? How much has it risen? Have there been other periods in our history when inequality was as great as it is today? Has the middle class really declined? Is it happening elsewhere, like in the United Kingdom and Japan?

The purpose of this book, therefore, is to answer many of these questions, *without* entering the debate over what should be done about it or the legitimacy of the "worry" over growing income inequality. The method consists of a straightforward review of the statistical trends in inequality over the last century and some of the relevant literature on the subject. Hopefully, this will provide readers with an improved perspective on the income inequality situation as it exists today. As mentioned at the outset, the United States stands on the threshold of the next century, for the most part optimistic and expectant of what lies ahead. To the extent that growing income inequality may or may not represent some dark clouds on the horizon, it is hoped this book will furnish the means by which to evaluate the significance of those clouds.

Popular Impressions

In the early 1980s economists and other researchers began reporting that the average earnings of American workers had not grown much since the early 1970s and that the distribution of their earnings was becoming more un-equal.[5] One explanation for this development was the employment shift in the industrial composition of the nation (deindustrialization) away from manufacturing industries to service-producing industries (average earnings in the latter are less than in the former and more dispersed).[6] The implica-tion of this development for the breadwinners from middle-class families was obvious, and soon journalists in the print media were spreading the news that the middle class in the United States was declining, even though there is no official definition of the middle class.[7] Additional concern over growing income inequality emerged in the mid-1980s with the publication of Frank Levy's book, *Dollars and Dreams: The Changing American In-come Distribution.*[8] Levy sounded the alarm that Americans were now facing an "increasing inequality of prospects" in attaining a middle-class lifestyle.

Since that time, scholarly investigations into economic inequality have mushroomed, as have media reports that brought the disquieting economic news to the public. By the end of the 1980s, related issues such as deterio-rating job quality, falling wages of low-skilled men, and corporate downsizings were hitting the front pages of newspapers and were the lead stories on the nightly news. With the onset of the 1990–91 recession, the economic news, of course, only grew worse. And because this particular recession affected so many more highly paid white-collar workers than ever before, the spotlight on stories related to inequality widened. Even well into the 1990s major newspapers were preparing feature stories on the changes taking place in corporate America and its work force.[9]

The public has been exposed to much information about the changes taking place in the job market—and the impact they have had on the income distribution and income inequality. Even though in the past few years or so such news stories have diminished as the economy roared ahead, popular impressions about growing income inequality have taken hold in the public's mind. In the following pages, some of these popular impressions have been condensed into tighter analytical topics so they can be examined in the context of the actual income distribution statistics (these topics will be explored in greater detail in subsequent chapters).

Figure 1.1 **Percentage of Households by Income Class, 1996**

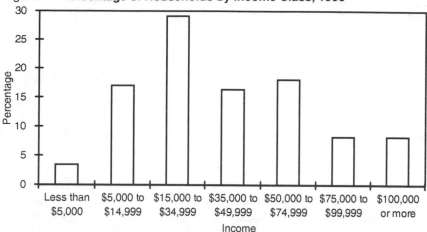

Source: U.S. Bureau of the Census, Annual Demographic Survey, CPS.

A Nation of Haves and Have Nots

It is hard to know how the typical American envisions the shape of the income distribution. One might suspect, however, that given all the media reports about "the haves and have nots," they would picture a bimodal distribution, that is, one with a lot of persons in the lower-income classes, relatively fewer in the middle, and a lot in the upper-income classes. This, of course, is not the case. Even for those who do know that the distribution is skewed to the right, they might not know the relative density of the distribution across all income classes.

Figure 1.1 displays the distribution of income (before any taxes have been paid) of the 101.0 million households in the United States in 1996 across income classes. There are, of course, many sources of income data, but the primary source used in income inequality research comes from a survey of the nation's households called the Current Population Survey (CPS) conducted by the U.S. Bureau of the Census. CPS income data are used in the figure, and more will be said about the CPS and income data in Chapter 2.[10]

The first problem one confronts in looking at the data is what do we mean by high-, middle-, and low-income classes? This is a difficult question and one that is highly subjective. For the purposes of this early discussion, we consider households with incomes of less than $15,000 as low, those with incomes between $15,000 and $75,000 as middle, and those with incomes above $75,000 as high. One could object in many ways to these

Figure 1.2 **Percentage of Aggregate Income Received by Each Quintile of Households, 1996**

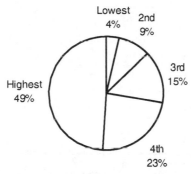

Source: U.S. Bureau of the Census, Annual Demographic Survey, CPS.

income classifications, but for the sake of exposition at this point let us proceed. Under this classification scheme we found that the majority of households were in the middle-income class, or 63.2 percent of all households. The high-income class contained 16.4 percent and the low-income class 20.4 percent. This depiction of the income distribution does not appear particularly unequal.

Another way to examine these data is to again arrange households from the lowest income recipient to the highest, and then divide this distribution into equal quantiles, for example, quintiles or fifths. Doing this makes it possible to calculate how much of the total, or aggregate, income goes to each quintile of the distribution. The results of such an exercise (which the Census Bureau performs) for the 1996 income distribution are displayed in Figure 1.2.

The data in the figure show that while the lowest fifth of households received only 3.7 percent of the aggregate household income in 1996, the highest fifth of households received almost half, or 49.0 percent. Consequently, the middle three income quintiles received, by definition, 47.3 percent of all the income flowing to households in 1996. The dividing line between the lowest quintile and middle three was $14,768, while the dividing line between the middle three and the highest quintile was $68,015—dividing lines somewhat similar to the income classes defined above. When the income distribution is viewed in this manner, it looks considerably more unequal, especially in terms of the shares of income going to the lowest- and highest-income households.

The middle of the income distribution—or those in between—is still quite large, however, regardless of the figure being examined.[11] More will be said about the middle of the income distribution and the "middle class" later.

Figure 1.3 **The 95th-to-20th Percentile Household Income Ratio, 1967–1996**

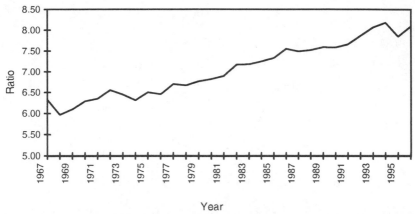

Year

Source: U.S. Bureau of the Census, Annual Demographic Survey, CPS.

The Rich Get Richer and the Poor Get Poorer

Perhaps the most common of the popular impressions of growing income inequality is that the rich have been getting richer over time while the poor have been becoming poorer. Again, one must be careful in using terms such as "rich" and "poor." For example, in the discussion above, high-income classes were defined as households with incomes in 1996 beginning at $75,000 and higher, and in that group would be Bill Gates's household as well as a household with an income of $85,000 a year situated in the suburbs. "Rich" like "poor" can mean different things to different people.

Despite this problem, the Census data can provide some insight into how the incomes of households have changed at different points in the income distribution over time. In Figure 1.3 are displayed the ratios of the incomes of households at the 95th percentile of the household income distribution to the incomes of households at the 20th percentile between 1967 and 1996. (It is important to note that the households at these points in the distribution are not necessarily the same households from one time period to another, such as 1967 and 1996. There is much movement in the income distribution over time as life's circumstances change.) This is only one of many measures of income inequality that economists have used in their research.

As shown in Figure 1.3, the long-term trend in the ratio has been upward. In 1967 it was 6.33 and by 1996, 8.09. By 1996 incomes of households at the 95th percentile were eight times the size of the incomes of households at the 20th percentile. The income gap had widened a little in the 1970s and then accelerated in the 1980s and 1990s, indicating quite different rates of income growth for those households at these points of the distribution.

What were these growth rates? Between 1967 and 1996 household incomes adjusted for inflation—or "real" incomes— at the 95th percentile had risen from $82,124 to $119,540, or by 45.6 percent; at the 20th percentile of the distribution, real household incomes rose from $12,967 to $14,768, or only 13.9 percent.[12] To provide some additional perspective on these trends, the real median household income in the United States (the income at the 50th percentile) rose from $30,874 in 1967 to $35,492 by 1996, or 15.0 percent. Clearly, the incomes of households at the top end of the distribution had grown much faster than incomes for those at the lower end of the distribution and for those households in the "statistical" middle of the distribution.

A Declining Middle Class

Another popular impression is that our nation's middle class has been eroding because a middle-class life style in the United States has become more difficult to achieve with each passing year. It has been reported that housewives are now forced to work in the labor market, husbands now have to work as much overtime as possible, and everyone has to scrimp and save more than ever before. But this is another impression that, unfortunately, is beset with a definitional question. What is the middle class?

While there is no official definition of the middle class, many definitions have been devised for the purposes of economic analysis, legislation, and marketing strategies, among other things. But they too all involve a certain amount of subjectivity. Alan Blinder, the Princeton economics professor and former Federal Reserve Board member, once said (perhaps facetiously) his definition of the middle class in America was anybody with an income below the 99th percentile of the income distribution.[13] And the Census Bureau, "the fact finder of the nation," has never defined the middle class. Still, the term is used every day—from people in the street to the president.

According to Webster's dictionary, the middle class is defined as: "The social class between the aristocracy or very wealthy and the lower working class: people in business and the professions, highly skilled workers, well-to-do farmers, etc. are now generally included in the middle class."[14] Using this definition as a guide and looking back to Figure 1.1, one might argue that this sounds like households with annual incomes in the range of $25,000 to $99,999. Obviously, one can take issue with this purely statistical definition (as one can take issue with any income-based definition of the middle class), but for the sake of argument, let's see what happened to the middle class if we use this definition.

Figure 1.4 **Percentage of Households in Low-, Middle-, and High-Income Classes, 1967–1996** (in 1996 dollars)

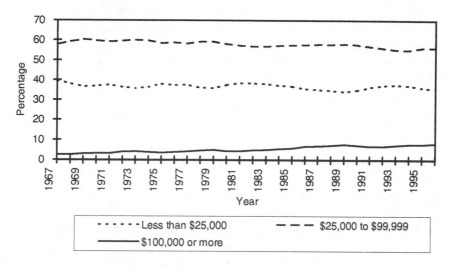

Source: U.S. Bureau of the Census, Annual Demographic Survey, CPS.

Figure 1.4 contains the proportions of all households with incomes between $25,000 and $99,999 (in 1996 dollars) in the 1967–1996 period (top line). The figure shows that the proportion has tended to drift downward, but rather slowly. Based on this definition of the middle class, therefore, the middle class has declined in a relative sense, but not to the extent often suggested in the media. Indeed, in an absolute sense what has happened is that the growth in this country's middle class has slowed down. Between 1967 and 1977, the number of households with incomes (in 1996 dollars) between $25,000 and $99,999 increased from 35.2 million to 44.3 million, almost 9.2 million households. Between 1977 and 1987, the number of households in this income range increased by 8.4 million—a somewhat smaller absolute gain (and smaller percentage gain). In the last period, from 1987 to 1996, almost a ten-year period, households in this income range increased by only 4.0 million (a much smaller percentage gain).

The astute reader, of course, will immediately ask: "If this is what has happened to the middle class over the last thirty years or so, what's happened to the lower class and upper class?" Again, if we accept this purely income-based definition of the middle class, we automatically have defined the other two classes. As can be seen in Figure 1.4, the proportion of all households in the country with annual incomes above $100,000 has almost tripled over these years, from 2.6 percent of all households in 1967 to 8.2

percent by 1996. The proportion of households in the lower class—annual incomes below $25,000—over the 1967–1996 period has drifted slightly downward from 39.6 percent to 35.6 percent.[15] With respect to the lower- and upper-income classes, it should be pointed out that because of the broad definitions used here, it is not evident whether or not greater proportions of households are now clustered at the extreme tails of the distribution.

The foregoing analyses provided a statistical background on the changes that have indeed occurred in the income distribution. Hopefully, they will have anchored some of the more popular impressions about income inequality floating around in the media.

One's Position in the Income Distribution

At the basis of the concern over growing income inequality lies the income distribution itself. For centuries economists have pondered the determinants of income and the income distribution and theoretical explanations have been developed. One thing is certain: As the civilization of man evolved over the centuries—from the age of cavemen to the information age—the process of income determination has become considerably more complex. Indeed, the Nobel Prize–winning economist Kenneth Arrow once remarked that the income distribution is the outcome of a complex assortment of lifetime choices.[16] Many of these choices produce or result in certain economic, social, and demographic characteristics that are associated with one's position in the income distribution.

Income statistics over the years have revealed well-known relationships between certain economic, social, and demographic characteristics of persons, families, and households and their income levels. For example, it is well known that, on average, men earn more than women, white families have higher incomes than black families, and people with a college education earn more than people who dropped out of high school. Numerous relationships of this kind, based on averages, exist.

Relationships of this kind are not necessarily deterministic in the sense they "cause" a certain income level to come about, although some certainly do. Rather, these relationships should be thought of as associations. But this is not to say these associations do not contain useful information with regard to one's position in the income distribution. Indeed, thought of this way, these associations take on a probabilistic quality. That is, if you happen to be a white man with a college education who is the head of a family, it is likely that your position in the income distribution will be much higher than that of a black woman who is a high school dropout and who is the head of a family.

These associations, of course, change over time. For example, we know that the gender pay gap and the income gap between the races has closed in recent years, while the relative wage differential between a college graduate and a high school dropout widened in the 1980s and 1990s. Nevertheless, these associations, at a point in time, have useful information content when used with other associations and can help identify one's probable position in the income distribution.

This approach to understanding the income distribution is also helpful in understanding the idea that incomes are outcomes. To the extent that we make choices about many things in life, such as, How much education do I want? Should I take this job or that job? Should I get married? and so on, some of these choices become very important in the income level that one will ultimately attain.[17]

Naturally, there are many characteristics that don't involve choice but they too have implications for our incomes. There's not much one can do about one's sex or age or race and so on, but these "nonchoices" also carry certain useful information regarding one's probable income level. For example, the age-earnings profile of men is quite informative.[18] By knowing a man's age and nothing else, one has a general idea where he is in the profile. So, even these nonchoice characteristics can be useful in identifying one's likely position in the income distribution.

Table 1.2 presents various economic, social, and demographic characteristics, or, as they will be referred to henceforth, factors.[19] The list should not be considered exhaustive. Many of the factors contain subfactors that add further definition to the particular factor. As shown in the table, some are person-specific and others are family- and household-specific. Therefore, they can be used when thinking about either the family or household income distribution (discussed in Chapter 3) or the earnings distribution of individual workers (discussed in Chapter 4). The following is a discussion of some of these factors.

Economic Factors

Labor market earnings continue to represent the principal source of income for Americans.[20] Consequently, the decision to work, and how much to work, is a critical one. The occupation of an individual, obviously, contains a great deal of information with respect to one's position in the income distribution. Doctors and lawyers earn considerably more than do truck drivers and assembly line workers. In addition, persons in the same type of

Table 1.1

Economic, Social, and Demographic Factors Associated with Income Levels

Economic	Social	Demographic
Individual Work/No Work Occupation Industry union status	Individual Education Marital Status	Individual Age Sex Race/Hispanic Origin
Household/Family Household Earners wife works Income Sources	Household/Family Type married couple single parent	Household/Family Size Urban/Rural

occupation can have quite different earnings because of their involvement or lack of involvement with certain technologies requiring unique skills and aptitudes. Consequently, a possible subfactor under occupation is the level of technological "know-how" involved in the occupation.

A worker's industry of employment, while not providing as much information as his or her occupation, can still be useful, especially when subfactors are considered. For example, industries with high capital-to-labor ratios will pay higher wages because of their investment in technologies and capital equipment. In addition, certain industries might be more prone to import competition than others and, in consequence, adjust pay scales accordingly

A subfactor under both occupation and industry is union status. It is well known that union members have higher relative wage levels than nonunion workers, and some occupations and industries are more unionized than others. Even though union membership has declined in recent years, it is still a useful piece of information.

All of the above factors and subfactors are also important in the context of the family and household, especially when they relate to the primary earner. But they are also important for additional earners in the family and household. Indeed, the number of earners in a household is an important subfactor. The entrance of women into the labor force, in particular married women, has been one of the more dramatic labor force developments in the second half of this century. Furthermore, the impact of wives' earnings on family incomes has been the topic of much research in recent years.

One last economic factor that provides much information about the position in the income distribution of a family or household is the sources of income. That is, is all the income derived through the labor market, or are there nonmarket sources of income, such as dividends, interest, royalties, transfer payments, and so on? Obviously, if the only source of income for a particular household is Social Security, then its position in the distribution is fairly evident, just as a household's whose sources of income are multiple and involve a mixture of labor market earnings and income derived from a variety of assets.

Social Factors

A very important social factor in income determination is one's education level. The relationship between education and earnings is well known and is interpreted in terms of human capital theory. Educational attainment has risen rapidly in this century and is often cited as a principal reason for the United States's rapid economic growth.

Along with this broad social factor, however, are some important sub-factors. The first is the nature of the education. There are great differences in the earnings levels among those with degrees in engineering or medicine (e.g., electrical engineers earn more, on average, than civil engineers, and brain surgeons earn more than general practitioners). But the amount of education, of course, is not always directly related to the years of education completed or degrees received. Consider the difference in earnings between religious ministers with advanced theological degrees and stockbrokers with bachelor of science degrees in business administration.

A second is the quality of the education. A bachelor of arts degree from Harvard, in all probability, is of greater value in the labor market than one from most state universities. Similarly, there are differences in high school educations and technical school educations. Consequently, it is useful to know something more than just the number of years an individual attended school in assessing his or her position in the income distribution.

And another subfactor related to the above is "unmeasured" skills. It is well known that within certain education and work experience groups (e.g., college graduates with fifteen to nineteen years of work experience) earnings variation not only exists but has increased over the past decades. In other words, traditional education measures are not exact proxies for human capital accumulation and the wage premiums some workers earn. These unmeasured cognitive skills may be related to the use of new information-age technologies, such as computers, or other kinds of activities for which a person has a unique capability. Consequently, a useful subfactor would be information relating to the kinds of skills workers bring to their jobs.

Household composition—that is, whether a household consists of a married couple (with or without children), a single parent (male or female), or a single individual (or a group of single individuals)—has also become an important characteristic for identifying one's position in the income distribution. The greater incidence of marital disruptions and births out of wedlock, along with the increasing age at first marriage, has had a profound effect on society's living arrangements and, ultimately, incomes. Married-couple families today constitute a much smaller proportion of all households than they did years ago, while single-parent families and single-person households make up a larger proportion of all households. The former typically have higher incomes than the latter so household composition is another useful factor in understanding the income distribution.

Demographic Factors

Three basic demographic factors—age, sex, and race—contain useful information. Age identifies one's place in the life cycle and, given what is known about behavior with respect to school, work, retirement, and other activities, it is possible to relate this to income position. Similarly, the gender difference with respect to remuneration in the job market is well known, even though these differences have narrowed. And, of course, black–white differences (as well as Hispanic–non-Hispanic differences) with respect to income are still evident.

Other revealing demographic factors about the household and family are the size and type of residence. Typically, households and families with four persons in them have the highest incomes while those with one person have the lowest. The former, on average, reflects the traditional married-couple family, and the latter either a retired person or an unmarried, separated, or divorced individual, many of whom tend to be young. Households with residences in the suburbs of large metropolitan areas, on average, have the highest incomes while the lowest incomes are in households located outside metropolitan areas.

From the above, it is apparent that one's income level is associated with many economic, social, and demographic factors. The strengths of these associations vary. Many of these factors are determined by the choices of individuals (i.e., endogenous), while others do not involve choices (i.e., exogenous). It is through the interaction of these factors that one finds his or her probable position in the income distribution.

How the Income Distribution Changes

The income distribution has been treated as an outcome of choices and events, or as a static phenomenon. It is most commonly measured on an annual basis, and occasionally on a subannual basis. However, the income distribution can be thought of in a dynamic way as well. From one point in time to another there are significant movements of households between different positions in the income distribution. Some are moving up, others are moving down, and yet for others, incomes are not changing. In this section, the "dynamic" aspects of the income distribution are examined, or how the distribution changes over time, and how, and to what extent other economic indicators reflect changes in the distribution.

Dynamic Aspects

Economists and other researchers interested in the income distribution typically rely on point-in-time, or cross-sectional, surveys of households for their income data to assess changes in the income distribution. The income data from the Current Population Survey (CPS) of the Census Bureau, discussed in the beginning of this chapter, are from a cross-sectional survey. Changes in the data from surveys of this type reflect "net" changes in households with incomes at particular points in the income distribution.

The CPS has taken a "snapshot" of the number of households with incomes in each calendar year since the 1940s, and then classified these incomes by income intervals, for example, households with incomes between $20,000 and $29,999. The change in the number of households in any interval between two years, therefore, reflects only the net change, because during any two years households may have moved into and out of each interval, or not moved at all. What is not captured in these cross-sectional surveys, therefore, are the gross flows into and out of the intervals. The example in Table 1.2 illustrates this concept.

In this example, the number of households with incomes in the $20,000-to-$29,999 range increased by 1,000 households between 1995 and 1996. This is the net change. It was accounted for, however, by a gross change of 3,000 households—2,000 households flowing into this particular interval from other intervals and 1,000 households flowing out. In other words, there were many more households moving in and out of this income interval than is reflected by the net change.

This gross flow information is very useful in understanding the dynamic nature of the income distribution. It becomes even more useful when we know where the inflow originated and the outflow went. For example, if the

Table 1.2

Gross and Net Income Changes: An Example

	1995	Change	1996
Households, $20,000 to $29,999	9,000		10,000
Net change		1,000	
Gross change		3,000	
Inflow		2,000	
Outflow		1,000	

2,000 households representing the inflow had come from lower intervals and the 1,000 households representing the outflow had gone to higher intervals, this would be good economic news. If the reverse had been true, that is, the 2,000 household inflow had come from intervals above and the 1,000 household outflow had gone further down, that would be bad economic news, even though the net change is the same.

In the past thirty years or so, surveys have been developed that capture gross flows such as the above. These surveys are called "longitudinal" surveys because basically they involve repeated interviews of the same individuals and households over a period of time. In this way they track the changes that occur in incomes and other characteristics of the households. While the cross-sectional surveys can be likened to snapshots of the situations of households, longitudinal surveys can be likened to panoramas.

The data from longitudinal surveys are very powerful analytically. Typically, not only is economic information collected in the interviews, but social and demographic information as well. This means it becomes possible to identify the correlates of income changes, both when household incomes are on the rise and on the decline. One of the disadvantages of these types of surveys, however, is the problem of sample attrition, or the reduction in the number of survey participants. Many participants in these surveys refuse to be interviewed over long periods of time and if respondent attrition is not random, the resulting sample becomes less and less representative of the population, causing the resulting data estimates to be biased. Nevertheless, attempts are made through various statistical techniques to lessen the effects of these biases.

One of the first and most widely used longitudinal surveys is the Panel Study of Income Dynamics (PSID) conducted by the Survey Research Center of the University of Michigan—Ann Arbor. This survey was begun in 1968. The data from it have been used to study not only the income distribution but other topics such as household compositional change, the retirement process, and many public policy issues.

Of the many income studies based on the PSID, a relatively recent one has particular relevance for the study of growing income inequality. Duncan, Smeeding, and Rodgers used the PSID to study what was happening to the middle class during the 1980s.[21] Based on their analysis and definition of the middle class, they concluded that the number of adults with after-tax household incomes between $18,500 and $55,000 (in 1987 dollars) did indeed decline during the 1980s. According to their data, the probability of falling from this middle-income group into the lower-income group increased relative to the probability of moving into the higher-income group.

The Census Bureau during the 1980s began its own longitudinal household survey called the Survey of Income and Program Participation (SIPP). It was designed for the purposes of collecting higher-quality income data and monitoring the extensive transfer income programs of the federal government. The SIPP involves interviewing the same individuals in households every few months over several years and collecting information from them on a variety of topics relating to their economic well-being. The Census Bureau produces periodic reports relating to the income distribution based on this survey, showing the proportions of persons in the population with changes in household incomes of 5 percent or more from year to year.[22]

In its report for 1992–93, the Census Bureau showed that while 40 percent of the population experienced a 5 percent or more increase in their incomes, another 40 percent experienced a 5 percent decline or more—both changes reflecting the large amount of movement that occurs in the income distribution from year to year. They also showed that the upward movement in incomes was frequently associated with workers beginning full-time (35 hours or more a week), year-round (50 to 52 weeks) jobs, the creation of new households through marriage, and the addition of adults (who presumably work) to the household.

Despite the analytical potential of longitudinal databases and their usefulness in understanding how the income distribution changes, most research into growing income inequality in recent years has been based on cross-sectional surveys, especially the CPS. This is because of the CPS's historical database and its reliability. In years to come, however, longitudinal databases will be used more in income distribution research.

The Interaction of Economic, Social, and Demographic Factors

As pointed out above, the simple fact that a member of a household decides to work full time, year round instead of only part time can make a large difference in the household's position in the income distribution. Similarly, the decision to get married typically means that the number of potential earners in one's household will automatically double, thereby possibly raising income. As the Census data above implied, changes of these types are common in American society.

To understand why the income distribution is changing, however, more than one factor must usually be considered. Indeed, an array of economic, social, and demographic factors (and their subfactors) can be involved. A job layoff for the chief breadwinner, for example, has an important effect on economic well-being. But the rest of his or her circumstances are also important in determining the family's eventual position in the income distribution. That is, what is the education or training level of the chief breadwinner, are retraining opportunities available, does anyone else work in the family, are there other sources of income available to the family? Other circumstances involve where one lives (i.e., an urban or rural area), the state of the job market in that area, the number of persons in the household the chief breadwinner has responsibility for, and so on. And it is also of importance if the chief breadwinner is a man or woman, young or old, white, black, or Hispanic. The important point is this: The choices one has made during one's lifetime, as well as one's unchangeable characteristics, are all important in determining how the chief breadwinner adjusts to a job layoff and where ultimately the new position in the income distribution will be.

The income distribution and changes in it, consequently, must be considered in the context of the economic, social, and demographic structure of society. When any one factor produces a change in the income-creating potential of a household, other factors must be taken into account as to where the new income level will be in the distribution. In other words, linkages exist between these factors at any point in time.

Many of these linkages between the factors (and subfactors) are not well understood in terms of causation. Over time the economic, social, and demographic structure of society is subject to change and this in turn changes the nature of the linkages. It is well known, for example, that the economy today is subject to more global competition than ever before; that society's living arrangements have become more diverse; and that our population is aging rapidly. These very general examples of change imply changes to the linkages between factors and subfactors.

Lester Thurow, in a recent book, wrote about how certain changes in the world are shaping the future of capitalism. He likened these forces to the tectonic plates which lie beneath the earth's surface and, on occasion, shift, producing changes in the earth's topography.[23] Similarly, one might think of the economic, social, and demographic factors described here as tectonic plates upon which rest the income distribution of the United States. Shifts in these plates (which are brought about by the actions of humanity) in recent years have resulted in growing income inequality. It is the job of the economist to understand these dynamic shifts so as to explain why the income distribution, in static terms, has changed.

Other Indicators of Income Distribution Change

At the beginning of this chapter, certain statistical measures were used to verify popular impressions about what was happening to this country's income distribution. All of them, despite their crudeness, provided statistical insights into growing income inequality. There are many other measures of inequality that have been used in recent research, as will be shown in the following chapter, and some of these tend to be more technical in nature.

In addition to measures of income inequality, there are other statistical indicators related to income inequality that often are seen in the media and help form popular impressions of what's happening to the income distribution. The following is a brief description of some of the more popular ones.

Poverty

The federal government has an official definition of poverty and the Census Bureau makes estimates of the poverty population in the United States from the CPS.[24] The poverty definition obviously has a relationship to the income distribution in that it relates to those persons with low or poverty-level incomes. Persons living in families below federal government poverty income lines, or thresholds, are considered to be officially poor. These lines, which are updated each year for inflation, relate to the cost of an economy food plan developed by the Department of Agriculture in 1955. The poverty lines vary by family size, age of householder, and number of related children under 18.[25]

At the end of the 1960s, the poverty rate, or the proportion of the population living in families and households with incomes below the poverty line, was 12.1 percent. It moved even lower in the 1970s and by the end of that decade was 11.7 percent. During the next decade, however, poverty increased and by 1989 the rate was 12.8 percent. The poverty rate rose with the onset of the 1990–91 recession and reached 15.1 percent in 1993. Since then, however, the rate has dropped and in 1996 was 13.7 percent. To the extent that income inequality has increased in the 1980s and 1990s, the trends in poverty and income inequality are somewhat similar and reflective of growing income differences.

Low-Wage Workers

Another topic frequently discussed in the newspapers and broadcast media relating to growing inequality is the percentage of workers involved in low-wage employment. During the 1980s many economists said that among the millions of jobs the economy was creating, a large proportion were low-wage jobs. Indeed, a significant amount of research has been conducted into the falling wages of unskilled workers, especially young men.[26]

The Census Bureau, in the early 1990s, developed a statistical series presenting the proportion of full-time, year-round workers whose annual earnings fell below the federal government's poverty line for a four-person family (in 1994 this line was $13,828).[27] In other words, these data reflect employment that has yielded less than the amount needed by a family of four to reach the federal government's poverty line. The proportion of low-earners—or workers earning "poverty-level wages"—among all full-time, year-round workers rose from 12.1 percent in 1979 to 14.1 percent in 1989. By 1994, the proportion had reached a level of 16.2 percent—or nearly one out of every six full-time, year-round workers. As will be shown, the percentage of low-wage workers among young workers and those with low skill levels and poor educations increased significantly during these years.

Single-Parent Families

The increase in the number of single-parent families brought about by divorce, separation, and childbearing out of wedlock has been associated with rising income inequality. According to the Census Bureau, in 1979 the proportion of all families headed by a single parent was 17.5 percent and in 1996 it was 23.7 percent (in 1969 the proportion was only 13.9 percent).[28]

Many single-parent families have no labor force participants because the majority are headed by women who have small children. Even among those in which the mother does work, working schedules are constrained by the duties involved with caring for the family. In addition, many of these mothers have low skill levels and poor educations. In consequence, the annual earnings of single-parent families are much lower than for married couples. In 1996, the median income of families headed by women was $21,564 compared to the median of $49,858 for married-couple families.[29]

With a growing proportion of families headed by single parents, it follows that the proportion of families composed of married couples has declined.

This also has had implications for growing income inequality, one of which is discussed below.

Working Wives

One of the most significant labor market developments in the second half of this century has been the increase in the labor force activity of women. The upward trend has also been very evident in recent years for wives, both those with and without small children. The percentage of married-couple families with a wife in the paid labor force rose from 49.3 percent in 1979 to 62.0 percent by 1996.[30]

Historically, the impact of working wives on the income distribution has been to lower income inequality among families.[31] This occurred because of the relatively small earnings variation that wives experienced and the fact that wives with husbands with low earnings tended to participate in the labor market to a greater extent than wives whose husbands had higher earnings. Researchers have recently found evidence that this effect may have moderated in recent years, at least in the context of the overall household income distribution.[32] This is because women have sought both to have careers in the labor market as well as to improve the economic situation of their families. Recent research suggests that there is a growing correlation between the earnings of husbands and wives and this also has led to greater income inequality.[33]

Earnings Differences

There are yet other indicators which are frequently seen in the print and electronic media and have been associated with growing income inequality. One that has been especially popular in recent years (and was referred to earlier) is the compensation received by the CEOs of major corporations. Many news stories have reported the sizable compensation packages received by CEOs and compared them to the pay of their employees.[34] According to these reports, these relative earnings differentials have widened enormously in the last two decades and exacerbated the income gap. The impact of the CEOs' remuneration on income inequality, however, has been disputed, most recently by the President's Council of Economic Advisers. According to the Council, because CEOs represent only a tiny fraction of the work force, their impact on earnings inequality is minimal.[35]

Related to these earnings differentials are those between workers of different education and skill levels. While these do not capture the attention of those of CEOs and their employees, they are important in explaining growing income differences. One of the most commonly used relative wage differential is that between college-educated workers and high school dropouts. During the 1980s this differential increased dramatically as the demand for highly educated and skilled workers shifted upward and the demand for poorly educated and unskilled workers plummeted.

News accounts of the rising number of millionaires and highly paid athletes and entertainers have also become increasingly popular in recent years. For example, a well-known television show in the 1990s was "Lifestyles of the Rich and Famous." While good data on the number of millionaires and the super-rich are difficult to find, the stories about their lives and lifestyles also reinforce popular impressions about growing income disparities in America.

Summary

Concern over the growth in income inequality in recent years, despite the sustained economic growth through much of the 1990s, continues to linger. Differences in the growth of household incomes between the upper and lower halves of the income distribution over the past thirty years or so have produced large "dollar differences" between the rich and the poor. But the middle class, when defined as those households with incomes between $25,000 and $99,999 a year, has surely not disappeared. It has only grown more slowly.

The reason or reasons for the growth in income inequality are still not completely understood, reflecting the complex process of income determination. As was shown, a variety of economic, social, and demographic factors are associated with one's position in the income distribution. While changes in the way the labor market operates have been shown to be most important, other changes in American society and the world are important as well.

2

Concepts and Methods of Inequality Analysis

The topic of income inequality in our society today is often misunderstood and confused with other economic issues. This is because it is one of those slippery economic terms with moral, conceptual, and empirical aspects that are not necessarily intuitive. For most economists, however, income inequality has a specific meaning. To them it means how the total income of a country or geographical entity is distributed among its citizens. In this chapter, the concepts and methods of inequality analysis that economists follow are presented.

Measuring Income and Income Inequality

Some basic measures of income inequality were presented in Chapter 1—the proportion of households in various income classes, the shares of aggregate income received by household quintiles, and the ratio of incomes at the 95th and 20th percentiles of the income distribution. These measures were based on income data from the Current Population Survey, or CPS, a survey of households conducted by the Census Bureau. By using CPS data, certain conceptual questions regarding the measurement of income and income inequality were automatically answered.

First, the Census Bureau's concept of income was used, a concept that differs from that of other federal government agencies involved with collecting information on income. Second, the income data were before any federal, state, or local taxes had been deducted. Third, the incomes related to the year 1996, a one-year period, but as everyone knows, income is accrued continually over time. Fourth, the Census data relate to persons (or an individual) living in households, that is, persons living together and sharing resources (this includes families as well as groups of individuals not related to one another). And fifth, no adjustments to the Census income data were made for differences in the number of persons residing in households, or household size. The following discussion elaborates on these five topics and by doing so reveals the significance of each for income inequality measurement.

Defining Income

Income, in its broadest sense, is the value of the goods and services that society produces through the interaction of the factors of production—land, labor, capital, and entrepreneurship. Economists have typically distinguished between two types of income distributions, the "size" distribution of income and the "functional" distribution of income. The former shows how income is distributed among the owners of the factors, in other words, people; the latter shows how income is distributed according to the factor services provided in the production process. So it is how the size distribution of income is determined that we are interested in.

But what really is income when thought of in the context of a person or family or household? When economists think of income this way, they often think of it as the access and control over economic resources, another rather loose and vague definition. Certainly, one's take-home pay is part of income as are the dividends and interest received from certain investments, but what about the contributions employers make for their workers' health insurance or the inheritance one receives from his or her parents? Or what about the implicit returns homeowners receive on the equity in their homes? Are these also components of income? Or is income what the Internal Revenue Service (IRS) says it is after taxpayers figure out their annual federal income tax liability? Economists and statisticians have wrestled with the specifics of the income definition for years.

Income inequality measurement can be very sensitive to how income is defined. For example, measured income inequality (as the Census Bureau measures it) today would probably be greater if the "perks" (e.g., limousine service, country club memberships, stock options) received by the very wealthy were included. On the other hand, it is lower if the value of certain income transfer payments (e.g., subsidized housing, food stamps, health benefits) received by the poor are included in their incomes. Consequently, in reviewing reports on income inequality, it is important to know what is and what is not included in the income data.

Two federal government sources of income data other than the Census Bureau's are the IRS (mentioned earlier) and the Bureau of Economic Analysis (BEA).[1] We all know how and why the IRS collects its income information, but perhaps the function of the BEA is not as well known. The BEA produces estimates of the National Income and Product Accounts, the most popular estimates being gross domestic product and personal income. The income concepts of both the IRS and the BEA are somewhat different than the Census Bureau concept.

The income concept used by the Census Bureau in its CPS is the narrowest of the three. It is the narrowest because it relates only to "money" income: It is defined as the sum of wages and salaries, net income from self-employment, Social Security or railroad retirement income, Supplemental Security Income, public assistance or welfare payments, interest, dividends, income from estates and trusts, rental income, veterans' payments, unemployment and worker's compensation, private and government pensions, alimony and child support, regular contributions from persons not living in the household, and other periodic income. Money income does not include income in the form of noncash benefits, such as food stamps, health benefits, rent-free housing, and goods produced and consumed on the farm; nor does it include the noncash benefits received by some persons in the form of access to transportation services and recreation facilities, medical, health, and educational services, and payments made for retirement purposes. Capital gains and lump sum inheritance or insurance payments are also not included in the Census income concept (though it does provide experimental estimates of the former, as will be discussed below).

The BEA income concept is more inclusive in that while it includes nearly all the income items in the CPS concept (BEA does not include workers' contributions for social insurance), it also includes many nonmonetary transactions taking place in the economy. These transactions involve such things as in-kind payments for work, whether they be in the form of food, clothing, or housing. In addition, Medicare, Medicaid, and certain employer-provided benefits (e.g., health insurance) are included in their income estimate. Another important inclusion is the net rental value of owner-occupied housing, that is, the implicit return to homeowners' equities. Because of these inclusions, estimates of personal income are much higher than the estimate of aggregate money income from the CPS.

The IRS income estimates differ from both the Census Bureau's CPS and the BEA's because tax laws exclude income from certain sources, for example, veterans' disability payments and interest received on tax-exempt bonds. In addition, many persons with low incomes are not required to file tax returns, while at the same time many persons with high incomes can either defer certain income receipts or avoid tax liability altogether.

From the foregoing, an important distinction between income and labor market earnings should be evident, as well as the distinction between income and wealth. Earnings from work (whether in the form of wages and salaries or self-employment income) are a part of income, in fact usually the largest part. In the context of the factors of production, economists view earnings as the return to labor (as well as to capital insofar as self-employment income is generated with the assistance of physical capital). With respect to income and wealth, economists tend to think of income as a "flow" variable in that income is continually being produced; in contrast, wealth is viewed as a "stock" variable, that is, such things of value as the houses, automobiles, and jewelry owned by individuals.

Before-Tax and After-Tax Income

Taxes are a fact of life for everyone. While many Americans are unhappy about how their tax dollars are spent, tax revenues are presumably used for the general good of society—education, health, roads and bridges, national defense, and so on. The income that is left after all taxes are paid is what we have to either save or spend, or our disposable income.

There are all kinds of taxes, of course, that are levied for different purposes in our society. The one that perhaps comes to mind first is the federal income tax. This tax is considered to be progressive in that tax rates rise as income rises, thereby having a redistributive effect on the income distribution. But other taxes, like a flat state sales tax, are proportional in the sense that everyone is subject to the same tax rate. Obviously, this tax has a somewhat opposite effect from the federal income tax on the income distribution.

Whether or not to measure income inequality before or after all taxes have been deducted from incomes does make a difference in the level of measured income inequality. The Census Bureau publishes, in addition to its official income distribution statistics which are based on before-tax incomes, a series of experimental distributions. These distributions have been adjusted for the payment of certain taxes as well as for the value of certain noncash benefits and the inclusion of capital gains.[2] These adjustments are made through the use of econometric modeling and this is why these data are considered to be experimental.

One of the distributions excludes the payment of three taxes: federal income taxes, state income taxes, and workers' payroll taxes. Using the ratio of household incomes at the 80th percentile to the 20th percentile as a crude measure of inequality, this ratio, after taxes were excluded from the official income distribution in 1996, was 3.97, or incomes at 80th percentile were four times as large as those at the 20th percentile. When the same ratio is calculated using the official Census Bureau's income distribution (before taxes), the ratio rises to 4.60.[3] More will be said about these experimental income distributions in the following chapter.

Most of the research into growing income inequality has been based on income data before taxes have been excluded. More than anything else, this reflects researchers' reliance on the Census Bureau's CPS official income data for their research and the fact that actual after-tax income data are difficult to come by. This is because of the great variety of taxes (as well as fees) that exist at various levels of government.

The issue of whether to use either before or after tax income data only highlights a greater and more significant problem in both income distribution and income inequality measurement. Ideally, researchers would like to have at their disposal the most comprehensive income distribution possible and by that is meant one inclusive of all actual tax payments as well as all money and nonmoney income items. The Census Bureau has led the research into the development of such an income distribution with the development of its various experimental income distributions.

Monthly, Annual, and Lifetime Incomes

The Census Bureau's income data, of course, relate to a calendar year. Other sources of income data also typically relate to a calendar year. And when people think of incomes, as in the case of wondering about how much "so and so" makes or earns, they do so typically in terms of a year. Why? More than anything else, the measurement of incomes on an annual basis is simply the result of convention and tradition. But incomes could be measured over any time period and sometimes are. What are the implications for measuring income inequality?

Generally speaking, the amount of dispersion in an income distribution diminishes as the time period used in the measurement is lengthened. This is logical if one simply thinks a little bit about the income-producing process. Life is not a smooth, event-free process—there are bumps in the road now and then. Income flows can be interrupted by illnesses, job layoffs, job changes, retirements, stock market crashes, and so on. At any point in time, society is experiencing many of these events, but over time the ups and downs of the income flows even out, or are averaged out.[4] Consequently, income differences in society will be smaller over long periods of time than short periods.

Because of these variations in income across time, some economists believe that the ideal measurement of inequality should be carried out over the lifetimes of individuals and their families.[5] In other words, it would be best to follow the same cohort of people through time and then measure the amount of inequality in the "lifetime" income distribution. (Many economists have pointed out that the annual income distributions of the Census Bureau can be misinterpreted because the families or households in the top or bottom of the distribution—or any part of the distribution—from year to year or over a span of years are not necessarily the same.) This would not only eliminate income variations due to the random shocks of life, but also eliminate the inequality existing in the distribution only because of simple age variations in the population (i.e., young persons have lower incomes than middle-age persons). Unfortunately, income data that track lifetime incomes are hard to come by. This is because people move and change addresses as well as oftentimes are unwilling to be involved in lifetime surveys. This makes the measurement of lifetime income inequality very difficult.

Despite the economists who believe that the only meaningful time period by which to measure inequality is a lifetime, the preponderance of the literature and research into inequality has been carried out using income and wage data of the Census Bureau, which are annual data. As was mentioned earlier, these data represent essentially one-year snapshots of the income distribution and, therefore, include the random "ups and downs" of income flows as well as those components of inequality due to life-cycle differences of our existing population in a one-year period. To the extent that growing income inequality has been due to factors other than those mentioned above, the task of economists is all the more challenging.

Income Recipients

The income data of the Census Bureau referred to previously relate to households. Why not families or persons? The simple answer is that data for families and persons could also have been shown and the Census Bureau does report on income inequality among families and earnings inequality among persons as well. Households are featured, however, because income inequality can (and usually does) involve judgments regarding economic well-being and personal consumption. Since income is often shared in a household, the household is the most appropriate income recipiency unit in a study of income inequality.

The Census Bureau has a very precise definition of a household.[6] A household is defined as a house, apartment, or other group of rooms regarded as a housing unit which is occupied by an individual or group of individuals. In featuring the household as their primary recipiency unit of income measurement, the Bureau assumes that income is pooled or shared for the purposes of consumption. Obviously, in this day and age of diverse living arrangements there are many households in which persons not related to one another may or may not share incomes for consumption. For example, two recent college graduates who rent an apartment together would be considered a single household, even though they might not share their incomes for personal consumption purposes. The household, therefore, is not the perfect unit for inequality measurement, but because households account for everyone in the civilian noninstitutional population it is a convenient unit.

Families are a subunit of households. They are defined as a group of two or more persons related by birth, marriage, or adoption who reside together. Because of the rise in divorces, marital separations, births out of wedlock, and alternative living arrangements, the family has lost some of its relevance in income inequality measurement because it relates to an increasingly smaller part of the overall population. It is relevant, of course, in analyses that are family-specific.

Income inequality (as measured by the Census Bureau) tends to be higher among households than families. This is because many households are composed of young persons and elderly persons with low incomes. Researchers have used both households and families as the recipient units in their analyses. In addition, they frequently make adjustments for differences in household and family sizes through the use of equivalence scales, about which more is said below.

Adjusting Incomes for Differences in Household Size

The Census income data mentioned so far relate to households with different numbers of persons living in them. Some were households consisting of only one person, such as that of an elderly widower or young single person, and others contained more than one, such as that of a single-parent or married-couple family.

A common practice among economists studying income inequality is to adjust the household or family income data for differences in the number of persons in a household or family. This is done because of the presumed economies of scale which occur as the number of persons in the household or family increases. In effect it is adjusting for the old adage, "Two can live as cheaply as one."

The necessity for the adjustment has immediate appeal, especially when it is considered in another light. If two households have identical annual incomes of $40,000, and one is composed of two members and the other four, there is an obvious difference in the income available to each member of the household. In other words, the household incomes are the same but certainly the amount of economic resources available to each household member differs greatly.

To compensate for these apparent differences in "per capita" income, as well as the assumed economies of scale inherent in increasingly larger families and households, economists have devised equivalence scales. Basically, an equivalence scale is an index by which family or household in-

Table 2.1

Equivalence Scale Implicit in the Federal Government's Poverty Lines, 1996

Size of family	Poverty threshold	Equivalence scale
1 person	$ 7,995	1.000
2 persons	$10,233	1.279
3 persons	$12,516	1.565
4 persons	$16,036	2.010
5 persons	$18,952	2.370
6 persons	$21,389	2.680
7 persons	$24,268	3.040
8 persons	$27,091	3.390
9 or more persons	$31,971	3.999

Source: U.S. Bureau of the Census, *Poverty in the United States: 1996* (P60-198) (Washington, DC: USGPO, September 1997), Table 1, p. 1.

comes are adjusted for each extra family and household member. One of the more popular equivalence scales is the one implicit in the federal government's poverty lines, which, as was discussed earlier, vary by family size and are based on an economy food plan that assures a minimally nutritional diet. Table 2.1 shows the poverty lines in 1996 for families ranging in size from one to nine persons as well as the equivalence scale, or index, which is nothing more than the poverty lines for households of sizes one to nine or more persons divided by the poverty line for a one-person household.[7] In other words, the poverty line for a one-person household was $7,995 in 1996 and for a two-person household it was $10,233, which yields an equivalent income deflator of 1.279, and so on up to the nine-or-more-person household and its deflator of 3.999.

Table 2.2 shows how these deflators would work in a hypothetical society of five households of different family sizes and incomes. Based on actual incomes, the Wilsons' and Clarks' households had equal incomes, but after their household size has been factored in, it can be seen there is a very large difference in their adjusted incomes, suggesting there is a very large difference in economic well-being. Or consider the Smith household where actual income was $22,000 and consisted of just one person and the household of the Joneses in which actual income was $37,000 but there were four people living in it. Even though there was a $15,000 difference in household income in favor of the Joneses, once household size is considered it is shown that the Smiths' household has more "adjusted" income, but not as much as implied on a per capita basis.

Table 2.2

Hypothetical Equivalence Scale Adjustments to Family Incomes

Household	Actual income	Family size	Equivalence scale (deflator)	Adjusted income
Smith	$22,000	1	1.000	$22,000
Jones	$37,000	4	2.000	$18,408
Wilson	$40,000	5	2.370	$16,878
Clark	$40,000	2	1.279	$31,274
Hill	$90,000	3	1.565	$57,508

As was indicated, the equivalence scales used here were based on those implicit in the federal government's poverty guidelines which are based on food requirements. Economists have developed other scales based on more comprehensive requirements for modern day life which incorporate more sophisticated relationships between income and consumption expenditures. These are based on actual income and consumption patterns. But as becomes quite clear after thinking for a while about this problem of adjusting actual incomes for apparent economies of scale and per capita income differences, normative issues soon arise, that is, strong assumptions between income and needs.[8]

The composition of households varies widely—some have only adults in them, others are comprised of adults and children. It is very difficult to know the exact consumption needs of similar individuals. For example, two individuals of the same age, sex, weight, and height may have very different needs in terms of health care; they may have different needs in terms of clothing because they live in different parts of the country; they may have different food needs because of differences in their jobs (or even their metabolisms); and their consumption patterns may vary significantly because of the different consumer prices they face in the areas they live. In addition to not having information on specific consumption needs (other than the very basic necessities of life) of households, there is also the problem of personal preferences. For example, in the hypothetical case above, both the Clarks' and Wilsons' households have identical incomes, but because of the different household sizes and the equivalence scales used to adjust actual incomes, the Clarks were found to be almost twice as "well off" as the Wilsons. For the sake of argument, let's assume that the Wilsons' household has three children that they love and adore, while the Clarks' consists of a married couple with a dog that they love and adore. It is most unlikely that the Wilsons would give up their three children for a dog so as to equalize their adjusted income. In other words, while equivalence scales can be used perhaps to adjust incomes for differences in household and family sizes based on the basic necessities of life, it is exceedingly difficult to go beyond this point (indeed, there are some economists who would suggest that there is no universal consensus on what constitutes the basic necessities of life).

In a very important theoretical article almost two decades ago, two economists suggested that it is very difficult to make welfare comparisons (which is often the case when income inequality is at issue) using equivalence scales.[9] The basis of their article is that equivalence scales involve interpersonal or interfamily comparisons of welfare. This means that in cases when incomes are being adjusted for family size differences, there is an implication that we know the values that have been given to additional members (typically children) of families or households. Or, as they illustrate, do we really know how much money or income would be needed to make families with three children as well off as those with two children and $12,000? It depends on how strongly people desire additional members (typically children) in their families and households.

This is perhaps one of the thorniest conceptual issues in the measurement of income inequality. It is further complicated by the fact that average family and household sizes have also declined in recent decades, presumably freeing up additional income for household members. Shouldn't current income data be adjusted to reflect this demographic dividend? The problem is that other things have changed in our society and demography over time and while our average families and households have changed, so too have our needs. Consider how indoor plumbing slowly turned from a quasi luxury to a necessity over the decades or how telephone usage has changed. In short, adjusting income for one kind of difference (and change) invites adjustments of other kinds, many of which are too difficult to translate into monetary amounts.

The Census Bureau publishes household income data classified by the size of the household, in addition to many other classifications such as age of the householder (or head of household), race, employment status, residence, and so on. While most of its measures of household income inequality are not based on income data adjusted for household size, they do publish a series that implicitly makes such an adjustment. This series is referred to as the ratio of family income to the family's poverty line—the income-to-needs ratio—about which more will be said in the following chapter.

Inequality Measures

Over the years, economists have used a variety of measures to determine the amount of inequality in an income distribution. Some of these are well-

Table 2.3

Income Inequality Measures, 1979 and 1989

Measure	1979	1989	Percent change
Household Income Classes (in 1991 dollars)			
Less than $25,000 (percent)	29.8	27.9	NA
$25,000 to $74,999 (percent)	56.5	52.5	NA
$75,000 or more (percent)	13.7	19.6	NA
Household Income Shares (in 1991 dollars)			
Lowest quintile (percent)	5.2	4.6	NA
Middle 3 quintiles (percent)	52.1	49.8	NA
Highest quintile (percent)	42.7	45.6	NA
Top 5 percent	16.3	18.6	NA
Percentile ratios			
90th-to-10th	6.85	7.91	15.4
90th-to-50th	2.18	2.36	8.3
10th-to-50th	0.32	0.3	−6.2
Coefficient of Variation	0.775	0.909	17.3
Variance of Natural Logarithm of Income	0.685	0.782	14.2
Gini Index	0.376	0.410	9.0
Theil Index	0.243	0.297	22.2
Atkinson Index (epsilon = 0.5)	0.119	0.142	19.3
Atkinson Index (epsilon = 2.0)	0.882	0.907	2.8

Source: Author's calculations of March 1980 and March 1990 Annual Demographic Survey data from the CPS.
NA—Not applicable.

known statistical measures of dispersion and others have been developed by statisticians, mathematicians, and economists for the purposes of gauging the degree of inequality in an income distribution.

A few simple measures have already been presented, but there are many more, both simple and complicated. In this section, we discuss the nature and properties of the measures most frequently seen in the income inequality literature as well as the media. Table 2.3 shows what these various measures registered when applied to the household income distributions for 1979 and 1989.[10] This table is presented to give the reader a flavor for the particular "metric" of the measure and to demonstrate how they differ in their recording of dispersion in the income distribution. It is important to remember that there is no official measure of income inequality.

Income Classes

Perhaps one of the most basic measures of income inequality that the general public thinks of when this topic comes up are the number (or percentage) of households or families in particular income classes. If pressed, most people would come up with some idea of what income range is "middle class," or "poor," or "rich." To use these income ranges across time, of course, they have to be adjusted for changes in consumer prices, or inflation.

In Table 2.3 three household income classes are presented, households with incomes of less than $25,000, those with incomes of $25,000 to $74,999, and those with incomes of $75,000 a year or more. The inequality metric is obviously a percentage. Aside from the problem of arbitrariness in defining the income ranges (i.e., one person's income range for the middle class may be different from another's), ranges mask the location of households within the range. Although the changes in the proportions of households in each income class suggest an overall upward movement, the data do not reflect what happened within each range. Maybe there was an increase in the proportion of households with incomes of less than $7,500 between 1979 and 1989? Or maybe there was a larger proportion of households with income above $100,000?

The data are silent on these questions. Consequently, this form of inequality measurement can only be considered one of the crudest measures of inequality (and that may even be stretching it).[11]

Income Shares

One of the inequality measures the Census Bureau uses in its annual reports on the income situation of Americans is referred to as income shares. In simplest terms, this measure involves arranging the incomes of households from the lowest to the highest, dividing this distribution into quintiles, or fifths, and then calculating how much income each fifth received (the Census Bureau also calculates how much income goes to the highest 5 percent of households).

The metric involved in this measure is the percentage of total income received by each quintile (the distribution, of course, could be divided on the basis of any quantile, such as deciles, ventiles, or percentiles). The table shows that between 1979 and 1989 income shares going to the lowest quintile (or 20 percent of households) and the three middle quintiles fell, while the top quintile share of total income rose from 42.7 to 45.6 percent. As is also shown, most of the gain at the top was garnered by the top 5 percent of households.

This measure has great intuitive appeal because 1) with basically five numbers we can tell what share of the "income pie" goes to different segments of the distribution and 2) with an additional five numbers for another year we can tell whose shares are growing, shrinking, or not changing. The story told by these shares between 1979 and 1989, and shown in Table 2.3, has been the familiar one heard most often in recent years: growing income inequality!

Related to this measure is the well-known Lorenz curve which graphically shows the relationship between the cumulative percentage of households along the horizontal axis and the cumulative percentage of income received by those households along the vertical axis. A hypothetical Lorenz curve is displayed in Figure 2.1.; crude Lorenz curves for the United States in 1979 and 1989 could be drawn on the basis of the income shares going to each quintile of the income distribution; as the Lorenz curve bows further out toward the lower right-hand corner of the figure, inequality increases because a growing proportion of the income pie is being concentrated in the upper end of the income distribution. The diagonal line in the figure is a Lorenz curve representing perfect income equality since each segment of the population receives the same amount of income; perfect income inequality would be represented by a Lorenz curve lying on top of the x-axis and right-hand boundary of the figure since all income is received by only 1 percent of the population. More will be said about Lorenz curves below.

Ratios of Percentiles

Another method of income inequality measurement is to calculate percentiles of the income distribution and then measure the distances between these percentiles using a ratio (the metric) as was done in the opening chapter. Table 2.3 shows the income ratios between the 90th and 10th percentiles of the income distribution, the 90th and 50th, and the 10th and the 50th in 1979 and 1989 (but any percentiles could be used to gauge the dollar distance of households located at various points of the distribution).

This measurement approach has been used extensively (especially in the earnings and wage inequality literature). By using a combination of income ratios based on percentiles, such as in the table, it is possible to see where in the distribution dispersion is occurring.[12] Table 2.3 shows that indeed the distribution was pulling apart between 1979 and 1989, and that most of the greater dispersion was taking place in the upper half of the distribution.

Figure 2.1 **A Hypothetical Lorenz Curve**

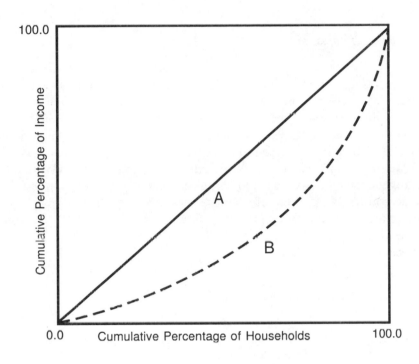

The three measures of inequality just discussed—income classes, income shares, and percentile ratios—while simple and straightforward do require the examination of several statistics at once to reach some judgment as to what is happening to the income distribution. Consequently, summary measures—single valued measures—have been developed of dispersion in an income distribution. Because of the way these measures are constructed (see Appendix A for their mathematical constructions), however, each has their own properties and problems of interpretation.[13] While the metric in all these summary measures will register 0 when there is perfect equality of incomes, they will differ substantially when income inequality is present. To understand these properties, economists have employed the Principle of Transfers, a principle which says that inequality should be reduced if a small amount of income is transferred from a person with more income to another person with less income and the amount of the inequality reduction is dependent upon where in the income distribution the income transfer takes place.[14]

Coefficient of Variation

The coefficient of variation is simply the standard deviation divided by the mean, or average, of the income distribution. This is a relative measure of dispersion and the metric is devoid of units. The coefficient of variation will always register a decline in inequality when an income transfer (from a richer person to a poorer person) takes place. Because of the way it is constructed, the coefficient of variation is more sensitive to relative income differences among high-income households than low-income households, and therefore more sensitive to changes in the upper end of the income distribution. According to the coefficient of variations shown in Table 2.3, inequality rose from .775 to .909 (or 17.3 percent) between 1979 and 1989.

Variance of the Natural Logarithm of Income

The variance of the natural logarithm of income is represented simply by the formula for the variance of a distribution, except expressed in terms of natural logarithms. Because incomes are expressed in logarithms, high incomes are compressed so that deviations from the mean income are accentuated at the bottom of the distribution. Consequently, changes in the bottom half of the income distribution will have a greater impact on this measure than those in the upper half. In addition, at very high income levels the transfer of income will not always register a decrease in income inequality. Between 1979 and 1989, this measure increased by 14.2 percent, or from .685 to .782.

The Gini Index

This measure of income inequality has been used by the Census Bureau for many years. Developed by the Italian mathematician Corrado Gini, this measure is related closely to the Lorenz curve pictured in Figure 2.1. What this measure does is estimate the area between the Lorenz curve of perfect equality (a diagonal line) and another Lorenz curve reflecting a certain amount of inequality (the bowed line). In simplest terms, this area—A—

when divided by the total area under the Lorenz curve of perfect equality—A + B—yields the Gini index. By definition, the Gini index can vary between 0 (perfect equality) and 1 (perfect inequality).

Changes in the Gini index are most sensitive to changes (or income transfers) taking place in the middle of the distribution because it is based on the Lorenz curve which reflects the cumulative percentage of incomes received by households. An income transfer of a certain amount will have a much greater impact in the middle because there are more households involved than a similar transfer of income at the lower or upper ends of the distribution. The Gini index increased between 1979 and 1989 by 9.0 percent, or from .376 to .410.

The Theil Index

The Theil index was developed by the economist Henri Theil. This index too has an inherent weighting scheme in that each household's income is related to the mean of the distribution. It has been used by economists to decompose the overall increase in inequality occurring because of changes between groups and within groups (about which more will be said).

Income transfers taking place in the income distribution will have their greatest impact on the Theil index when they occur in the lower end of the distribution, which is similar to the situation when the variance of the natural logarithm of income is used. As can be seen in Table 2.3, the change in the Theil index was from .243 to .297, or 22.2 percent.

The Atkinson Index

Another inequality measure was developed by the economist Anthony Atkinson to overcome a problem inherent in Lorenz curves. It is possible that Lorenz curves can intersect (as one can picture in Figure 2.1), and when they do, the resulting Gini indexes are ambiguous with respect to measured inequality. Atkinson devised a measure that permits one to select the area of the income distribution to be the most sensitive to changes in income, or income transfers. The formulation of the Atkinson index contains a parameter called an "epsilon," which allows one to decide in which part of the income distribution changes (or income transfers) will be the most sensitive. As the value of the epsilon rises, the index becomes increasingly sensitive to changes occurring in the lower end of the distribution. As shown in Table 2.3, the Atkinson index based on an epsilon of 0.5 rose by 19.3 percent between 1979 and 1989 while the Atkinson index based on an epsilon of 2.0 rose only by 2.8 percent. This difference reflects the fact that rising income inequality in the 1980s was being driven more by income gains at the top of the distribution than at the bottom.

From the above discussion it is clear that the measurement of income inequality can be a complicated affair (as well as confusing).[15] As was shown, for the period of 1979 to 1989 the various summary measures all registered increases in income inequality, but to varying degrees. Indeed, even the simpler measures yielded somewhat ambiguous results. Economists who have studied the subject of growing income inequality tend to admit that there is no one preferred measure of inequality.

Data and Data Issues

Income data that can be used in income inequality research are difficult to obtain because people are often reluctant to divulge income information unless required to. In addition, while some income information is often obtained by law, the data are frequently difficult to use in income inequality research because they are not accompanied by other economic, social, and demographic characteristics of the individuals. For example, the IRS and BEA income data referred to earlier lack this necessary correlating information.

Household surveys like the CPS, on the other hand, do collect an abundance of background information about the household which supplements the annual income data. While other household surveys conducted by other government agencies and private institutions have been used to study both earning and income inequality, the CPS is the chief source of income data for analyses. In this section, therefore, attention is focused primarily on the CPS.

Some Background

The CPS had its origins in the late 1930s when there was widespread unemployment due to the Great Depression. Up until then, there was simply no mechanism by which to measure unemployment. In 1937 the Works Project Administration (WPA) attempted to count the country's unemployed through the use of a postcard survey.[16] This initial survey was soon to be improved by statisticians who drew a national sample and designed a questionnaire to ascertain the actual activity of household members each month vis-à-vis the labor market. The WPA, of course, eventually was terminated and this new sample survey was taken over by the Census Bureau to administer in the early 1940s. This is when the survey received its formal name, the Current Population Survey.

It was soon realized that the monthly CPS could be used periodically to collect other information relating to the economic well-being of the country.

In the mid-1940s, a few supplemental questions about income were added to the monthly labor force questionnaire in the spring of each year. These additional questions would eventually become what is formally known today as the March Annual Demographic Survey of the CPS (the number of questions concerning income expanded from just a few in the 1940s to a battery of questions in the mid-1990s, reflecting the growth in the diversity of income sources over the last fifty years).

The income data from the CPS, of course, are used for various purposes besides the measurement of income inequality. Because they are supplemented by extensive demographic detail, they are used, for example, by businesses for marketing purposes and by economic forecasters who are tracking the course of the economy. One of the major governmental uses is the measurement of the nation's poverty population.

Operation

The CPS is a monthly household survey of around 50,000 households. Each month trained CPS enumerators either visit or telephone household respondents and initially inquire about each household member's (15 years of age and over) activities in the week containing the 12th of the month. In March, they also ask the battery of questions relating to the work experience and income of the household and its members in the previous calendar year. Up until the early 1990s, a paper questionnaire was used in the interview process and responses were recorded by pencil. After that time computer-assisted survey information collection (CASIC) was initiated by the Census Bureau in which all CPS questions (including those about income) were administered from a computer (either a laptop or a computer located in a centralized telephoning facility).

Over the fifty years or so that income data have been collected in the CPS, many changes have taken place in the CPS methodology aimed at improving the quality of the data, the most significant in recent years being the introduction of CASIC. A more periodic change involves the CPS sample design. Each decade after the decennial census is taken, the Census Bureau randomly selects a new sample of geographic areas that will represent the nation's population. Sample weights are based on the decennial census information and these new weights were introduced in survey years 1973, 1982, and 1994 (based on the 1970, 1980, and 1990 censuses, respectively).

The processing of the CPS income data is a complex procedure. Not only does it involve the editing of nonsensical responses to certain questions, but it also involves the imputation of income amounts for those respondents who do not answer certain questions. The procedure the Census Bureau uses is called a "hot deck" procedure and involves imputing information from a "donor," or someone with similar characteristics to the respondent with the missing information. Improvements in these procedure over the years have affected the data quality. For example, in 1989 the hot deck procedure was changed (for those missing the entire income supplement) so that all income items were supplied from the same donor, and, along with the addition of a more detailed imputation system, the aggregate level of CPS income increased relative to independent benchmarks.

Limitations

One of the major limitations of the CPS income data alluded to earlier is they are based on a money income concept. While this concept was quite relevant back in the 1940s, it became less so with the growing importance of noncash income items associated with the many social programs aimed at low-income households and the changes in workers' compensation packages. To the extent that these noncash components of income are missing, income inequality measurements become biased. In addition, the omission of capital gains from the CPS money income concept also distorts inequality findings, especially in periods like the mid-1990s when the stock market soared to record highs.

Even the money income data that are collected in the CPS are subject to limitations. Because the data are based on a probability sample of households, all CPS estimates are subject to sampling errors. In addition, the income estimates are known to contain nonsampling errors due to such things as noninterviews, undercoverage, inaccurate responses, and missing data. The underreporting of income is a serious problem for income inequality analysis because both the receipt and the amounts of certain income items vary across the distribution, especially at the very top and the very bottom of the distributions. And these are the areas of great interest to economists and policy makers alike. The CPS in 1990 collected about 88 percent of aggregate income as derived from independent estimates, but this masks great variation depending on income source: with respect to wages and salaries the CPS collected 97 percent, but for dividend income it collected only 33 percent and only 72 percent of Aid to Families with Dependent Children.[17]

Another problem inherent in the CPS is the problem of truncation bias that results from the use of top codes in the collection of the data. Income amounts reported by respondents that are above certain levels are suppressed in order to reduce the effects of interviewer error and to provide confidentiality to survey respondents. This creates problems in periods of rising inequality when the source of the inequality is the rising incomes at the top end of the distribution. The top codes will bias downward inequality measurement because these very high incomes will be suppressed. Top codes are increased from time-to-time to accommodate rising incomes, the most recent increase occurring in March 1994 (income data for 1993). The most important top code that was increased related to earnings from a person's longest job or business in the previous year, which was raised from $299,999 to $999,999. The previous time this top code was changed was in March 1986 (income data for 1985). Top codes are lower on the CPS public-use files, and magnify the truncation bias problem.

Despite these limitations, the CPS income data have three major advantages over income data from all other sources. First, they do reflect (at least) the money income situation for the nation, and they have done so for the last 50 years or so. Second, although changes have been made to the CPS methodology over the years, the quality of the income data is always being monitored and consistency and continuity of the data have been of paramount importance. And third, the income data are supplemented by a wealth of other economic, social, and demographic information.

Analytical Issues

Economists, to their credit, have done a fairly good job in monitoring the trends in income inequality and attempting to understand why income inequality has increased. In reviewing this effort, however, it appears they have struggled with—and have been perplexed by—two analytical problems.

The first problem involves selecting an income inequality measure. While this may not appear to pose a problem for analysis, it is a problem. As was just shown, there are many measures of income inequality from which to select and they can provide different results with respect to the trend in inequality. Most economists agree that there is no preferred measure. Consequently, while there may be agreement that income inequality has risen in recent years, the extent of the increase and the nature of the increase often depend on the inequality measure being used.

A case in point involves the topic of the declining middle class, which was popular in the 1980s. This development was presumably the result of a polarization in the income distribution in which households were moving from the middle to the lower and upper parts of the distribution. Many of the inequality measures mentioned cannot distinguish this form of inequality from inequality caused, for example, by a growth in incomes only among households at the very top of the distribution. The problem of measure selection thus has important ramifications when the topic is addressed by policy makers, let alone for a public that has grown uneasy over the reports of growing inequality.

The second problem involves attempts to understand why inequality is growing and, more specifically, the flow of causation. While there are certain economic phenomena with well known, identifiable causes, there are other phenomena where the flow of causation is less clear. That is, it is difficult to distinguish cause and effect. Many factors that have been mentioned as possible causes of growing income inequality fall into this category. An example of this is the growth in the number of single-parent families and, more specifically, unwed mothers. These parents are typically very young, live in large urban areas, and have low incomes. Some researchers suggest their low incomes and generally poor economic prospects (the effect) are the result of early childbearing, or wrong moral choices (the cause). Other researchers would argue that their early childbearing (the effect) is really a viable economic option arising from their poor economic situation (the cause). This very specific analytical problem is common in other factors related to the process of income determination and poses a formidable challenge for those researchers attempting to understand income inequality.

Conclusion

Four facts about the analysis of income inequality trends should be evident from the preceding discussion of the concepts and methods of inequality as well as the discussion of the first chapter.

- The subject can be provocative.
- The subject is conceptually complicated and elusive.
- There are many ways to measure income inequality.
- The nature of the trend in income inequality (i.e., its rate of change, the timing of changes) often depends on the measure being used.

These facts make the review of trends in income inequality a difficult task and perhaps less "scientific" than other topics in economics. The review of trends in other economic phenomena, such as unemployment, inflation, and economic growth, do not involve as much ambiguity or arouse as much feeling. Anyone involved in an analysis of the trends in income inequality, therefore, must be aware of these aspects of the subject.

3

Inequality in the Post–World War II Era

The immediate fact that stands out when one looks back across the past century is how much things have changed. Whatever dimension we look at, whether it be the scientific, economic, demographic, or cultural, it is very evident that this is not the same country it was a hundred, fifty, or even twenty-five years ago.

The degree of income inequality in our society also has undergone significant change throughout the past century, as will be shown. If one thinks about it for a moment or two, it is only natural to expect change in the income distribution. As the world around us changes, the outcomes of our productive endeavors can be expected to change because so many different aspects of life are involved to varying degrees in the creation of income.

In this chapter the trends in income inequality since World War II (WWII) will be reviewed. Because of improvements in our country's statistical system, we can keep close track of the changes that have occurred in recent years. As will be shown in a later chapter, fewer and poorer income statistics in the first half of the century make it more difficult to discern trends in income inequality. However, the evidence is sufficiently robust for economists to make some judgments about what was happening to the income distribution in those years also.

An Overview

Many analyses of income and earnings inequality trends have appeared in the economics literature as well as the popular press. As with all of these, the authors had to make certain choices with respect to the source of data to analyze and the methodology to employ. Given this author's background and experience, the choices were easy.[1]

The source of the annual income data for the following analysis of income inequality trends since WWII is the Census Bureau's CPS for the years 1947 to 1996. Unless otherwise stated, these data are available to the public either through the Census Bureau's publications or its electronic home page at http://www.census.gov. The income recipient unit is the household and/or family, and three basic measures of inequality will be used, each to supplement the other: ratios of incomes at selected percentiles of the income distribution, shares of aggregate income received by quintiles of the income distribution, and the Gini index. Other statistical measures will be used to support and illustrate the three basic measures. As was mentioned, these are the basic measures that have been used over the years by the Census Bureau.

While familiarity may appear to be a weak reed upon which to rest one's justification for using a certain database and methodology in an analysis of this type, especially after the admonition of the last chapter, it really is not. The Census Bureau does not have any one official measure of inequality, but it does indeed collect and produce the "official" household and family income statistics upon which the federal government bases much of its social policies and programs as well as makes its annual measurement of the poverty population. In its role as "fact finder for the nation," the Census Bureau has used the Gini index and the shares of aggregate income received by quintiles as measures of inequality since the 1940s. It has also expanded its measures of inequality and the income distribution (as will be discussed later) in response to the growing interest in inequality. Consequently, while these inequality measures may not be official, they certainly have been used in conjunction with the official income statistics of the U.S. government, which does provide some substantive justification for their use here.

The Census Bureau's income statistics reveal distinctive trends in the real (in 1996 dollars) median incomes of families and households in the post–WWII era. These trends are shown in Figure 3.1. With respect to the trend for families between 1947 and 1996, two distinct periods of income growth can be seen in the figure. Between 1947 and 1973, the median rose from $19,651 to $40,059, or 2.7 percent a year.2 However, between 1973 and 1996, the median fluctuated with swings in the business cycle and at $42,300 in 1996 had only grown at an average annual rate of 0.2 percent a year. Clearly, the income growth of families over these two periods was distinctly different.

The statistical series for households begins in 1967. Median household income is considerably lower than the median for family households. In 1996 the median for households was only $35,492, or only 84 percent as high as that for families. This is because of the large number of young and elderly persons living alone with low incomes who are included in the count of households, but not of families. Back in 1967, median household income was about 90 percent as great as the median for all families.

Figure 3.1 **Real Median Family and Household Income, 1947–1996**

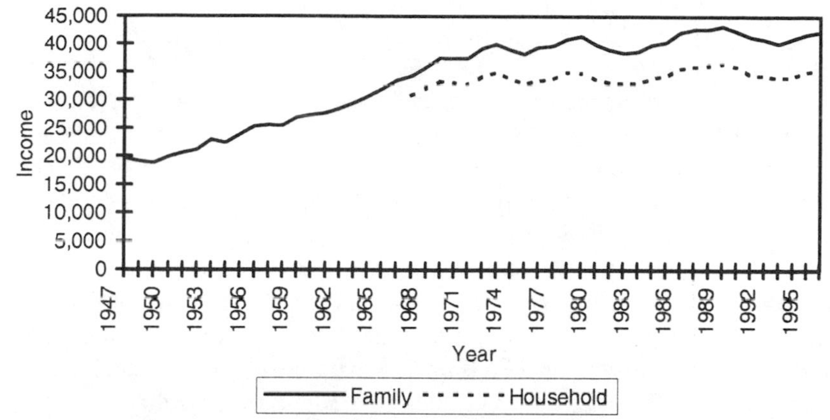

Source: U.S. Bureau of the Census, Annual Demographic Survey, CPS.
Note: Real income is in 1996 dollars.

The real median income for households between 1973 and 1996 did not grow much and paralleled the trend in incomes of families. Over this twenty-three-year period, the median rose only from $34,943 to $35,492. Between 1967 and 1973, on the other hand, it increased by slightly more than $4,000. Consequently, the poor income performance for families in the 1973–1996 period was matched by that of households as well. It is most likely that the income-growth pattern for households was similar to that for families between 1947 and 1973 because "nonfamily" households were not as common then as they have become in recent decades.

In terms of income growth, therefore, the post-WWII period can be broken into two distinct time periods with the early 1970s (usually 1973) representing the dividing line. This dividing line is significant for it was then that the underlying structure of the nation's income distribution—or the economic, social, and demographic tectonic plates—were beginning to shift. For the average American, this period will be remembered because of Watergate, the final days of the Vietnam War, and gas lines, but the more significant events for their long-run economic futures were beginning to be played out deep within the structure of their society.

Throughout most of the 1947–1973 period, the trend in income inequality attracted very little attention. Indeed, the subject of the income distribution was an obscure topic investigated by only a handful of economists and graduate students working on their Ph.D.s. The reason was that not much was happening to the income distribution and by 1980 Alan Blinder concluded that the most obvious characterization one could make about it in the post-WWII period was its constancy.[3] There had been a tendency for inequality to rise slightly during periods of economic downturns and to decline slightly in periods of economic expansion, but by and large, the long-run secular trend was flat.

The "constancy" of the income distribution in the two or three decades after WWII also confirmed another famous economist's long-term views of income inequality. Simon Kuznets, who made the study of the income distribution his life work, believed that inequality tends to increase in the early stages of economic development, but then declines as an economy matures.[4] Given the great income disparities that were assumed to have been in existence at the end of the 1920s and into the decade of the Great Depression, the lack of change in the income distribution in the decades following WWII tended to confirm Kuznets's beliefs.

It was within this frame of reference that economists in the late 1970s and early 1980s greeted rising measures of income inequality. As mentioned in a previous chapter, the first signs of growing inequality were in the labor market where earnings and wage distributions were becoming more dispersed. In the 1980s, income inequality accelerated and the increases were unexpected because previous research had demonstrated that economic growth typically helped the poor more than the rich, leading to *lower* amounts of inequality and reductions in poverty.[5] Subsequent research was to show that the economic growth of the 1980s seemed to have much weaker redistributive effects than in earlier decades.[6]

Gini indexes based on the family and household income distributions between 1947 and 1996 are displayed in Figure 3.2. Between 1947 and 1973, the period when family income was rising rapidly, inequality as measured by the Gini index was fairly stable or declining. This meant that incomes were rising no matter where one's family was located in the income distribution. In the 1973-to-mid-1990s period, on the other hand, when both real median family and household incomes were growing slowly, inequality in both distributions was clearly on the rise. Between 1973 and 1996, the Gini index for families increased from .356 to .425 and for households it increased from .397 to .455. The slow growth in real median incomes, along with rising income inequality, meant that the incomes of some families and households were growing faster than others.

Before moving in to take a closer look at income inequality trends in the post-WWII era, it would be useful to observe the average income trends from another source, the BEA. The slow growth in average family and household incomes after the early 1970s, as reported by the Census Bureau, received much attention in the media during the 1980s. It did so not only because it meant "bad news" for millions of Americans, but also because it

Figure 3.2 **Gini Indexes for Families and Households, 1947–1996**

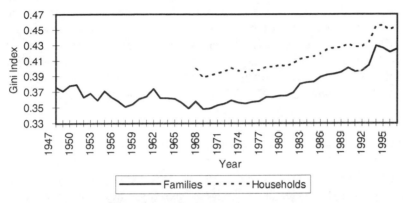

Source: U.S. Bureau of the Census, Annual Demographic Survey, CPS.

conflicted with other statistical series that measured incomes.[7] The series in question was one generated from BEA's National Income and Product Accounts and called real per capita personal income (related to it was the BEA's real per capita disposable personal income, an after-tax income measure). This series, which is based on administrative data and uses a more comprehensive income concept than in the CPS (as was pointed out in the previous chapter), rose at an average annual rate between 1975 and 1985 of 2.1 percent compared to 1.0 percent for average, or "mean" family income as measured by the CPS (real median family income, according to the CPS, increased by 0.5 percent a year and real median household income increased by only 0.4 percent).

Efforts were made to statistically reconcile the disparate growth rates and by and large they were successful, but the fact remained that one series was growing more than twice as fast as the other. Were Americans' real incomes rising or were they virtually standing still? An answer to this question was supplied by two economists who saw it as related to rising inequality. Frank Levy and Richard Michel believed that rising real per capita income in the 1970s and 1980s was largely fueled by more workers and not higher wages, which up until the 1970s had been the usual source of rising incomes.[8] Dramatic increases had occurred in the proportion of the population that worked during these years at the same time that wages began to stagnate. Young married wives entered the work force in the millions and many young persons born in the baby boom years of 1946 to 1964 were moving into the labor force. Levy and Michel went on to contrast this development with what had occurred in the 1950s when the source of income growth was rising wages and the proportion of the population that was working had remained constant. They summarized their argument by saying that the period between 1973 and 1984, when our major income measures were registering different developments, "revealed just how much of postwar society was predicated on the assumption of rising real wages."[9]

This digression into the divergent income trends of the CPS and BEA during the 1970s and 1980s and the Levy-Michel interpretation of it sets the stage for the following discussion of income inequality trends in the 1947–1973 and 1973–1996 periods.

1947 to 1973: Rapid Income Growth, Stable Income Inequality

For nearly thirty years after the end of WWII, U.S. incomes rose rapidly and the income distribution exhibited marked stability, suggesting that every family in the country was sharing in the income-producing capacity of the economy. The nation's income pie was getting bigger and everyone was helping themselves to a larger and larger piece of the pie. Simply by looking at the trend in real median family income in these years, one would have to conclude that these were the "golden years" with respect to income growth.

It was a period of time, however, that was not without its economic and social problems, as many of us can remember. Recessions punctuated the period, the Korean War and Vietnam War disrupted the lives of countless Americans, and the racial and cultural revolutions caused citizens to look inward as much as they caused them to look outward. As can also be seen in Figure 3.1, real family incomes faltered in the late 1940s, in 1954 and 1958, and then again in the late 1960s and early 1970s. (Income data for families rather than households are examined here because income data for households were not compiled by the Census Bureau until 1967.) But if one drew a line through all the years in that period, the income trend would point in only one direction: up!

Widespread Income Gains

But it wasn't only good news for the families with incomes at the median, or 50th percentile, of the distribution. Real incomes were advancing at all points of the income distribution. Table 3.1 shows real incomes for families (in 1996 dollars) at the 20th, 40th, 60th, 80th, and 95th percentiles of the family income distribution, as well as at the median, in 1947, 1957, 1967, and 1973. The average annual growth rates in family incomes between 1947 and 1957 suggest that the income distribution was narrowing because average annual growth was greater in the lower half of the distribution than at the very top. Family incomes were rising by 2.2 percent a year at the 20th

Table 3.1

Real Family Income at Various Percentiles of the Income Distribution, 1947, 1957, 1967, and 1973

Percentiles	1947	1957	1967	1973	Average Annual Growth Rates (in percent)		
					1947–57	1957–67	1967–73
20th	$10,270	$12,799	$17,760	$20,214	2.2	3.3	2.2
40th	16,572	21,781	29,154	33,355	2.7	2.9	2.2
60th	22,472	28,777	39,095	46,538	2.5	3.1	2.9
80th	31,886	38,608	53,597	64,000	1.9	3.3	3.0
95th	52,335	59,128	86,118	99,774	1.2	3.8	2.5
Median	19,651	25,546	34,289	40,059	2.6	2.9	2.6

Source: U.S. Bureau of the Census, Annual Demographic Survey, CPS.
Note: Real incomes in 1996 dollars.

percentile and 2.7 percent at the 40th, while at the 95th percentile incomes were rising by only 1.2 percent a year. In the 1957–1967 period, income growth speeded up, as reflected by the median, and the growth rates at all the percentiles over this ten-year period were higher than in the previous ten years. Indeed, real income growth near the very top of the distribution—the 95th percentile—was approaching 4.0 percent a year. This upward movement across the distribution continued on into the 1970s as well.

Because of the relative similarity of income growth among families of all income classes, relative dollar distances between them remained fairly constant over the 1947–1973 period. In 1947, as the country moved out of its wartime setting, incomes of families at the 50th percentile of the income distribution were almost twice as large as incomes of families at the 20th percentile and about 40 percent as large as incomes of families at the 95th percentile. As the country exited from the Vietnam War twenty-six years later, these income relationships were about the same. For the average family at the 50th percentile of the distribution some comfort could be taken in the fact that neither were the poor falling further behind nor were the rich running away from them.

The nation's economy had grown substantially in twenty-six years, propelled by ever-increasing labor productivity which translated into higher wages for the nation's workers. To use a popular expression made famous by President John F. Kennedy and now often found in the inequality literature (in either a positive or negative form), "a rising tide had lifted all boats." Economists pointed to a number of factors responsible for this post-

Table 3.2

Percentage of Income Received by Each Quintile of Families, 1947, 1957, 1967, and 1973

Quintile	1947	1957	1967	1973
Lowest	5.0	5.1	5.4	5.5
2nd	11.9	12.7	12.2	11.9
3rd	17.0	18.1	17.5	17.5
4th	23.1	23.8	23.5	24.0
Highest	43.0	40.4	41.4	41.1
Top 5%	17.5	15.6	16.4	15.5

Source: U.S. Bureau of the Census, Annual Demographic Survey, CPS.

WWII surge in productivity growth. The backlog of innovations built up during the depression of the 1930s and WWII finally came into public use, demilitarization unleashed a well-trained and experienced labor force ready to go to work for their own pursuits, and expanding markets both at home and abroad released a pent-up demand for goods of all kinds. The ingredients for rising incomes and long-term prosperity were in place: new technologies, a well-trained labor force, and sustained consumer demand.

The "Solid" Middle Class

Because of the widespread gains in real family incomes in these years, the idea of a constantly growing and prospering middle class became entrenched in the American psyche. Living conditions improved tremendously for almost everyone. New automobiles, new houses, and consumer durables like televisions, washing machines, refrigerators, and freezers became the hot ticket items. The formula for attaining the American Dream was simple: Get as much education as you can, work hard, and do the right things!

To gain some perspective on the solidity of the middle class in this period, one only has to think of the ever-growing size of the national income pie and the middle classes' "constant" share of it. The statistics are impressive. As shown in Table 3.2, if one assumes that middle-class families in America could be defined as those with incomes in the middle three quintiles (or 60 percent of all families) of the income distribution, then in 1947 these families received 52.0 percent of aggregate income. Twenty-six years later in 1973—approximately a generation—these three quintiles received 53.4 percent of aggregate income.

Upon a closer look at the data in the table, one could even make the case

Figure 3.3 **Changes in Family Income Inequality, 1947–1973** (Percent Change in Gini Index vs. 1968)

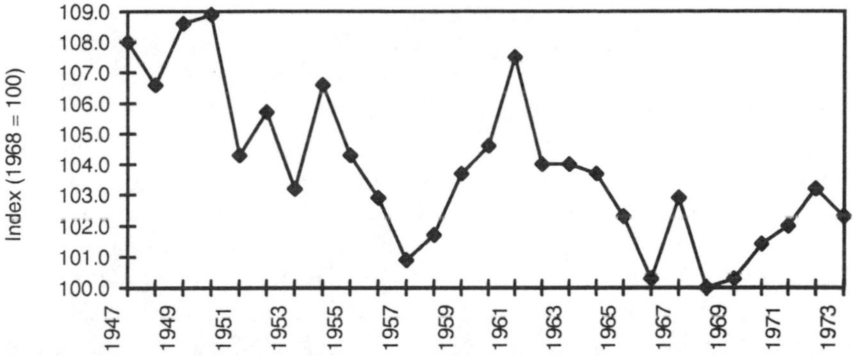

Source: U.S. Bureau of the Census, Annual Demographic Survey, CPS.

that the middle class as well as the lowest quintile had gained relative to the richest 5 percent of families. The latter's share of the aggregate income pie fell from 17.5 percent in 1947 to 15.5 percent by 1973, and three-quarters of this reduction was picked up by the middle three quintiles of families—the middle class—and one quarter was received by the lowest quintile of families.[10]

All of these statistics are suggestive of a very stable income distribution, one in which the level of inequality had not changed or, if anything, became a little less unequal. What do all these statistics mean when they are summarized into a single measure of income inequality?

The Inequality Trend . . . and Poverty

As we saw in Figure 3.2, the long-term trend in the Census Bureau's Gini index indicated that income inequality was fairly stable or possibly declining between 1947 and 1973. Indeed, the Gini index for the family income distribution in 1947 was .376 and by 1973 it was .356, indicative of a decline in inequality in the income distribution, no doubt brought about by the downward shift in income received by the top 5 percent of families.

The trend line in Figure 3.3 displays the trend differently. The Gini index is indexed equal to 100 in 1968—its lowest point in the second half of this century—and all subsequent readings are measured relative to it. The figure reveals that this summary index of inequality "bounced around" considerably in the 1947–1973 period, but the trend was downward.[11] Perhaps the largest variation occurred in the years between 1957 and 1966 when the index moved up from .351 in 1957 to .374 by 1961 and then moved down to .349 by 1966. The increase is associated with the slowdown in economic activity and the recessions of the late 1950s and early 1960s; the decrease is associated with the subsequent economic recovery of the mid-1960s. Initially, income shares for the lowest quintile declined from 5.1 percent of aggregate income in 1957 to 4.7 percent by 1961 while the share for the highest quintile of families rose from 40.4 to 42.2 percent; in the economic recovery, the income shares for these two groups returned to their approximate positions in 1957.

Movements in inequality such as these were the basis for economists' notion that changes in inequality were countercyclical, that is, as the economy slumped the incomes of the lower-income classes would be proportionally more affected than the upper-income classes and inequality would increase. On the other hand, as the economy recovered and prosperity resumed, income inequality would decline. Indeed, the income redistributive effects of business cycles, as proxied by the rate of poverty and rate of unemployment, have been estimated. For example, one estimate based on the experience of the 1950s through the 1970s indicated that for a one-percentage-point reduction in unemployment, the poverty rate would fall by one percentage point.[12]

By 1968 the Gini index for family incomes had reached its post-WWII low of .348—and it would never be that low again in this century. So, it could be said that between 1947 and 1968, inequality in America had dropped by almost 8.0 percent in terms of the change in the Gini index. In terms of relative income differences (another metric), while in 1947 the income of the family at the 95th percentile was 5.10 times as large as the income of the family at the 20th percentile, by 1968 the differential had fallen to 4.53 times as large.

It was during the early 1960s, of course, that national concern rose over poverty, which eventually led to President Johnson's much celebrated War on Poverty. It may appear odd today, with our concern over growing income inequality, that at a period of time when income inequality was near its post-WWII low such a crusade to wipe out poverty would be launched. However, what this most emphatically demonstrates is that inequality and poverty can be viewed as unique economic phenomenons.

The difference between both phenomenons can be illustrated with the use of a diagram provided by the economists Eugene Smolensky and Robert Plotnick and shown in Figure 3.4.[13] The figure contains two distributions at two periods in time and a hypothetical poverty line which divides the population into the poor and nonpoor. While the Gini index (or some other summary inequality measure) tells us how much inequality is contained in the distributions, the poverty rate (derived by dividing the poor by the sum of the poor and nonpoor) tells us the proportion of the population that is below the poverty line. In the figure, both distributions have the same

Figure 3.4 **The Poverty Rate and Inequality**

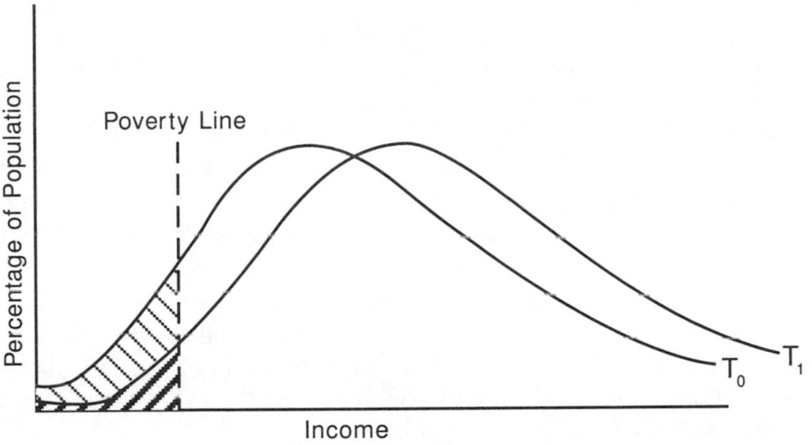

Source: Eugene Smolensky and Robert Plotnick, "Inequality and Poverty in the United States: 1900–1990," University of California, Berkeley, July 1992 (unpublished paper).

amount of inequality in them, but different poverty rates. Consequently, if the distribution kept moving further and further to the right while not changing its shape (its degree of inequality), the poverty rate would become smaller and smaller. (Of course, this relationship depends on the nature of the poverty measure. In this example, the poverty line was assumed to be an absolute measure, but it also could have been defined in terms of a relative measure, for example, some fraction of the median income.)

One might jump to the conclusion that this is what happened between 1947 and 1973 but poverty data for the entire period is unavailable. It is known that between 1959 and 1973, the poverty rate in the nation was cut in half (from 22.4 to 11.1 percent), while the Gini index went from .361 to .356—a very small change. In other words, the situation depicted in Figure 3.4 was probably prevailing over this period of time, and most likely earlier.

What all this illustrates is this: concern over income inequality reflects the social judgments of the day. Income inequality by all measures was very low in the 1960s (and especially by today's levels), yet a groundswell of popular support for eradicating poverty arose.

In part, this concern about poverty was fueled by rising unemployment associated with the recessions of the late 1950s and early 1960s along with the discovery (by some popular journalists) of pockets of poverty in urban and rural America.[14] In other words, although real incomes for Americans had increased smartly, some had been left behind and "the rising tide had not lifted all boats," even then. Again, the perception of a maldistribution of income had come into being at a time when measured income inequality was approaching its post-WWII low (perhaps its century low). The topic of poverty, and its relationship to income inequality, will be further examined in this chapter.

The history of the late 1960s and early 1970s, of course, is well known. These were times of turmoil across society, both because of what was going on at home as well as abroad. Many people don't want to look back at these years. From the standpoint of economic developments in this country, however, and especially with respect to developments in the nation's income distribution, these years must be looked at for they represent a watershed. Significant economic changes were about to take place that would have implications for changes in the income distribution that economists are still trying to understand. Not only would the war in Vietnam come to an end and not only would President Nixon resign and not only would we be standing in gas lines, but the growth in productivity, wages, and incomes that most Americans had become accustomed to—and shared—would slow dramatically.

1973 to 1996: Slow Income Growth, Rising Inequality

The story of growing income and wage inequality in the United States since the early 1970s has been the topic of countless articles, books, television and radio documentaries, and so on. Less than twenty years ago, one would have been hard-pressed to find any discussion of this topic in the popular media, or in the economics journals, for that matter.[15] Today, while interest in the topic has waned to some extent because of the sustained economic expansion since the early 1990s, the topic of inequality still lingers on the minds of many, especially when the multimillion-dollar salaries of CEOs or Wall Street bankers are mentioned or when we hear about a downsizing, a plant closing, or a plant relocation to another part of the country or another nation. These are some of the aspects of today's rhetoric over growing income inequality that can strike a nerve in the average American.

In this section, not only the trends in income inequality between 1973 and 1996 will be presented, but also what "growing income inequality" means today or, in other words, what are the social judgments surrounding the perception of income differences. As was shown in the previous section, in the early 1960s the existence of poverty amidst a generally prosperous nation led to significant changes in social policies directed at families with low incomes. Today's perceptions of growing income differences have led to certain social judgments as well. There is a concern about the middle class and their children. Both political parties in mid-1997 fought over the nature of a tax-cut bill aimed at families with children as well as tax reductions on capital gains. These debates have all grown out of the perception in the early 1990s that something profound had happened to the income distribution over the past couple of decades and that as some families and households were enjoying the fruits of their hours in the labor market others were not. Passage in 1996 of the legislation leading to a higher federal minimum wage, for example, was a response to reported changes in the income distribution and what the nation's citizens and legislators perceived to be remedies.

Unlike the review of income inequality trends in the 1947–1973 period that focused on the situation for families, in this section we will examine trends for both families and households, but with more emphasis on households. The income data for households, which includes incomes of families and persons living in other social arrangements, first became available in 1967. Around that time, the Census Bureau fully recognized that the traditional four-person, Ozzie and Harriet–type family of the 1950s was becoming passé. Sweeping changes were taking place in America's social and demographic setting. For example, the baby boom generation was maturing and marrying much later than previous generations, divorces, marital separations, and children born out of wedlock were becoming more common, and the aging of the population were all producing a variety of living arrangements that differed radically from the typical family model of the 1950s. These changes, of course, have continued to diminish the significance of the family as the only unit for income inequality analysis.

In addition to examining the trends for both families and households in this section, income distributions will be examined that have been adjusted for the payment of certain taxes and receipt of certain noncash payments. The Census Bureau, in the 1980s, developed experimental income distributions to analyze the impact of the government's tax and income transfer programs. Finally, income-to-poverty ratios for families and households in the quintiles of the distribution will be examined to see how they have changed in recent years. In effect, these ratios adjust the income distribution for family and household size differences and the assumed economies of scale arising from multiperson households.

It Started in the Seventies

With the advantage of twenty-five years of hindsight, one can now see that the seeds of growing income inequality were sown in the 1970s.[16] After 1973, income growth for families and households began to stagnate, reflecting the recession of 1974, which was particularly severe, and the slowdown in wage growth. Figure 3.1 shows that for both families and households, real median incomes peaked in 1973, the former at $40,059 and the latter at $34,943 (in 1996 dollars). It would not be until the end of that decade that

Table 3.3

Real Household Income at Various Percentiles of the Income Distribution, 1973, 1979, and 1989

Percentile	1973	1979	1989	Average Annual Rate of Change (in percent) 1973–79	1979–89
20th	$14,686	$14,861	$15,305	0.2	0.3
40th	27,900	27,638	29,102	–0.2	0.5
60th	41,386	42,458	44,729	0.4	0.5
80th	59,785	61,693	67,960	0.5	1.0
95th	94,768	100,639	116,093	1.0	1.4
Median	34,943	34,902	36,575	–0.02	0.5

Source: U.S. Bureau of the Census, Annual Demographic Survey, CPS.
Note: Real incomes in 1996 dollars.

family and household income would reach and surpass those levels. Real average income growth had been sharply curtailed.

Even more disturbing was how incomes were changing across the distribution. In the 1947–1973 period, real incomes at the 20th, 40th, 60th, 80th, and 95th percentiles of the family income distribution were growing similarly, but after 1973 this pattern changed. As shown in Table 3.3, between 1973 and 1979 the average annual growth rate for households at the 20th percentile was a paltry 0.2 percent a year, and for those at the 40th percentile real incomes were declining by that much a year. At the upper end of the income distribution, incomes had also slowed relative to the 1960s and early 1970s, but they were still rising. At the 95th percentile, for example, real incomes were growing at an average annual rate of 1.0 percent a year.[17]

These differential rates of income growth did not attract much attention at that time; rather what did receive attention was the slowdown, indeed stagnation, in average household incomes. As some may recall, during this period the economic problems confronting the country were weak economic growth, relatively high unemployment, and persistent inflation, all topped off by plummeting productivity growth. The oil shortage of 1973–74 (and the resulting price increases) was one of the events that is often pointed to for explaining the slowdown in productivity growth as is the influx of baby boomers and women into the labor force (both with little work experience), and the establishment of more government regulations that impeded efficient business operations. But the definitive explanation for the slowdown in productivity growth in the 1970s has yet to be agreed upon.

Table 3.4

Percentage of Income Received by Each Quintile of Households, Selected Years

Quintile	1973	1979	1989	1992	1993	1996
Lowest	4.2	4.2	3.8	3.8	3.6	3.7
2nd	10.5	10.3	9.5	9.4	9.0	9.0
3rd	17.1	16.9	15.8	15.8	15.1	15.1
4th	24.6	24.7	24.0	24.2	23.5	23.3
Highest	43.6	44.0	46.8	46.9	48.9	49.0
Top 5%	16.6	16.4	18.9	18.6	21.0	21.4

Source: U.S. Bureau of the Census, Annual Demographic Survey, CPS.

While attention then was focused on the sluggishness of average income growth, changes were beginning to be seen in the shares of aggregate income received by the quintiles of the distribution and to some extent the Gini index. Table 3.4 displays the shares for the 1973–1979 period. A very slight decline in income shares can be seen for the 2nd and 3rd quintiles. The Gini index on the other hand, as is shown in Figure 3.2, increased from .397 to .404, a modest increase of 1.8 percent but indeed an increase and a precursor of what was ahead.

Growing Income Inequality Accelerates

The next ten years—1979 to 1989—was the period in which a major shift in the income distribution occurred. It began with the recessions of the 1980–1982 period in which both inflation and unemployment swept the nation and millions of jobs were lost.[18] Inflation, according to the Consumer Price Index for Urban Consumers (CPI-U) of the Bureau of Labor Statistics (BLS), increased by 10.3 percent between 1980 and 1981 and by 6.2 percent between 1981 and 1982, while monthly unemployment, according to BLS, averaged 7.1 percent in 1980 and by 1983 was even higher at 9.6 percent. Between 1980 and 1982, the number of jobs in the manufacturing industry shrank from a level of 20.3 million to 18.8 million and many of these jobs were lost forever.

The impact of these economic events on family and household incomes was immense and lasted for several years. Real median family income plunged from $41,530 in 1979 to $38,459 in 1982 and real median household income fell from $34,902 to $33,105 over the same period. But the pain of these recessions was not being felt the same by everyone. Incomes

Figure 3.5 **Changes in Real Household Incomes at Various Percentiles of the Distribution, 1979–1987**

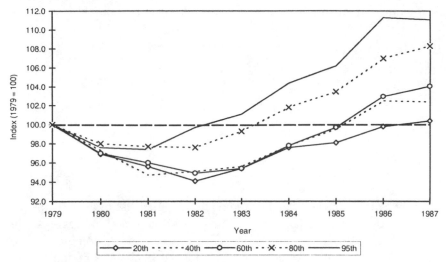

Source: U.S. Bureau of the Census, Annual Demographic Survey, CPS.
Note: Real income is in 1996 dollars.

among households at the 20th percentile, for example, were down by 5.9 percent between 1979 and 1982 (in real terms) but only 2.4 percent for households with incomes at the 80th percentile.

The differential impact of the recessions and the ensuing economic recovery on household incomes located at different percentiles of the income distribution can be seen in Figure 3.5. Real incomes at the 20th, 40th, 60th, 80th, and 95th percentiles in 1979 have been indexed to 100.0 and then real incomes in the 1980–1987 period have been converted to the index and plotted. Clearly, the impact of the recession was greatest—in terms of real income decline—on those who had incomes at the 20th percentile. And the economic recovery also had its weakest effect on those at the 20th percentile since it took until 1987 for their incomes to return to the level experienced in 1979. By way of contrast, households whose incomes were at the 95th percentile or 80th percentile declined less and recovered quicker. Their incomes slumped by at most about 2.5 percent and they had regained their 1979 income levels by 1983 (the 95th) and 1984 (the 80th). In other words, households at the upper end of the income distribution led the way out of the recessions and into the economic expansion of the 1980s.

The economic recovery of the 1980s had put a lid on inflation, cut unemployment rolls, and created millions of new jobs. By 1987 inflation had come down to a 3.6 percent annual rate, the nation's unemployment rate was dropping and averaged only 6.1 percent, and since 1982 12.6 million nonfarm payroll jobs had been added to the economy. But it was becoming increasingly apparent that the economic recovery had been uneven with respect to who was sharing in the renewed prosperity. One indication of this was the relatively small number of manufacturing jobs that had been added to employers' payrolls. Between 1982 and 1987 only 243,000 manufacturing jobs had been created. Another, of course, was how the shares of income received by quintiles of the distribution were changing during those years.

In attempting to understand why the economic expansion of the 1980s had such an uneven impact on incomes across the income distribution, the economists Rebecca Blank and David Card have offered a plausible explanation.[19] They suggested that the failure of rapid economic growth to lead to rising incomes in all segments of the income distribution might be explained by developments in the labor market as well as trends in family composition. As is well known, productivity growth during this period continued to be low relative to the pre-1973 level and wage growth was meager. At the same time, growing inequality in the wage distribution was occurring. These factors, when combined with differential changes taking place in the composition of households across the quintiles of the income distribution (i.e., the growing proportion of single-parent families and declining proportion of married-couple families), meant that the effects of economic growth would be shared differentially. This connection between growing wage inequality, changing household composition, and rising income inequality will be further discussed in a subsequent chapter.

Economic growth continued until the end of the 1980s when real median household income reached its highest level in 1989 ($36,575) since the series began in 1967 and real median family income reached its highest level ($43,290) since 1947. But signs that the expansion was coming to an end were beginning to appear. Growth in real gross domestic product slowed in 1989 and 1990 and at the same time the annual reductions in the nation's unemployment rate dried up.

Many households were simply fortunate to have household members whose skills and backgrounds were exactly what their employers required to remain competitive in both national and world markets. For them, the choices they had made in terms of jobs and educations, as well as the determination and hard work to improve themselves economically, paid off handsomely in the 1980s. For many others, the decade of the 1980s was like trying to walk up an escalator that was moving downward. Unwanted skills, poor educations, and, in some cases, bad attitudes, all led to low-paying jobs; for others, more hours in the work place only meant holding onto the economic lifestyle they had at the end of the 1970s.

The resulting shift in the income distribution and growth in inequality in the 1980s was, by standards of the 1960s and 1970s, monumental. As shown in Table 3.4, between 1979 and 1989 the share of aggregate money income accruing to the highest quintile had indeed increased while it decreased in all the other quintiles. Those in the highest income quintile saw their share increase from 44.0 percent to 46.8 percent, and most of that was experienced by the richest 5 percent of households in the distribution. The largest reduction in income shares was experienced by households in the third quintile where the share reduction was from 16.9 percent to 15.8 percent. In 1989, these were households with annual incomes (in 1996 real dollars) of between roughly $29,000 and $45,000—certainly what many Americans would consider to be middle-class incomes. In ten years the Gini index for households rose from .404 to .431, an increase of 6.7 percent.[20] While the relative income distance in 1989 between the 20th percentile ($15,305) of the household income distribution and the median ($36,575) had increased a little since 1979 (239 percent vs. 235 percent), the distance in 1989 between the median ($36,575) and the 95th percentile ($116,093) had widened considerably (317 percent vs. 288 percent).

The 1990s: Recession, Recovery . . . Stability?

Developments in the income inequality story in the 1990s are somewhat more difficult to relate. Methodological changes were made in the CPS by the Census Bureau beginning with the income data for 1993 (or the March 1994 CPS), which will be spelled out below.

As the economy slipped into the recession of 1990–91, plant closures, downsizings, and reduced work weeks seriously crimped the economic lifestyles of Americans, many from the middle and lower ranks of the income distribution who already had not shared the economic benefits of the 1980s. Unemployment increased to 6.7 percent in 1991 and then to 7.4 percent of the work force by 1992. Job growth, spectacular in the 1980s, shriveled. But this recession was also slightly different from the previous. Media reports of widespread layoffs of white-collar workers and middle managers from the United States's largest corporations now were beginning to unsettle families and households further up in the higher ranks of the income distribution. The federal government's BLS corroborated these reports that the recession was having an unusually harsh impact on the white-collar labor force.[21]

The median household income (in 1996 dollars) fell from $36,575 in 1989 to $34,261 by 1992, or 6.3 percent. Incomes in the first year—1989–1990—collapsed across the income distribution (see Figure 3.6), as they had in the 1980–82 recession. Unlike that period, however, the income decline continued at a significant rate into the next year, 1991, and the next year,

Figure 3.6 **Changes in Real Household Incomes at Various Percentiles of the Distribution, 1989–1996**

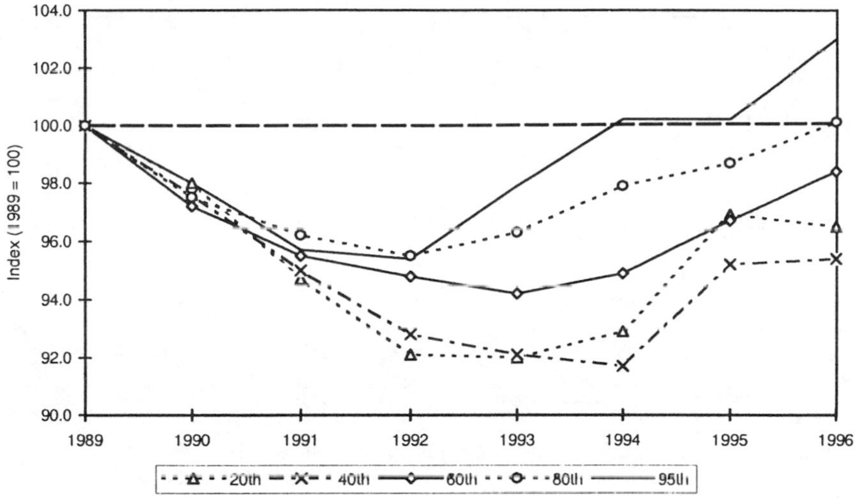

Source: U.S. Bureau of the Census, Annual Demographic Survey, CPS.
Note: Real income is in 1996 dollars.

1992, even for those households at the 80th and 95th percentiles of the income distribution. Indeed, by 1992, real incomes at the 80th percentile had fallen 4.5 percent, and at the 95th percentile by 4.6 percent. These declines were much more severe than in the 1980–1982 period reflecting the greater impact of the recession on the upper part of the income distribution.

Also reflecting a somewhat different recessionary impact on households at the high end of the income distribution was what was happening (or not happening) to the income shares of the various quintiles in the distribution as well as to the Gini index. It was during the 1980–82 recession that shifts were beginning to take place in income shares reflecting growing income inequality. In the 1990–91 recession by way of contrast, little change occurred on the inequality front, reflecting the more severe impact of the recession on upper-income households. As shown in Table 3.4, between 1989 and 1992 shares were virtually unchanged, except for a slight decline among the richest 5 percent of households. Their share of aggregate income slipped slightly from 18.9 percent to 18.6 percent. In consequence, the Gini index, which was .431 in 1989, moved slightly downward to .428 in 1990 and 1991—the heart of the recession—and then up to .434 in 1992.[22] In the previous recession of the early 1980s, the Gini index moved from .404 in 1979 to .403 in 1980, .406 in 1981, and .412 in 1982. The pattern of changes in the Gini index for households during these two periods can be compared in Figure 3.7.

Figure 3.7 **Change in Household Income Inequality, 1979–1982 and 1989–1992** (Percent Change in Gini Index, 1979 and 1989 = 100)

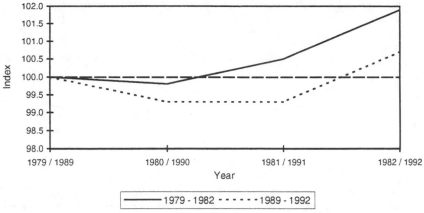

Source: U.S. Bureau of the Census, Annual Demographic Survey, CPS.

So, income inequality, which had accelerated through most of the 1980s, slowed in the early 1990s largely because of the unusually strong impact on incomes at the upper end of the income distribution brought on by the recession. Ironically, this slowdown was not the kind President Bush re-quired for his re-election bid. The news accounts of rising income inequality in the past represented the tinder for the sparks of growing unemployment, falling wages, and other maladies of a weakened job market.

Changes in the CPS

Between 1992 and 1993 when the economy was slowly recovering from the recession, methodological and operational changes were made in the CPS, clouding developments with respect to income inequality. Such changes in the CPS are not new, of course, and the major ones that have taken place since 1947 are briefly discussed in Appendix B. Presumably, all these changes repre-sent improvements in the quality of the data obtained through the CPS. One fact is certain, however; methodological and operational changes can result in statistical estimates that are different from the ones that would have been derived had no changes been made. The following describes changes that were made to the operation of the CPS, with particular emphasis on changes in the Annual Demographic Survey which is the source of the CPS income estimates.

During the 1980s and early 1990s, the BLS, with the help of the Census Bureau, was engaged in an effort to modernize and improve the monthly CPS, that is, the part of the survey in which employment, unemployment, and other labor market information is collected. The focus of the improvements was on redesigning the monthly labor force questionnaire and introducing a system known as computer-assisted survey information collection (CASIC). Beginning in January 1994, this redesigned monthly CPS was put into operation.

The redesign had implications for the Annual Demographic Survey conducted every March. Although the questionnaire used to obtain the income information (as well as the previous year's work experience information) was not changed from those of earlier years, the new CASIC system was used. This technology replaced the traditional pencil-to-paper transcription of survey respondents' answers. In that procedure, the Monthly Labor Force questionnaire (containing the labor force questions for March) and then the Annual Demographic Survey questionnaire (containing the income and work experience questions for the previous year) were filled out by the enumerator. In the CASIC system, in contrast, all the questions are administered from a computer (either from a laptop at the household or from a computer located in a centralized telephoning facility) as if only one questionnaire is in use. Unlike the past when CPS interviewers had to physically shift from the labor force questionnaire to the income and work experience questionnaire, the mechanics of CASIC avoided any significant interruption of the interview process.

Two other technical changes occurred in the March 1994 CPS that could have affected income data and the measurement of income inequality. First, and as happens after every decennial census of the population, data from Census Bureau surveys are reweighted according to estimates of the civilian noninstitutional population derived from the most recent decennial census. The CPS income data for 1993 reflected the new weights from the 1990 census, which were also adjusted for the notorious "undercount" of the population (i.e., for various reasons, some persons in the population were not counted at the time of the decennial census). The second change involved the top codes or upper-income limits used in the Annual Demographic Survey. As was discussed in Chapter 2, these top codes are occasionally increased to reflect rising nominal incomes and an increase occurred in these top codes between the March 1993 and March 1994 surveys. The most important top code that was increased related to the earnings of workers from their longest jobs or businesses. This was increased from $299,999 to $999,999, so the income data collected in 1992 was "capped" at the $300,000 level while that collected in 1993 was capped at $1,000,000. The last time such a change was made was between the March 1985 and March 1986 surveys when this top code was increased from $99,999 to $299,999.

An Interpretation

What were the effects of these changes on the 1993 income data and on income inequality? Before that question is answered it is useful to look at the changes in real median household and family incomes between 1992 and 1993 back in Figure 3.1 and the changes in the Gini indexes between 1992 and 1993 back in Figure 3.2.

While the income changes appeared to continue downward both for households and families, inequality according to the Gini index had surged! Real median incomes in 1993 for households and families hit their lowest points since the mid-1980s—$33,922 for households and $40,131 for families, respectively. The Gini index for households jumped from .434 in 1992 to .454 in 1993, an increase of 4.6 percent, the largest one-year increase on record, while the Gini index for families also surged from .404 to .429, an increase of 6.2 percent, the largest on record.

One Census Bureau economist who examined the effects of the changes in the CPS on the household income and income inequality estimates for 1992 and 1993 found that the reweighting of the estimates on the basis of the 1990 decennial census had little effect on estimates of income and income inequality, but that the increase in the top codes did.[23] If the new top codes had not been used, the Gini index for households in 1993 would have been only .447 instead of .454. In other words, the percentage increase in inequality according to the Gini index would have been only about 3.0 percent instead of the actual 4.6 percent, so that the change in top codes alone accounted for about one-third of the increase in the Gini index. Further analysis of the data for 1992 and 1993 by other Census Bureau economists corroborated this finding and they speculated about the effect on inequality of the shift from the pencil-and-paper method of conducting the survey questions to the CASIC procedures. They suggested that with the increase in top codes *and* the introduction of CASIC, the combined effect of the two could have accounted for more than one-half of the 4.6-percentage-point increase in inequality.[24] This means that the Gini index probably would have increased by at least 2.3 percent or from .434 in 1992 to .444 in 1993. Even so, this increase too would have been the largest one-year increase in inequality that has been recorded since the series began.

Suffice it to say that the changes in income inequality between 1992 and 1993 are difficult, at best, to interpret. No doubt there was an increase in inequality but there is also no doubt that the increase—which was gigantic relative to past changes—was overstated. Consequently, care must be taken when examining changes in the shares of income received by each quintile of the distribution as well as changes in the real incomes at the upper percentiles of the income distribution. For example, between 1992 and 1993 the share of income going to the richest 5 percent of households increased from 18.6 percent to 21.0 percent (Table 3.4)—an unprecedented, and almost unbelievable, increase.[25]

So to explain the sizable, but seemingly unquantifiable, increase in inequality between 1992 and 1993, one is left with what was happening in the economy in those years. As we know, unemployment was falling, and although job growth was sluggish for a while, it was beginning again. One analysis of this period suggests that the employment growth that was occurring was at both the bottom end and top end of the earnings distribution.[26] The large numbers of highly paid workers in middle management jobs of corporate America who lost jobs in the 1990–91 recession were finding their way back into the workforce, and some of them, at least, at fairly good pay levels. At the same time, the pattern of employment growth in low-paying jobs also resumed. Together, these two labor force developments probably resulted in a temporary spurt (if not surge) in income inequality—but exactly how much is still a matter of speculation. As was the case in the recovery from the recessions of the 1980–1982 period, it was the households from the upper end of the income distribution whose incomes recovered the fastest. But the difference with the recession of the early 1990s was that because the incomes of the households at the far end of the distribution had fallen so much in this recession, when they recovered to their previous levels they had to increase so much more. This represented the "extra" energy for the increase in inequality between 1992 and 1993. While this is speculative due to the above-mentioned changes in the CPS, there is some evidence that inequality was on the rise in the 1991–1992 period, before the CPS methodological changes took place. Both the share of income received by the top 5 percent in the income distribution increased (from 18.1 to 18.6 percent) as did the overall Gini index (from .428 to .434).

Between 1993 and 1996 (years in which the CPS was conducted without any major methodological changes), the income distribution appeared to stabilize again—but this time, as the economy was expanding. As shown in Table 3.4, the shares of aggregate income received by the quintiles of the household income distribution changed very little over these years. Recall that during the end of the 1980s and early 1990s—the period in which the economy was contracting—the Gini index for the distribution had changed very little as well (this theme of income distribution stabilization will be returned to later).

One of the statistical explanations for the apparent leveling off in inequality between 1993 and 1996 was the pattern of income growth across the income distribution. As can be seen in Table 3.5, income growth at the

Table 3.5

Real Household Income at Various Percentiles of the Income Distribution, 1993–1996

Percentile	1993	1996	Average Annual Percent Change
20th	$14,080	$14,768	1.6
40th	26,797	27,760	1.2
60th	42,122	44,006	1.5
80th	65,475	68,015	1.3
95th	113,618	119,540	1.7
Median	33,922	35,492	1.5

Source: U.S. Bureau of the Census, Annual Demographic Survey, CPS.
Note: Real income is in 1996 dollars.

bottom of the distribution was about as fast as at the top, a reversal of what had been the experience before the 1990s. While real incomes at the median were rising by 1.5 percent a year, they were rising by 1.6 percent a year at the 20th percentile and 1.7 percent at the 95th percentile. The Gini index was virtually unchanged—.454 in 1993 and .455 in 1996.

Despite this apparent halt in growing income inequality, the general public, after having just gone through a period of economic sluggishness when incomes had dropped and job security was on their minds, remained uneasy about growing income differences in America. Continued news reports about the compensation packages of CEOs, the downsizings, and corporate restructurings only piqued their interest in "inequality" stories. And, of course, the Census Bureau data were there to dramatize the change that occurred in the country's income distribution in just one generation. While middle-income households had seen their real annual incomes rise by only $550 between 1973 and 1996 (from $34,943 to $35,492), the households at the 95th percentile had experienced almost a $25,000 increase (from $94,768 to $119,540). So it didn't matter whether inequality had leveled off or not.

But the 1993 to 1996 stability in the income distribution is not something to ignore. Indeed, it may be a sign of things to come. If one looks closely at the trend in income inequality since the late 1980s to the mid-1990s, and ignores the change that took place between 1992 and 1993, the trend is remarkably flat. As shown in Figure 3.2, the Gini index for households rose from .427 in 1988 to .434 in 1992, or just 1.6 percent, while between 1993 and 1996, the Gini index was little changed. Consequently, although income inequality has increased over the long run, the rate of increase may be slowing down.[27]

Table 3.6

**Average Family Income-to-Poverty Ratio by Income Quintiles,
Selected Years**

Quintile	1973	1979	1989	1992	1993	1996
Lowest	1.12	1.11	1.01	0.89	0.88	0.96
2nd	2.27	2.28	2.30	2.15	2.10	2.22
3rd	3.15	3.25	3.43	3.26	3.19	3.37
4th	4.19	4.38	4.79	4.55	4.60	4.78
Highest	6.99	7.18	8.90	8.39	9.07	9.55
Gini Index	0.356	0.365	0.401	0.404	0.429	0.425

Source: U.S. Bureau of the Census, Annual Demographic Survey, CPS.

Adjusting Incomes for Differences in Family Size

Many of the analyses of growing dispersion in the income distribution are based on family or household income statistics that have been adjusted for the number of members in the income recipient unit. The Census Bureau does not make any direct adjustment for family and household size differences to their income estimates. They do, however, publish a statistical series which shows the average income-to-poverty ratio for families by income quintile that makes an "implicit" adjustment for family size changes because the federal government's poverty thresholds are embodied in the statistic.

The average income-to-poverty ratios are computed by dividing the mean income of families in each quintile of the distribution by the poverty thresholds that would apply to the families and then averaging the ratios in that quintile.[28] The following is an example of what the average income-to-poverty ratio means. In 1996, the income-to-poverty ratio for a four-person family with two related children under 18 and an annual money income of $55,000 would be 3.46, since the poverty threshold for this family in 1996 was $15,911. If family income had increased by almost $10,000 because of the husband's pay raise and at the same time the family had another child, the income-to-poverty ratio would have remained approximately the same because not only did income go up, but the poverty threshold went up as well (to $18,725). If a child had not arrived, the ratio would have been 4.09, and if the pay raise had not occurred but the new child had arrived, the ratio would have fallen to 2.94. As with all equivalence scales of this kind, judgments must be made about the value of additional family members.

Table 3.6 displays the movement of the average income-to-poverty ratios in the quintiles of the family income distribution for selected years between

1973 and 1996. Between 1973 and 1979, the ratios in the lowest and second highest quintiles of the family income distribution were unchanged while in the next three quintiles there was some increase. These changes are indicative of growing inequality. In the 1979–1989 period, the ratios in the top three quintiles continued to rise (with particularly sharp increases in the fourth and fifth quintiles), while the ratio in the lowest quintile fell. This is consistent with an acceleration in income inequality. From 1989 to 1992, income-to-poverty ratios dropped across the quintiles (with the largest drop in the lowest quintile) and from 1993 to 1996 the ratios rose (with the largest relative increase occurring in the bottom quintile). These changes are fairly consistent with how the Gini index for families (unadjusted for changes in family sizes) recorded rising inequality in the 1973–1996 period.

Adjusting Incomes for Taxes and Transfers

In recent years, the Census Bureau has published experimental measures of the income distribution based on fourteen different definitions of income.[29] Basically, what these measures represent are statistical simulations of income distributions that reflect adjustments for certain taxes paid by families and households as well as their receipt of government transfers and other noncash benefits. These taxes and transfers have not been taken into account in the official statistics even though it is well known that they affect income levels and the shape of the income distribution. Consequently, these experimental distributions are an attempt by the Census Bureau to develop a more comprehensive distribution of income.

By the use of various statistical techniques, three kinds of taxes are deducted from official household income statistics collected in the CPS. These are federal individual income taxes, state individual income taxes, and payroll taxes. Cash values are also estimated for various noncash benefits received by certain households, such as food stamps, school lunches, housing subsidies, Medicare, Medicaid, employer contributions for health insurance, and the net imputed return on the equity in owner-occupied houses.[30]

The Census Bureau's research in this area has shown that the official distribution of income would be more equal under a broader definition of income. Table 3.7 contains the Gini indexes and the income shares of the quintiles for five of the fourteen simulated income distributions as of 1996. Definition 1 shows the Gini index and income shares for the official distribution of income (the Gini index and shares are slightly different from that shown elsewhere because the Census Bureau computes these estimates from grouped data which is statistically more efficient to do so when dealing with multiple-income distributions).

Table 3.7

Percentage of Income Received by Household Quintiles and Gini Index by Experimental Definition of Income, 1996

	Lowest	Middle 3 Quintiles	Highest	Gini Index
Definition 1	3.7	47.3	49.0	0.447
Definition 4	0.9	45.7	53.4	0.511
Definition 8	1.2	48.7	50.1	0.483
Definition 11	3.9	50.2	45.9	0.416
Definition 14	4.9	50.1	45.0	0.398
Definition 15	5.1	50.3	44.6	0.392

Source: U.S. Bureau of the Census, Annual Demographic Survey, CPS.
Note: Def.   1—Official definition.
        Def.   4—Def. 1 less government cash transfers plus capital gains and employee
                health benefits.
        Def.   8—Def. 4 less taxes.
        Def. 11—Def. 8 plus nonmeans-tested government cash transfers.
        Def. 14—Def. 11 plus means-tested government cash transfers.
        Def. 15—Def. 14 plus return on home equity.

Inequality rises sharply once government cash transfer payments (both means- and nonmeans-tested) are eliminated and capital gains and employee health benefits are added to the official distribution as is shown in income definition 4.[31] The cash transfers that are eliminated include Social Security payments, unemployment compensation, Aid to Families with Dependent Children, and Supplementary Security Income. Capital gains are included in the definition plus health insurance payments made by employers. The share of income going to the richest quintile rises from 49.0 percent to 53.4 percent and the Gini index in 1996 rises from .447 to .511. This distribution, presumably, would be similar to the income distribution generated by the private sector of the economy alone.

The effect of taxes on the income distribution is shown in income definition 8. Clearly, inequality falls, as measured by the Gini index, reflecting the redistributive effect of the income taxes. But as definition 11 shows, the effect on inequality is much greater when certain nonmeans-tested cash transfer payments are added back into the distribution. These transfers include some of the ones previously taken out—Social Security, unemployment insurance, and workers' compensation. Inequality falls from .483 to .416, and the shares of income going to the lower part of the distribution increases.

Inequality drops further with the addition to the income distribution of means-tested cash and noncash benefits such as Aid to Families with De-

Figure 3.8 **Gini Index for Households Based on Experimental Income Definition 15 and the Official Income Definition, 1979–1996**

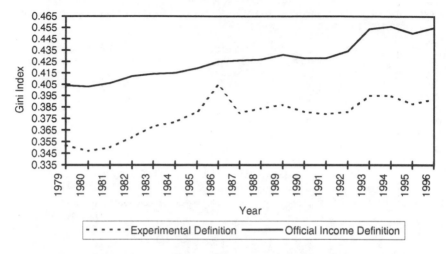

Source: U.S. Bureau of the Census, Annual Demographic Survey, CPS.

pendent Children, Supplementary Security Income, Medicaid, food stamps, rent subsidies, and free or reduced-price school lunches. The share of income going to the lowest quintile rises from 3.9 to 4.9 percent and the Gini index drops somewhat more to .398. And the last definition of income, definition 15, includes the net imputed value of one's equity in their house, which reduces the Gini index somewhat further to .392. As can be seen in Table 3.7, therefore, as the income definition becomes broader, shares of aggregate income shift from the highest income quintile to the lower quintiles.

The experimental distributions of the Census Bureau have been helpful in understanding the nature of the tax and transfer policy of the government. Indeed, they demonstrate that government transfers have a much greater redistributive impact than the tax system.[32] The obvious question is, how did these experimental distributions track the rise in inequality since the late 1970s? The answer to that question can be seen in Figure 3.8, which shows the trend in the Gini index for the most comprehensive income distribution series. It is obvious from the figure that the trend is very similar to the trend which is based on incomes before tax and transfer payments. As Daniel Weinberg of the Census Bureau recently concluded in speaking of the trend in inequality between 1979 and 1994 (as measured by one of its broadest definitions), "this alternative perspective does not change the picture of increasing income inequality over the 1979–1994 period."[33]

Trends in Other Indicators

For many Americans, income inequality is such an elusive concept that it has many different meanings and manifestations to them. In this section of the chapter, we examine some of the statistical indicators often associated with these concerns which are thought to be related to rising income inequality. Some of them, as will be shown, have a more direct relationship than others.

Middle-Class Worries

The middle class has become the topic of much attention in recent years because of the perception that the middle class in the United States is "not so solid" as it once was. Indeed, at the heart of the debate over the tax cut in Washington in the summer of 1997 was how to provide tax relief to the middle class. And a few years earlier during the Presidential elections we heard the constant refrain that the middle class was working harder only to stay in place.

As was shown in Chapter 1, the middle of the household income distribution, that is, households with incomes between $25,000 and $99,999 (in 1996 dollars), has not grown as rapidly as it had in earlier years. In addition, the experience during the early 1990s was particularly traumatic on this portion of the income distribution. In 1989, before the recession of the early 1990s, 58.1 percent of all households had incomes of between $25,000 and $99,999 (in 1996 dollars). Five years later in 1994 the proportion was down to 55.1 percent. This relative decline in the proportion of households in this income range, brought about by the business downturn in the early 1990s, translated into a very meager net increase of households in this income range—just over 300,000.

What happened, of course, was that many households from the middle of the income distribution moved down into the lowest income category of less than $25,000 a year. The proportion of households in this income category between 1989 and 1994 rose from 34.2 percent to 37.2 percent, an actual increase of 4.9 million households (the proportion above $100,000 was unchanged at 7.7 percent). These statistics were shown in Figure 1.4 of Chapter 1.

Growth in the proportion of households in the middle-income range of from $25,000 to $99,999 started to pick up in 1995 and 1996 (a net increase of 2.2 million households since 1994). But for households in this income range during the 1989–1994 period, growing income inequality immediately translated into the possible threat of slipping out of the middle class. Concerns over job loss from plant closings and downsizings, the loss of health insurance coverage, and, at best, the eventual employment in a low-wage job were what headlines about growing income inequality meant to them.

For these reasons, many of the statistics appearing in the media relating to the labor market—such as those below—have had particular relevance to the middle class (others, like unemployment, are discussed later).

Job Displacement

After the recessions in the early 1980s the federal government began to collect data on persons who reported they had lost or left jobs because of a plant closing, an employer going out of business, a layoff from which they were not recalled, or other similar reason. Another supplement to the monthly CPS (like the Annual Demographic Survey in March) was used and the results have been analyzed by the Bureau of Labor Statistics (BLS).[34] These statistics have been very useful for economists in studying the labor market implications of corporate downsizings and restructurings that have taken place in recent years.

The data show that as of the last survey in February 1996, a total of 4.2 million persons had permanently lost their jobs in which they had been employed for three years or longer over the period from January 1993 to January 1996 (another 5.2 million had lost jobs but had less than three years of job tenure). This was a period, of course, when the economic recovery from the recession was under way. In the heart of the recession—from January 1991 to January 1993—job displacement was more severe with 4.6 million persons permanently losing their jobs. Before the recession, job displacement was less severe, especially considering that the survey period was much longer—from January 1985 to January 1990. Approximately 4.3 million tenured workers lost jobs permanently in the second half of the 1980s.[35]

The data on job displacement also reveal how the 1990–91 recession hit white-collar workers so much differently than in the recessions of the early 1980s. Table 3.8 shows that job displacement rates (i.e., the number of displaced workers divided by the estimated level of employment for a specific group) for managers and professional workers, although considerably lower than for semi-skilled operatives and plant workers, were much higher in the 1990–91 recession and recovery than was the case a decade earlier. The same effect can be seen when job displacement rates in manufacturing are compared to those in the finance, insurance, and real estate industries. In manufacturing the rates were much lower in the 1990–1991 period than in the early 1980s, but in the finance and related industries just the reverse was true.

Table 3.8

Job Displacement Rates (in percent) by Workers' Occupation and Industry Attachment, Selected Years

Characteristic	1981–83	1991–93	1993–95
Total	9.0	8.2	8.0
Managers, Prof. Wkrs.	4.9	6.2	6.0
Operators, Fabricators	18.9	11.8	12.1
Service Occ.	5.0	6.1	6.2
Manufacturing	17.4	12.9	11.1
Finance, Insurance	3.6	8.7	8.4

Source: U.S. Bureau of Labor Statistics, CPS Supplements.
Note: These rates relate to workers 20 years of age and over with no restriction to years of job tenure.

Health Insurance Loss

One of the central concerns over job security in recent years has been the possible loss of health insurance coverage because of a job loss. Federal legislation was passed in the 1980s (the Consolidated Omnibus Budget Reconciliation Act of 1985) allowing workers who had lost their jobs to continue paying for their health insurance for a limited amount of time. Nevertheless, the threat has worried many workers in recent years.

The realization that a fairly significant proportion of Americans, at any point in time, have no health insurance coverage prompted the Clinton administration in the early 1990s to propose a comprehensive health insurance program for all citizens. This, no doubt, was also prompted by growing concerns over losing health insurance coverage because of a job loss. Consequently, for many families, reports of growing income differences became associated with the fear of going without health insurance. Table 3.9 displays information on the extent of health insurance coverage in the United States that is also collected by the Census Bureau each March in the CPS. As can be seen, the proportion of the population without health insurance coverage rose significantly between the late 1980s and early 1990s, probably because of the recession, and it has only been in the mid-1990s that the proportion appeared to stabilize somewhat. Between 1987 and 1996, the proportion increased from 12.9 percent to 15.6 percent, or from 31.0 million to 41.7 million persons.

The health insurance issue is very complicated and is still the focal point of much public policy debate. Because of the national attention focused on

Table 3.9

Health Insurance Coverage Status of the Population, 1987–1996

Year	Population (thous.)	No Coverage (thous.)	No Coverage (percent)
1987	241,187	31,026	12.9
1988	243,685	32,680	13.4
1989	246,191	33,385	13.6
1990	248,886	34,719	13.9
1991	251,447	35,445	14.1
1992	256,830	38,641	15.0
1993	259,753	39,713	15.3
1994	262,105	39,718	15.2
1995	264,314	40,582	15.4
1996	266,792	41,716	15.6

Source: U.S. Bureau of the Census, Annual Demographic Survey, CPS.

it, health care providers, employers, and others in the health care industry have attempted to constrain health care costs. From the standpoint of employers' desires to cut costs, many have increased their hiring of contingent workers, part-time workers, and consultants so as to avoid paying for health care benefits. The broad, and sometimes elusive, concept of growing income inequality for some workers has a very practical and direct meaning for their economic well-being.

Low-Wage Employment

For many workers who lost jobs in recent years because of downsizings and then found new jobs, especially during the last recession, new paychecks were considerably smaller. One study relating to the 1990–1992 period showed that for men age 25 to 54 who left a full-time job and then reentered one, average weekly earnings plunged by about 20 percent (from $529 to $423).[36] And this was just "on average."

As was mentioned in Chapter 1, the Census Bureau produced a statistical series on low earners in the early 1990s. This was in response not only to the earnings erosion connected with the job losses taking place in the recession, but also to the assertion that although the economy in the 1980s had created millions of new jobs, most of them were low paying. For many Americans, therefore, the reality of growing income inequality was employment in a low-wage job.

Table 3.10 presents some of the data from this statistical series for the

Table 3.10

Percentage of Workers Who Worked Full-Time, Year-Round with Low Earnings by Selected Characteristics, Selected Years

Characteristic	1979	1989	1992	1994
Total	12.1	14.1	16.3	16.2
Men	7.7	10.1	12.4	12.7
Women	20.4	20.4	21.8	21.4
Age 18 to 24	22.9	33.9	41.9	42.5
Age 35 to 54	9.9	10.6	12.3	11.9
Less than High School	22.2	30.1	38.1	37.7
College Graduate	4.3	4.6	5.7	5.5

Source: U.S. Bureau of the Census, Annual Demographic Survey, CPS.
Note: Low earnings are defined as annual earnings of less than the poverty threshold for a four-person family.

years 1979, 1989, 1992, and 1994 for men and women, young workers and middle-age workers, and high school dropouts and college graduates. Low earners are defined as workers who worked full-time year-round and had annual earnings that fell below the federal government's poverty threshold for a family of four persons (in 1994 that threshold was $13,828, or approximately $6.91 an hour). The data reveal that during the 1980s there was an increase in the percentage of fully employed workers who had low earnings, and that this was particularly so for men, young workers, and high school dropouts, which paralleled the rise in income inequality. The situation was exacerbated for these groups during the recession of the early 1990s and did not improve much by 1994 during the early phase of the recovery.

The growing incidence of low earnings among certain groups with low skills and poor educational backgrounds was widely reported in the media. The appearance of statistics like these confirmed the views of many workers from the middle class that job security and job skills were important for economic survival in the labor market of the 1990s.

Poverty

One economic statistic that probably comes to mind for the average citizen when the topic of income inequality comes up is poverty. The federal government has been measuring the size of the poverty population for over thirty years, and although it is a much criticized measure and one that some people would consider to be obsolete, the topic still receives attention in the

Figure 3.9 **Rates of Poverty and Unemployment, 1947–1996**

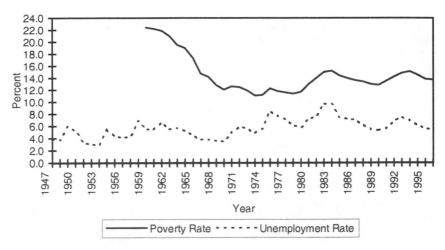

Year

Poverty Rate · · · · · · Unemployment Rate

Source: U.S. Bureau of the Census, Annual Demographic Survey, CPS; U.S. Bureau of Labor Statistics, Monthly CPS.
Note: The poverty rate is expressed as a percentage of the civilian noninstitutional population and the unemployment rate is expressed as a percentage of the civilian labor force.

media. Because it suggests the absence of economic resources it has a natural connection with income inequality.

The relationship between poverty and income inequality is not necessarily a strong one. Back in the early 1960s when the poverty rate was nearly 20 percent, income differences in society were relatively small and measured income inequality had almost reached its all-time low for the century. Nevertheless, there remains a link between poverty and income inequality in the public's mind.

Figure 3.9 shows the official rate of poverty as measured by the Census Bureau between 1959 and 1996.[37] Poverty today is far below the levels of the late 1950s and early 1960s. Indeed, poverty prior to this period was probably above 30 percent in the late 1940s and probably exceeded 60 or 70 percent at the beginning of the century, although using the current poverty definition on these bygone eras may be questionable.[38]

The data in Figure 3.9 do show, however, that despite the long-run decline in poverty during the 1960s and 1970s, the poverty rate gradually inched upward thereafter, indicating some relationship to the growing dispersion of incomes. The poverty rate (as officially defined in the early 1960s) hit its lowest level of 11.1 percent in 1973 but moved up slowly during the rest of the decade and then accelerated with the onset of the recessions in the early 1980s. By 1983, the nation's poverty rate hit 15.2 percent. It did respond to some extent to the economic recovery (but not to the extent that was expected) and by 1989 had slipped back to 12.8 percent. With the economy slumping into another recession at the beginning of the 1990s, the incidence of poverty increased each year until 1993 when it reached 15.1 percent. Since then it has eased down to 13.7 percent.

Unemployment

Another statistical series that people associate with growing income inequality no doubt is the country's overall rate of unemployment. This is natural because when workers lose jobs, earnings drop, and household incomes decline. Because economic slowdowns and recessions typically have had a harsher effect on workers in the lower part of the income distribution, income differences would tend to be magnified in these periods. A close look at the trend in the Gini index for families since 1947, shown in Figure 3.2, would tend to confirm the fact that inequality typically rises in periods of recession.

As was pointed out earlier, however, the 1980s appeared to be an anomaly. Inequality did indeed rise during the recessions in the 1980–1982 period, but then it kept on rising well into the economic recovery when the nation's unemployment rate was dropping. Consequently, the relationship between unemployment and income inequality has changed in recent years as well.

The average monthly rate of unemployment in the 1947–1996 period is displayed in Figure 3.9 (along with the poverty rate for the 1959–1996 period). The unemployment rate is still very sensitive to the economic health of the nation, as reflected in the business cycle. Its long-term trend in the post-WWII period, however, has been upward and after each recession it appeared to level off at higher level than in the past. This pattern was broken in the 1980s. By 1989, the nation's unemployment rate had dropped to 5.3 percent, its lowest level since 1973 (5.2 percent) as the economic expansion of the 1980s was coming to its end. As is well known by now, income inequality had accelerated throughout the 1980s and income differences by 1989 were at all-time highs in the second half of this century. It was clear to many economists at the time that growing income inequality was not necessarily being fueled by joblessness as thought of in the past, but rather the kinds of jobs the economy was generating.

Despite this changing relationship, many Americans still associate the problem of growing income inequality with joblessness and, to the extent that good-paying jobs are lost, they are correct. In the labor market of the last fifteen to twenty years, the jobs unemployed workers moved back into often paid much lower wages than their previous ones. So it is understandable that unemployment, much of it brought about by downsizing and other business practices to cut labor costs, is still associated with growing income inequality by many individuals, even though the nation's unemployment rate in the mid-1990s was at a relatively low post-WWII level.

Summing Up

This chapter has explained how approximately halfway through the second half of the twentieth century, the shape of the income distribution slowly began to change. Up until this time, most everyone's real incomes were rising and income differences were of little consequence. But as the nation emerged from the Vietnam War and the social strife of the civil rights movement, average income growth began to falter—and incomes began to grow more dispersed. By the 1980s, differences in real income growth rates between households at the bottom and top of the income distribution began to widen significantly and income inequality accelerated. Growth in America's solid middle class had slowed in less than a generation. As income differences continued to widen, the media began to report that something had happened to the American Dream—and fairness.

4

Trends in Earnings and
Earnings Inequality

Growing income inequality in the United States over the past quarter century is linked closely to growing dispersion in workers' earnings brought about by changes taking place in the labor market. This should not come as a big surprise given the way the majority of households in this country generate income, that is, by working. But interestingly, it was not the rise in income inequality that prompted economists to initially look to the earnings distribution. It was the other way around.

Issues relating to economic inequality, indeed, economic injustice, have always been the purview of the political left. It was not by the "luck of the draw" that the War on Poverty was born out of a Democratic administration in the 1960s. Many commentators viewed it as only a continuation of this political party's tradition of concern for the working class which really began with the Great Depression and the presidency of Franklin D. Roosevelt. As a result, a segment of society had grown increasingly sensitive to the plight of the poor, the economically disadvantaged, and the economic problems of the workers, even during times of overall prosperity.

This was the context in which the first signs of change in the earnings distribution were reported in the early 1970s. Most analyses of earnings inequality before that time were purely scholarly exercises explaining why the labor market generated earnings differences. Interest in the trends in earnings inequality was limited by the lack of reliable wage and earnings data with sufficient demographic detail and by the simple fact that real average earnings levels until the early 1970s had continued to increase, masking the deeper changes taking place within the distribution.[1]

Peter Henle, in 1972, was the first economist to point to a change in the shape of the earnings distribution of men between 1958 and 1970, or as he characterized it, "a slow but persistent trend toward inequality."[2] Using the Gini index as his metric of inequality, Henle showed that over the period earnings inequality for men had risen from .328 to .356, or 8.5 percent. His finding, which was reported in the *New York Times,* did not, however, result in a stampede of economists to investigate it further.[3] But it did represent the initial inquiry into a topic that would eventually consume the research time of many economists, not only in this country but around the world.

It would not be until the early 1980s, after growth in real average earnings for American workers almost came to a standstill in the mid-1970s, that the issue of rising earnings inequality became the subject of serious investigation.[4] Once the floodgates had opened, however, it became one of the major research topics in labor economics in recent decades, far surpassing inquiries into growing income inequality. And this was a fortuitous development because unlike the study of income inequality, labor economics provided a more developed theoretical framework for attempts to understand why the distribution of earnings had changed.

The Changing Nature of the Labor Market

The labor market of the mid-1990s is much different than the labor market of the mid-1950s, to say the least. The changes have occurred along many dimensions. For the sake of simplification, these dimensions can be categorized into three broad areas: the nature of the labor supply, the nature of the job, and the nature of wage-setting practices, or the rules and regulations under which the labor market functions. Aspects of each are discussed below, and some of the data relating to them appear in Table 4.1.

Labor Supply

Two major changes in the labor force that occurred in the last half century had important implications for income and earnings inequality. The first was the movement of women into the labor force and the second was the overall increase in the educational level of the labor force.

The proportion of the nation's civilian noninstitutional population age 16 and over participating in the labor force has increased gradually in the post-WWII period from just shy of 60 percent in 1955 to almost 67 percent by 1995. This increase in labor force activity was due primarily to one of the major transformations of the labor force in the second half of this century: the entry of women into the labor force.

The groundwork for women's entry into the work force was laid in the years of WWII when the demands of the military seriously constrained men's labor force activity. Slightly more than 30 percent of women age 16 and over participated in the labor force in the late 1940s, and by the late 1950s their participation rate had expanded to about 37 percent.[5] This spurt

Table 4.1

Changes in the Nature of the Labor Market, Selected Years

LABOR SUPPLY	1955	1965	1975	1985	1995
Labor Force Part. Rate—Total					
(percent)	59.3	58.9	61.2	64.8	66.6
Labor Force Part.					
Rate—Women (percent)	35.7	39.3	46.3	54.5	58.9
Less than High School					
Education (percent)	57.3	51.0	37.5	26.1	18.3
College Education or More					
(percent)	7.5	9.4	13.9	19.4	23.0
JOBS					
Manufacturing (percent)	33.3	29.7	23.8	19.8	15.8
Service-Producing Industries					
(percent)	59.5	63.9	70.6	74.5	79.3
Prof., Technical, and					
Managerial (percent)	17.3	18.9	21.4	27.2	31.4
Blue Collar (percent)	41.1	37.7	33.9	26.6	25.3
Supplements to Wages and					
Salaries as a Percent of					
Total Compensation	5.9	9.0	14.4	17.7	18.7
WAGE-SETTING PROCESS					
Minimum wage					
Current dollars	1.00	1.25	2.10	3.35	4.25
Constant 1995 dollars	5.60	6.05	5.95	4.74	4.25
Union membership (percent)	33.2	28.4	26.50	20.5	16.7

Source: U.S. Bureau of the Census, U.S. Bureau of Labor Statistics, U.S. Department of Labor, U.S. Bureau of Economic Analysis.

Note: Education data relate to persons 25 years of age and over; data for 1955 are actually for 1957.

Occupation data for 1955, 1965, and 1975 are actually for years 1950, 1960, and 1970 and are not exactly comparable to the data for 1985 and 1995 due to occupational classification changes which occurred in the early 1980s.

Current and constant dollar minimum wages for 1955 are actually for 1956.

Union membership data for 1955 and 1965 are based on biennial surveys of national and international unions by the Bureau of Labor Statistics and are percentages of total nonagricultural employment; the data for 1975 (actually 1977), 1985, and 1995 are based on estimates from the Current Population Survey and are percentages of total wage and salary employment.

in labor force activity was accounted for primarily by older women who had completed their childbearing. In the subsequent decade, younger women with young children would begin entering the work force in record numbers and by 1970 the women's participation rate was 43 percent. By the end of that decade, labor force participation of all women hit the 50 percent mark (1978 to be exact). In the late 1970s and into the 1980s, however, increases in work activity for younger women age 16 to 34 began to slow, causing a slight slowdown in the rate of increase for all women. By 1990 the rate had reached 57 percent, stabilized at that level until the economic recovery was into full swing, and then began to climb again. By 1996, the women's labor force participation rate averaged 59.3 percent.

The results of this enormous expansion in women's labor force activity, along with a modest decline in the participation rate for men (from 83 percent in 1960 to 75 percent in 1995), was their more equal representation (at least in numbers) in the American labor force. At the end of the first half of this century, women accounted for just about 30 percent of the labor force; by the mid-1990s they accounted for 46 percent.

The implications for earnings trends, earnings inequality, and family income inequality would be immense, as will be discussed more fully in the following chapter. At this point, two facts are worth noting. First, the rising real market wage for women was a major reason for their labor force entrance and, second, the women's earnings distribution was much different than the men's. The women's earnings distribution was considerably more compressed initially because of the narrow range of occupations they usually moved into (i.e., nurse, teacher, secretary), the activities of which had been once labeled "women's work." But because of this earnings or wage compression, the effect of married women's labor force activity on the overall distribution of family income was to lower inequality. As will be shown in Chapter 5, the full implications of the rise in the women's labor force on the household income distribution are still unfolding.

The second major change in the nature of the work force that occurred over the last fifty years is the rise in its educational level. It is well known that over time the improvement in the educational attainment level of the nation's population has had a significant effect on the economic growth of the United States. Part of this development was due to the G.I. Bill, which subsidized the educations of many veterans after WWII. According to the Census Bureau, and as is shown in Table 4.1, in 1957 over one-half of the population age 25 and older had less than a high school education and only 7.5 percent had a college education or more. By the mid-1990s, almost forty years later, the former percentage would drop to 18.3 percent and the latter would rise to 23.0 percent.

These were profound changes, which were reflected in the quality of the nation's labor supply. By 1991 over one-fourth (26.5 percent) of the civilian labor force age 25 to 64 had completed four years of college or more, almost double the proportion in 1970. At the other end of the education spectrum the proportion of the labor force that were high school dropouts had fallen from 36.1 percent to 13.0 percent.[6]

The connection between education and income, of course, has been well established. Indeed, the theory of human capital is an integral part of labor economics. As will be shown shortly, the demand for and supply of well-educated workers has played an important role in earnings inequality research. Relative wage differences between college-educated workers and high school dropouts, for example, widened dramatically in the 1980s as employers were willing to pay wage premiums for highly educated workers.

Not only have educational levels risen in past decades, but the kinds of education being acquired have changed as well. A growing proportion of college degrees conferred is in communication technologies, computer and information sciences, engineering and engineering technologies, and health sciences. In 1971, 10.5 percent of all the bachelor degrees and 13.6 percent of all the doctorate degrees were in these fields; in 1992 these proportions had jumped to 19.3 percent and 20.1 percent, respectively.[7] And the proportion of workers using computers at their jobs in 1993 was 45.8 percent, approaching one-half of the work force.[8]

The average American worker in the mid-1990s is no doubt different than the one of the mid-1950s in other ways as well. They are probably healthier, more mobile, better informed, and more concerned about their job responsibilities than ever before. But at the same time these changes were occurring, so too were changes taking place in their jobs.

Jobs

Most people are aware of the broad industrial and occupational transformation that has occurred in the United States during the past century. As the nation entered the twentieth century the economic base of the country was shifting from agriculture to industry and the production of consumer goods of all kinds. In the second half of the century, gradual shifting continued, this time away from goods production to service provision, and eventually to information processing. The nature of jobs, therefore, has undergone dramatic changes also.

The Bureau of Labor Statistics (BLS) has kept track of these shifts through their Current Employment Survey (CES), a survey of nonfarm business establishments that has been in operation for many years. As shown in Table 4.1, just over forty years ago in the mid-1950s, one out of every three (33.3 percent) nonfarm payroll workers worked in the manufacturing sector of the economy. By 1995 only one out of every six (15.8 percent) workers was a manufacturing worker. And it's not that this sector produces fewer manufactured goods. Indeed, personal consumption expenditures (in real terms) on manufactured goods more than tripled between

1950 and 1994.[9] What happened, of course, was that capital investments in technologies, management improvements, and other efficiencies led to greater productivity, enabling this growth in manufactured goods.

At the same time, the service-producing sector of the economy expanded, and by this is meant the broad collection of industries, such as retail trade, banking, transportation, health services, and government.[10] Their representation in nonfarm payroll employment between 1955 and 1995 rose from 59.5 percent to 79.3 percent. In other words, by the end of the century about eight out of every ten nonfarm workers in our country was involved in the production (creation) of a service for someone else. Personal consumption expenditures (in real terms) on services expanded by more than five times between 1950 and 1994.[11]

Over this half of the century then, along with the industrial restructuring of the economy came similar shifts in the kinds of occupations employers required. White-collar jobs were becoming more common relative to blue-collar jobs. The data in Table 4.1 provide a little more specificity to this occupational transformation. Persons working in professional, technical, and managerial occupations rose from 17.3 percent of the total in 1950 to 31.4 percent by 1995, while persons in craftsman, operative, and nonfarm laborer occupations dropped from 41.1 percent in 1950 to 25.3 percent by 1995.

These shifts in the industrial and occupational makeup of the American economy were also thought to have profound implications for growing earnings inequality. As was mentioned in Chapter 1, some economists in the early 1980s had pointed to industrial restructuring as the cause for the slow growth in earnings as well as the greater dispersion in earnings among workers.[12] The changing distribution of occupations in the United States resulting from shifts in occupational demand had also been associated with the widening gap in earnings differentials by education.[13]

Another important aspect of how the nature of jobs has changed in recent years is in terms of the nature of workers' compensation. Changes in legislation relating to the workplace as well as changes resulting from labor-management negotiations have increased the "supplements" to basic wage and salary payments of workers. These supplements include not only employers' contributions to government-mandated social insurance programs, such as unemployment insurance, but also the payments for employer-provided health insurance, life insurance, and pension programs.

As shown in Table 4.1, in 1955 these supplements accounted for only 5.9 percent of total workers' compensation but by 1975 the proportion had nearly tripled to 14.4 percent, and by 1995 it was up to 18.7 percent of total employee compensation. Obviously, these supplements represent costs to employers that affect their competitive position in the marketplace.

The BLS monitors such costs through their Employment Cost Index (ECI), a survey of nonfarm establishments' compensation practices. According to the ECI in 1994, the employer cost for employee compensation per hour worked in 1994 was $17.08 (and in manufacturing it was $20.72 an hour).[14] Of that amount, $12.14 consisted of basic wages and salaries and the rest—28.9 percent—was in the form of benefits. The legally required benefits paid by employers came to $1.60 an hour (9.4 percent) and the other benefits came to $3.34 (19.6 percent). These nonlegally required benefits were such things as paid leave (vacations and sick leave), health and life insurance, retirement contributions, and so on. Although ECI data are not available for the 1950s, there is no doubt that the average worker's benefit package back then did not resemble this package.

The issue of employer costs for employee compensation is an important one for earnings inequality and other economic issues because it impacts on employers' compensation practices. It has been reported that employers are hiring relatively more "contingent" workers (workers who are contracted out to employers) and part-time workers so as to hold down the rising costs of workers' benefit packages. And in Europe, where benefits are even greater, it has been alleged that their high costs prevent employers from hiring as many workers as they really need, resulting in unemployment rates well above those in the United States.

Jobs, of course, have been transformed in many other ways in this country. Workers are now often allowed more flexibility in setting their own work schedules and some are even permitted to work at home. Some commentators believe that average job tenure has declined, even though the empirical evidence suggests that average job tenure has not changed.[15] There is no doubt that jobs in the mid-1990s are different from those in the mid-1950s.

Wage-Setting Practices

Two fundamental changes have taken place in the last fifty years with regard to wage-setting in the United States, both of which have implications for earnings inequality and have been studied by economists. The first involves the real value of the minimum wage. As of September 1997, the federal minimum wage was $5.15 an hour, but only in recent years has the level been increased after a long period of decline in its real value.

Table 4.1 shows both the nominal value of the minimum wage between the 1950s and 1990s as well as its real value. From the mid-1950s to the end of the 1970s, the real value of the minimum wage (in 1995 dollars) ranged between $5.00 and $7.00 an hour, as the fraction of nonsupervisory employees whose jobs were covered by the minimum wage increased from 39 to 84 percent between 1960 and 1979.[16] But by 1985, the real minimum wage had fallen to $4.74 and by 1995 it was down to $4.25. Many politicians, as well as economists, have complained that the low minimum wage was one of the reasons for the increase in the number of low-wage workers over the years and the rise in poverty. Obviously, a change in the minimum wage does have some impact on the shape of the earnings distribution. In 1994 the number of workers paid at the minimum wage or lower totaled 4.1 million.[17]

Another significant change that has taken place in the labor market is the deunionization of the American work force. Back in the mid-1950s, union members accounted for approximately 33.2 percent of all nonagricultural workers, but by 1995 the percentage of total wage and salary employment represented by unions and labor organizations was 16.7 percent. It has been claimed that the loss of representation at the bargaining table has also had a negative impact on the earnings distribution in recent years. This factor also will be discussed in the following chapter.

Trends in Labor Market Earnings

If one were to rank the top ten economic disappointments of the U.S. economy in the second half of the twentieth century, most economists would place the trend in workers' real average earnings high up on this list. This is because real average earnings, after rising steadily for roughly twenty-five years following WWII, suddenly changed course in the early 1970s. This development had major implications for the income distribution. Before examining these trends, some concepts and definitions relating to earnings will be helpful.

The Basics of Earnings

Earnings refer to the money received by persons who work in the labor market, or as was discussed in Chapter 2, earnings represent the return to labor. Because there are many earnings series produced by the federal government, it is useful to become familiar with some of the terms associated with earnings. In this section, therefore, we will begin with the most basic terms and proceed to the more complex.

The "wage" is the most basic of all the terms used in reference to the return to labor. It is most often used in the context of economic theory and as the return to labor when considered as a factor of production. The "wage rate" is often used as the rate of pay received by a worker on the basis of some unit, such as an hour, a week, or a unit of product produced or sold.

The "wage level" is usually associated with an average level of wages of a certain economic sector, such as the wage level in manufacturing. However, when used this way it typically implies also the other components of one's pay, such as paid vacation time, health benefits, and so on. "Wages and salaries" is a term that is often used to combine the returns paid to workers who are paid on an hourly basis (or piece-rate basis) with those workers who have contracted with their employer on a weekly, monthly, or annual basis. Typically, this too includes certain supplementary payments to workers.

Although we have used the term "earnings" in a very broad sense, "earnings" does have a more specific usage. It is considered to be more inclusive than the wages and salaries paid by employers and includes workers who are self-employed as well. Earnings are usually thought of in terms of "gross" earnings (unless otherwise specified as "net" earnings) and include supplements to the basic wage or salary.

"Compensation" is regarded as the most inclusive of all earnings measures. It includes not only the wages and salaries paid to employees, but also bonuses, commissions, payments in kind, incentive payments, tips, and so forth. It also includes the supplements to wages and salaries, such as employers' legally obligated contributions for social insurance, but also for private pensions, health insurance, life insurance and any other payments employers make on behalf of their employees.

The remuneration of workers over the years has changed dramatically so it is essential that, when speaking of "earnings" from the labor market in the general sense, one knows the specific return to labor that is being talked about. In addition, and perhaps more important for the following discussion, most of the earnings series of the federal government are based on different concepts and defined uniquely (e.g., coverage, periodicity).

In theory, workers will tend to be paid an amount equal to the contribution they make to the value of their employer's output, or workers' productivity. It was not a coincidence that both productivity and real wage growth began to slow down in the early 1970s and why economists have attempted for so long to understand the causes of the decline in productivity growth.

Which Earnings Series?

One of the problems with the "number mills" in Washington, D.C., is that they sometimes churn out so many statistics purporting to measure the same thing (or nearly the same thing), that confusion ensues over which statistical series to believe. A case in point was discussed in the last chapter where the trend in real average family income and real per capita personal income began to diverge in the 1970s.

The same problem, but to perhaps a lesser degree, occurred to some of the federal government's measures of real earnings and their trends over recent decades. Indeed, the commissioner of the BLS, Katharine G. Abraham (and her co-authors), acknowledged as much in the mid-1990s in a paper in which they reviewed the long-term trends in four different real hourly earnings series.[18] According to their data, between 1973 and 1992 the real hourly earnings series from the Current Employment Survey (CES) of the BLS registered a 10 percent decline, two real hourly earnings measures from the March CPS and the monthly CPS had not changed much at all, and a real hourly wage measure developed from the National Income and Product Accounts (NIPA) increased by 10 percent.[19] These series pointed to differences in the earnings concepts used in each series, differences in the worker populations covered, and other methodological differences in the series.

In their paper, they indicated that while the media and the business community tended to focus on the real hourly wage measure from the CES, economists studying earnings trends and inequality have relied on the data from the CPS. There are two reasons economists have relied on the CPS. First, the CPS data are based on microdata, or the records of individuals that contain a plethora of information on the economic, social, and demographic backgrounds of workers and their households; the second reason, of course, is that these data can be arranged into distributions and then measured for the extent of inequality in them.

For the purposes of this analysis we will examine three of these series more closely and refer to them as the "most depressing" series, the "not as depressing" series, and the "least depressing" series. The most depressing series is the real hourly earnings series from the BLS's CES; the not as depressing series is the real annual earnings of full-time, year-round men and women workers as measured in the March CPS; the least depressing series is the BLS's Office of Productivity and Technology's real hourly compensation measure. This last measure is very similar to the NIPA measure used by Commissioner Abraham, except it is a total compensation measure while the others (including the NIPA measure discussed earlier) are wage and salary measures which only include certain supplements to workers' earnings.

The "Most Depressing" Series

Figure 4.1 presents the trends in three earnings series of workers in the 1960–1996 period. With a quick glance of the figure it is easy to pick out the least sanguine of the earnings series in the last thirty-five years: the BLS series on real average hourly earnings from the CES.

Figure 4.1 **Trends in Real Earnings Measures, 1960–1996** (1960 = 100)

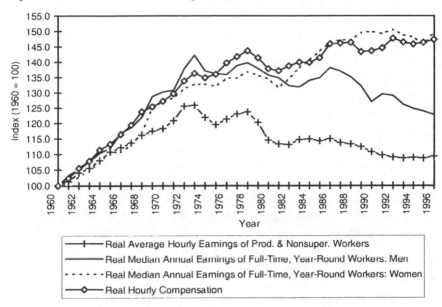

Sources: U.S. Bureau of Labor Statistics, Current Employment Statistics Survey and Quarterly Labor Productivity; U.S. Bureau of the Census, Annual Demographic Survey, CPS.

A few additional words about the background of this series are in order. The CES is a monthly survey of some 400,000 nonagricultural establishments by which the BLS measures nonfarm payroll employment and earnings. The CES is often referred to as the "establishment" survey. Unlike the CPS, it is not a probability survey, even though it has a mix of large and small establishments from each industry in its sample. The CES employment estimates are benchmarked annually to data from another one of BLS's programs (earnings and hours, however, are not benchmarked).[20] The representativeness of the CES has been questioned in recent years.

The establishment survey collects data each month on the total number of employees, the number of production or nonsupervisory workers, the payroll for production or nonsupervisory workers, and the number of hours that were paid for. The earnings and hours data apply only to production workers in the goods-producing industries (mining, construction, and manufacturing) and nonsupervisory workers in the service-producing industries (all other industries). Because of these definitions, an accountant in a manufacturing company would not be included as a production worker but an accountant in a bank would be counted as a nonsupervisory worker.

The earnings of production and nonsupervisory workers consist of the basic wage or salary before deductions for Social Security, unemployment insurance, union dues, and other deductions, and include pay for overtime, premiums for shift work, as well as pay for sick leave, holidays, and vacations. Bonuses, commissions, and other lump sum payments are not included nor are tips or payments in kind. The earnings data relate to workers employed full-time as well as part-time.

The trend in real hourly earnings for production or nonsupervisory workers between 1960 and 1996 is displayed in Figure 4.1. Hourly earnings are adjusted for inflation by the Consumer Price Index for Urban Wage Earners and Clerical Workers (CPI-W) of the BLS and have been indexed so that their value in 1960 equals 100.0. As shown there, real hourly earnings rose by almost 26 percent between 1960 and 1973, but then faltered in the 1970s. The recessions of the early 1980s pushed earnings further downward, from which they never recovered (indeed, gradually declined further), at least according to the establishment survey of the BLS. The average real wage for the American worker by 1996 was lower than it was thirty years earlier!

Clearly, if the trend in real average hourly earnings according to the BLS is to be believed, it is depressing. And, of course, this trend has not gone unnoticed by the media nor economists alike. With respect to the latter, one economist featured a similar dismal trend in real "spendable" hourly earnings based on the BLS earnings data.[21] This series was developed to replace the real spendable weekly earnings series which the BLS had discontinued in the early 1980s because of conceptual and measurement issues ("spendable" refers to the tax adjustment that is made to gross earnings to simulate take-home pay). Suffice it to say that one would only have to look at the official real hourly earnings series to become distressed over the trend in earnings of workers.

As even the BLS points out, however, the CES earnings data are subject to various limitations (in addition to the representativeness of the sample). For example, the average earnings estimates reflect shifts in the number of employees between high-paid and low-paid work as well as persistent long-term increases in the proportion of part-time workers in such industries as retail trade. The earnings estimates can also be affected by other long-term structural changes in the labor force.

The "Not as Depressing" Series

The earnings data collected in the March CPS have been used extensively by economists in examining trends in earnings and earnings inequality. Conceptually, the CPS earnings data are different than the CES data. They include not only wage and salary income but also income obtained through self-employment.[22] Commissions, tips, piece-rate payments, and cash bonuses are all included before any deductions are made for taxes, health insurance, union dues, and so forth.

Figure 4.1 displays the trend in the real median annual earnings of men and women who worked full-time, year-round between 1960 and 1996 (men and women who reported they usually worked thirty-five hours or more a week for fifty to fifty-two weeks a year).[23] The earnings of full-time, year-round workers are often examined because they provide a crude control for hours worked; the assumption is that these individuals have supplied approximately 2,000 hours of work (forty hours times fifty weeks) each year so that variation in annual earnings is due primarily to differences in hourly earnings and not hours worked.[24]

Let us focus attention on both the trend in real annual earnings for men and for women since, as can be seen in the figure, they have differed. Like the real hourly earnings series of the BLS, the real annual earnings for men increased strongly in the 1960s and into the 1970s, rising by over 40 percent between 1960 and 1973. After that, however, it was as if someone had stepped on the trend line. By the early 1980s, men's annual earnings were only 35 percent above the 1960 level (in contrast, the BLS series was only about 13 percent above its 1960 level). Men's real median annual earnings in the 1980s languished and then moved further downward with the onset of the recession in the 1990–1991 period. By 1996, their earnings were only 23 percent above their 1960 level, according to the CPS.

The earnings trend for women is more rosy. As shown in the figure, their earnings moved up by 33 percent between 1960 and 1973, and then also leveled off in the 1970s and early 1980s. In the 1980s, however, women's earnings began to rise again and by the end of that decade they were almost 50 percent higher than their 1960 level. Since the end of the 1990–91 recession the real earnings of women have remained relatively flat. The different earnings experiences for men and women, especially during the 1980s, would have implications for how the shape of their earnings distributions changed over these years.

One of the consequences of the different trends in earning for men and women, of course, has been the closing of the gender pay gap. While the women's median earnings level in 1960 was only 61 percent as high as the men's ($15,870 vs. $26,156 in 1996 dollars), by 1996 the women's median annual earnings were 74 percent as great as those of the men's ($23,710 vs. $32,144). As is well known, over this period growing numbers of women were entering high-paying professions and managerial positions.

The CPS annual earnings data are not without their limitations also (limitations of the CPS income data were discussed in Chapter 2). First, the data exclude a significant part of workers' compensation, such as employer-provided health insurance and other benefits employers provide their workers. Second, because the data are obtained via a household survey, there is a problem of nonresponse as well as the inaccurate reporting of earnings. It is well known that earnings nonresponse is particularly prevalent among high-income and low-income households, which tends to introduce biases into earnings distributions. In addition, respondents sometimes provide their net earnings rather than their gross earnings simply because it is the former they can recall easier. And third, there is the problem of truncation bias caused by the top coding of earnings responses, which was discussed in Chapter 2. All three tend to bias measures of earnings inequality downward because it is usually the earnings at the upper end of distribution that are most affected.

The "Least Depressing" Series

The least depressing series on the trend in workers' real earnings over the last thirty-five years or so is the BLS's series on real average hourly "compensation" in the nonfarm business sector. This series is produced and published by the BLS but it is based on estimates made by the Bureau of Economic Analysis (BEA) using data on wages, salaries, and benefits collected by the BLS. The real hourly compensation series is a part of the BLS's program on productivity measurement.

The real hourly compensation measure of the BLS is the most comprehensive measure of the returns to workers. It includes not only the wage and salary component of a worker's paycheck, but also employers' contributions to Social Security, health insurance, pension plans, vacations and holiday pay, and all other benefits. The series covers all workers (as well as self-employed workers) and the price deflator is the CPI-U of the BLS.

As shown in Figure 4.1, real average hourly compensation rose by 36 percent between 1960 and 1973, and, after dipping briefly in the 1973–74 recession, continued upward until 1978. Thereafter, it began to slip and, with the onset of the recessions in the 1980–1982 period, dropped back to its level of the early 1970s. In the 1980s, the series resumed its growth and at the end of that decade (1988) stood 46 percent higher than its 1960 level. Real hourly compensation fell again in the beginning of the 1990s and the ensuing recession but then recovered slightly and in 1996 was again 47 percent higher than in 1960.

The trend in this earning series is far different than the ones from the BLS establishment survey (only a 9 percent increase over the thirty-five-year period) and the one for men from the CPS (a 23 percent increase).

Some economists, for example, Marvin Kosters of the American Enterprise Institute, have favored the use of the real hourly compensation series as a measure of economic well-being over other measures because of its comprehensiveness.[25]

The real hourly compensation measure, although it is comprehensive, does have a basic shortcoming for earnings inequality analysis, just as does the real hourly earnings series from the BLS establishment series. They are based on administrative records and payroll data, and therefore do not include any information on workers' economic, social, and demographic characteristics.

The trends in real earnings for workers—the returns to labor—since 1973 have been generally lackluster relative to the years after WWII. How lackluster depends on the earnings series one wishes to examine. The March CPS annual earnings series has been the series of choice by economists examining earnings inequality in recent years, not so much because it represents superior data, but because other aspects of workers can be investigated at the same time, such as age, sex, education levels, occupation and industry of employment, marital status, and so on. It is in this sense that the CPS earnings data are superior and the reason that they shall be relied on in the following section for examining the trend in earnings inequality.

Growing Inequality in the Earnings Distribution

Studies of the growing dispersion in the earnings distribution of workers over the last fifteen to twenty years can be likened to a "cottage industry" for economists. The inquiry into growing earnings and wage inequality has spread to other industrialized countries, especially in western Europe. Unlike income inequality, the plethora of research on earnings inequality resulted in a thorough review article of the subject in the *Journal of Economic Literature* in 1992.[26]

This section of the chapter reviews some of the studies that have documented the trend in rising earnings and wage inequality in recent decades. Research into the causes of the trends will be discussed in the following chapter. Because some studies have both documented trends and explored the reasons, references to them will be found in both chapters.

As in the study of income inequality, many of the same conceptual and methodological issues apply to the study of earnings inequality. For example, earnings concepts may differ depending on the data being used. Measures of earnings inequality, which are basically the same as those used in income inequality analysis, can differ from study to study. Another problem that is not common in income inequality research, however, is the issue of the universe being covered. Universes may differ on the basis of work experience (i.e., full-time, year-round workers, all workers), period-of-earnings receipt (i.e., annual, monthly, weekly), and characteristics of workers (i.e., age, sex, occupation, industry). When all these issues are combined, there is the possibility, indeed likelihood, that conclusions regarding the magnitude, timing, and even direction of changes in earnings inequality will differ across studies.

Despite all these possibilities for differences to occur, however, the vast majority of studies have found that the amount of dispersion in the nation's earnings distribution has risen over the last twenty-five years or so. There is less agreement, however, as to how much it has risen and, most importantly, why it has risen. The following presents the major pieces of evidence documenting the growth in earnings inequality in the United States.

First Signs

The first indication of growing earnings inequality in the 1958–1970 period detected by Peter Henle in 1972 was largely ignored by the economic research community, perhaps because there were more pressing economic and political problems at the time, such as the productivity slowdown, the Mideast oil embargo, and Watergate. It was not until Henle's earlier work was updated (by himself and Paul Ryscavage) in 1980 that interest in growing earnings inequality picked up.[27] This research showed that growing earnings inequality for men of all work-experience categories appeared to have been concentrated in the 1968–1973 period, while no particular trend was evident for women earners.

Other economists soon began to take an interest. In 1982, Robert Plotnick found an overall increase in the dispersion of men's earnings during the 1958–1977 period, and Martin Dooley and Peter Gottschalk confirmed the finding of Henle and Ryscavage that the increase for men was particularly sharp in the late 1960s and early 1970s.[28] At this time, of course, the nation's economy was reeling from two back-to-back recessions. Unemployment had risen to nearly 10 percent of the workforce in 1982 (on an annual basis), and the manufacturing industry had lost over 2.0 million jobs between 1979 and 1982.

This mixture of bad economic news and growing evidence of earnings inequality, along with a perception that the Reagan administration's economic policies favored the rich, spawned a number of publications suggesting that the middle class was in trouble.[29] Two that were mentioned earlier, for example, were the book by Barry Bluestone and Bennett Harrison that discussed the consequences for middle-class jobs of the shift (the "deindustrialization") in the nation's industrial base from manufacturing to the service industries;[30] and, second, an article by Robert Kuttner warning that past industrial policies were leading to a decline in the middle class.[31] By the mid-1980s, the debate among economists, politicians, and journalists had been joined over the declining number of middle-class jobs.

Convincing Evidence

It would not be until later in the 1980s that documenting long-term trends in earnings inequality in the post-WWII period would become a popular endeavor among economists. One of the more comprehensive documentations of rising earning inequality in the United States (which is useful for discussion here) was conducted by the economist Lynn Karoly, who used CPS data to examine the trends between 1963 and 1989.[32] (The Census Bureau, while it has produced extensive historical data on household and family income inequality, has not done so with respect to the earnings inequality of workers.) Her estimation of the trends has been used by other economists, as well as international organizations monitoring earnings inequality in the United States.[33]

Karoly developed measures of weekly and hourly earnings from the March CPS from which inequality trends could be measured. The measures related to all wage and salary workers (she excluded persons who were self-employed). Because only annual earnings for the previous calendar year are collected in the March CPS, Karoly had to create her own estimates of weekly earnings and hourly earnings (she did this by dividing the number of weeks worked in the year and the number of annual hours worked in the year into annual earnings). In effect, these measures controlled for differences in weeks and hours worked by labor force participants.[34]

In her exposition of the trends in earnings inequality over the 1963–1989 period, Karoly used several ratios of earnings percentiles from the weekly and hourly earnings distributions, for all workers, men and women. For the purposes of our analysis, attention will be focused only on the ratio of weekly earnings at the 90th percentile to weekly earnings at the 10th percentile for men and for women. These ratios are shown in Figure 4.2.

According to Karoly's data the male worker in 1963 whose weekly earnings were at the 90th percentile earned about $920 (in 1996 dollars and before taxes) a week while his counterpart at the 10th percentile of the weekly earnings distribution earned $142 (in 1996 dollars), for a 90th-to-

Figure 4.2 **Ratio of Weekly Earnings at the 90th Percentile to the 10th Percentile of Wage and Salary Workers, by Sex, 1963–1989**

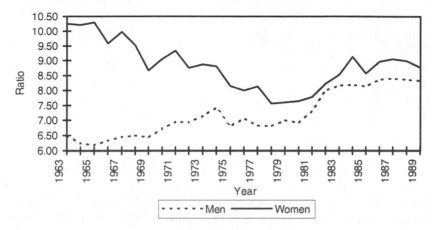

Source: These ratios were developed from data presented by Lynn A. Karoly, "The Trend in Inequality Among Families, Individuals, and Workers in the United States: A Twenty-Five Year Perspective," in *Uneven Tides: Rising Inequality in the 1980s,* Sheldon Danziger and Peter Gottschalk, eds. (New York: Russell Sage Foundation, 1993).

10th earnings ratio of 6.50 to 1. This ratio changed very little until the end of the 1960s and early 1970s when it began to rise. In 1974, it had risen to 7.42. For the rest of the 1970s, the ratio slipped downward to some extent and even by the end of that decade it was only at the 7.00 ($1,164 vs. $166, in 1996 dollars). The ratio shot up after 1980 and by 1986 was at 8.37 to 1, where it fluctuated in a narrow range until 1989.

Another way to gauge the growing dispersion in the earnings distribution—and specifically, its fits and starts—is by examining the average annual rates of change at percentiles of the earnings distribution. Table 4.2 shows these rates. Clearly, the 1960s were the "golden" years in that men's earnings were rising across the distribution. But then, as the nation entered the 1970s, average growth slowed and differences in earnings growth rates began to appear between the top earners and low earners. According to the CPS estimates of Karoly, the rest of the 1970s were marked by very slow wage growth. When the 1980s arrived, real earnings at the median began to decline as well as at the 10th and 25th percentiles. Earnings fell by over 1 percent a year at the latter two percentiles. Workers at the 90th percentile, however, continued to eke out modest gains in real earnings.

In a quarter of a century, real weekly earnings of men at the 90th percentile of the earnings distribution had risen by $321 to $1,241, or 1.2 percent a year on average. For those at the 10th percentile, however, the picture was

Table 4.2

Average Annual Percent Change in Weekly Earnings of Men and Women at Various Percentiles of the Earnings Distribution for Selected Periods Between 1963 and 1989

Period and Sex MEN	10th	25th	50th	75th	90th
1963–68	3.4	3.1	3.3	3.8	3.4
1968–74	−1.3	−1.0	0.1	0.5	0.9
1974–79	1.3	−0.3	0.1	0.7	0.2
1979–89	−1.1	−1.1	−0.7	—	0.6
WOMEN					
1963–78	3.4	2.0	1.4	1.3	1.4
1978–89	0.6	0.6	1.0	1.6	2.0

Source: Lynn A. Karoly, "The Trends in Inequality Among Families, Individuals, and Workers in the United States," Table B.2. See footnote 32.

much bleaker. Their real weekly earnings increased by only $7 to $149, or 0.2 percent a year.

The changes in earnings and earnings inequality for women over the 1963–1989 period are slightly more comforting, even though women's earnings are less than men's. In 1963, the real weekly earnings of women at the 10th percentile were $50 (in 1996 dollars) and earnings at the 90th percentile were $517.

As can be seen in Figure 4.2, the women's 90th-to-10th earnings percentile ratio declined slowly through the 1960s and 1970s from 10.25 to 1 in 1963 to a low of 7.56 to 1 in 1978. Thereafter, it began to accelerate reaching 9.13 to 1 in 1984 and then fluctuated between 8.58 and 9.06 through the rest of the 1980s. By 1989, the women at the 10th percentile had weekly earnings of $90 a week compared to $794 for the women at the 90th percentile.

To see further why these changes are somewhat more sanguine than those for men, one has only to look at the average annual rates of growth in the weekly earnings for women at various points in their earnings distribution over this quarter century. As can be seen in Table 4.2, during the 1960s and 1970s, real weekly earnings at the median were rising by 1.4 percent a year, the same rate as at the 90th percentile. At the bottom of the distribution, the 10th percentile, real earnings were rising over twice as fast—by 3.4 percent a year. Hence, the drop in the 90th-to-10th percentile ratio.

In the next period, however, a reversal occurred. Rates of growth faltered

Table 4.3

Estimates of Earnings Inequality in the 1963–1986 Period from Other Sources

Year	Gary Burtless—Gini Index; Annual Wage and Salary Earnings		Barry Bluestone—Variance of the Natural Log of Earnings; Annual Wage and Salary Earnings	
	Men	Women	Men	Women
1963	0.373	0.468	1.471	2.125
1967	0.369	0.458	1.354	1.867
1973	0.386	0.461	1.402	1.770
1979	0.389	0.432	1.430	1.852
1986	0.411	0.442	1.606	1.872

Source: See footnote 35 (estimates based on data from Annual Demographic Survey, CPS).

(although they did not decline) at the lower end of the distribution between 1978 and 1989, while those at the 75th and 90th percentiles picked up speed relative to the experience of the 1960s and 1970s. At the 75th percentile, real earnings were increasing by 1.6 percent a year and at the 90th, the rate was 2.0 percent a year. Consequently, earnings inequality for women, according to Karoly's estimates, increased.

The changes that occurred in the men's and women's earnings distributions over this period, both with respect to rates of increase at the median and at other percentiles of the distribution, then, were much different. This development will be examined further below.

The Evidence of Others

Other economists exploring the earnings distributions, of course, made estimates of the trend in earnings inequality from the CPS as well. The estimates of Gary Burtless, who used the Gini index as his measure of inequality, and those of Barry Bluestone, who used the variance of the natural logarithm of earnings as his measure, are displayed in Table 4.3 for the 1963–1986 period.[35] Their estimates were for men and women, but unlike Karoly's, were based on the actual annual wage and salary income of workers from the CPS rather than weekly earnings.

The estimates by Burtless for both men and women do, in a general way, mirror the trend in Karoly's 90th-to-10th percentile ratio over the period. The Gini index for the men rises in the 1967–1973 period, changes little in the remainder of the 1970s, and then shoots upward in the 1980s. For women, Burtless's Gini index tends to fall (much as Karoly's metric does) until the end of the 1970s and then moves up somewhat in the 1980s. The Bluestone estimates show inequality for men dropping in the 1960s, rising slightly in the 1970s, and then accelerating into the next decade. For women, the trend based on Bluestone's estimates is remarkably similar to Karoly's in that inequality falls to the end of the 1970s, after which it begins to rise.

The point of presenting this other evidence of rising earnings inequality is to show that although other measures and other types of earnings data have been used by economists, the same general conclusion is reached: Over the 1970s and 1980s the amount of dispersion in the earnings distribution had increased, especially for men. For women, earnings inequality appeared to be on a gradual decline in the 1960s and 1970s, but then began to increase during the 1980s. The exact timing and the amount of the increase, however, depends on which measures of earnings inequality are being examined.

Between and Within Group Inequality

One topic that is seen over and over again in the earnings inequality literature is the growing earnings inequality "between and within" groups. This terminology is common to the approach economists have taken in explaining growing earnings inequality, and is called an analysis of variance approach.

It was clear to many economists that between the 1970s and 1980s, relative earnings differentials between workers with different amounts of education and different amounts of work experience (age is usually used as a proxy for work experience) had changed. The data in Table 4.4, taken from the review article by Levy and Murnane, help to clarify this point.[36] The ratios appearing for the years 1971, 1979, and 1987 are based on the median earnings of men (from the March CPS) who worked full-time, year-round in those years, classified into two age groups (25 to 34 and 45 to 54) and two education groups (high school graduates but no college and college graduates). From these data one can calculate the relative earnings differential by education for both age groups of men. As the data shows, this education differential dropped for both groups in the 1971–1979 period but increased sharply in the 1979–1987 period. In other words, the earnings for more educated men relative to the less educated were changing more favorably in the 1980s than in the 1970s.

By calculating the earnings ratio of older high school–educated men to younger high school–educated men (and similarly for older and younger college-educated men), one can observe the effect of experience (i.e., age or work experience) on the ratio. For example, among the high school–educated men, the earnings of older workers were changing more favorably than for

Table 4.4

Ratios of Annual Earnings of Men Who Worked Full-Time, Year-Round: Relative Education and Relative Experience Earnings Differentials, 1971, 1979, and 1987

	1971	1979	1987
EDUCATION DIFFERENTIAL			
Men, Age 25 to 34, College vs.			
High School	1.22	1.13	1.38
Men, Age 45 to 54, College vs.			
High School	1.55	1.36	1.50
EXPERIENCE DIFFERENTIAL			
Men, High School, Age 45 to 54			
vs. Age 25 to 34	1.08	1.23	1.33
Men, College, Age 45 to 54 vs.			
Age 25 to 34	1.36	1.47	1.45

Source: Frank Levy and Richard Murnane, "U.S. Earnings Levels and Earnings Inequality," Table 5, Part 2. See footnote 36 (ratios based on earnings data from the Annual Demographic Survey, CPS).

younger workers throughout the 1971–1989 period. Among college-educated men, however, the experience differential rose in the 1970s and stayed high in the 1980s.

Changes in these relative wage differentials are helpful in explaining (at least statistically) a part of the rise in earnings inequality for men and women, but not all of it. It was evident that employers were willing to pay more for educated and experienced workers in the 1980s than they were in the 1970s. However, when economists ran regressions in which education and work experience (or age) were used to explain the variation in the earnings distribution, these "between" group characteristics could explain only a part of the increase in earnings inequality. The missing component had to be the rise in "within" group inequality. That is, even in the same education and experience (or age) group (e.g., college-educated men, age 45 to 54), inequality had increased. More will be said about this component of growing earnings inequality in Chapter 5. The important point is that the analysis of variance approach is the method economists have generally taken in their efforts to understand growing earnings inequality.

Inequality Among Men and Women

One aspect of the increase in earnings inequality for men and women that has not received much attention in the literature concerns how and why the

Table 4.5

Distribution of Net Changes in Employment of Men and Women Who Worked Full-Time, Year-Round by Earnings Classes, 1979–1989

	Men	Women
Total Net Change (in thousands)	6,710	8,201
Percent	100.0	100.0
Less than $12,000	19.7	17.6
$12,000 to $23,999	45.8	14.7
$24,000 to $47,999	−1.3	56.0
$48,000 to $59,999	16.7	7.4
$60,000 or more	19.0	4.3

Source: Paul Ryscavage, "Gender-Related Shifts in the Distribution of Wages," Table 4. See footnote 37 (data derived from the March 1980 and March 1990 Annual Demographic Surveys, CPS).

shapes of the earnings distributions of men and women were becoming more dispersed, especially in the 1980s. This is particularly relevant when raised in the context of the "job quality" and the "middle-class jobs" issue that was raging in the 1980s.

During those years millions of jobs had been created but the frequently heard complaint was that these jobs were low-paying. Most of them, it was alleged, were of the "hamburger flipping" variety, and this was especially the case for the kinds of jobs men were finding. One analysis of the kinds of jobs men and women were moving into during this period found that there were significant differences by gender.[37] As is shown in Table 4.5, of the 6.7 million net increase in full-time, year-round employment for men between 1979 and 1989, about 66 percent of it was in jobs that paid less than $24,000 (in 1992 dollars) a year, with the rest of the increase in jobs paying $48,000 (in 1992 dollars) a year or more. Employment growth for men in "middle wage" jobs was negligible; consequently there was some reason for the charge that the economy was generating low-wage jobs.

For women, however, there is less truth to the criticism. The table shows that of the 8.2 million net increase in full-time, year-round employment for women, 56 percent of it was in jobs paying between $24,000 and $47,999 (in 1992 dollars) a year. The fact that women were finding jobs in this wage range, but not men, raises interesting research questions. Apparently, employers' relative demand for labor was shifting quite differently for women than for men during this decade.

In terms of growing earnings inequality, it was apparent the men's and women's earnings distributions had grown more unequal in quite different ways. For men, there was an apparent "hollowing out" of the middle of the earnings distribution, but for women the same middle of the distribution was "filling in."[38]

Earnings Inequality in the 1990s

Assessing the trends in earnings inequality in the 1990s using the data from the March CPS is made difficult by the methodological changes made to the survey in March 1994. Paramount among these changes was the increase in the "top codes" relating to the earnings of workers on their longest jobs in 1993. (The Census Bureau does not record the actual earnings data provided by a sample member if it is above the top code; rather, it records those earnings at the top-coded value so as to protect the confidentiality of the respondent. The publicly released microdata of the March CPS are even further restricted.) These top codes were increased from $299,999 in 1992 to $999,999 in 1993 and, to the extent that a growing proportion of workers with very high earnings were no longer "capped" at the old top code, this meant that the upper tail of the earnings distribution would have more weight in inequality estimates simply through this change alone.

It is possible to obtain some insight on earnings inequality, however, from the monthly CPS since it obtains information on workers' usual weekly earnings (as well as information on their labor force status, which is the main purpose of the monthly CPS) from a portion of the monthly sample that was not affected by the increase in top codes in the March CPS. These data fall within the purview of the BLS and although the BLS publishes and reports on the usual weekly earnings data, they do not publish inequality measures based on the distributions. They do, however, make the data available for such purposes.

The Organization for Economic Co-operation and Development (OECD), an international organization of primarily industrialized nations based in Paris, France, has studied earnings inequality in member countries, including the United States. They used the usual weekly earnings data from the monthly CPS for the period of 1979–1995.[39] The data the OECD analyzed were ratios of earnings percentiles, specifically, the 90th-to-50th and 50th-to-10th, for men and women who were 25 years of age and over and worked full-time. Table 4.6 presents the ratios for the 1990s and selected years in the past for the United States.

The 90th-to-50th and 50th-to-10th earnings ratios for both men and women appeared to be slightly higher in 1994 and 1995 as compared to the ratios in the earlier part of the decade when the economy was moving through the years of recession and slow recovery. The fact that both ends of

Table 4.6

Percentile Ratios of Weekly Earnings of Men and Women Who Worked Full-Time (United States), 1979 and 1987–1995

	Men		Women	
Year	90th/50th	50th/10th	90th/50th	50th/10th
1979	1.73	1.84	1.73	1.77
1987	1.91	2.06	1.87	1.87
1988	1.99	2.05	1.77	1.99
1989	1.97	2.05	1.92	1.90
1990	1.96	2.02	1.92	1.91
1991	1.95	2.01	1.94	1.89
1992	2.00	2.04	1.96	1.90
1993	2.00	2.06	1.96	1.90
1994	2.01	2.13	2.03	1.98
1995	2.04	2.13	2.03	1.95

Source: Organization for Economic Co-operation and Development, *The 1996 OECD Employment Outlook,* Table 3.1. See footnote 39 (data from BLS's monthly CPS).

the distributions for men and for women were pulling further away from their respective median weekly earnings suggests that the forces producing greater earnings inequality were still present in the mid-1990s.

The data also tend to suggest that in the late 1980s and early 1990s, earnings inequality stabilized relative to the first half of the 1980s. Regardless of the measure and gender, the distributions had become more dispersed between 1979 and 1987. But then there was an apparent slowdown beginning a year or two later. This slowdown for men in the upper end of their distribution was evident between 1988 and 1991 where the 90th-to-50th ratio changed from 1.99 to 1.95 and in the lower end the 50th-to-10th ratio went from 2.05 to 2.01. Among the women the 90th-to-50th ratio moved up a little from 1.87 in 1987 to 1.94 by 1991, while the 50th-to-10th percentile ratio moved from 1.87 to 1.89. As was shown in Chapter 3, this was a period when income inequality was in a period of stabilization as well.

Again, it should be emphasized that assessing the inequality trends of the 1990s is more difficult because of the changes to the CPS Annual Demographic Survey in March 1994. The data relied on here (weekly earnings from the monthly CPS), as well as the inequality measures (ratios of percentiles), represent but one rendering of what was happening. Gini indexes based on the annual earnings of men and women working full-time, year-round in the 1993–1996 period (years providing comparable earnings data) from the March CPS show little change in earnings inequality. The Gini index for men had moved up from .386 in 1993 to .393 by 1996 and for women the Gini index went up from .326 to .334 (both changes are not statistically significant at the 90 percent confidence level). Consequently, the conclusion that earnings inequality in the mid-1990s was again beginning to increase must be considered to be tentative at best.[40]

Characteristics of High Earners and Low Earners

With as much interest as there is in the greater dispersion of the earnings distribution, it is useful to examine the incidence of employment in both high-wage and low-wage jobs. From the data developed at the Census Bureau concerning low-earnings employment discussed in the previous chapter, data are also available on the occurrence of employment in high-paying jobs.[41] High earners have been defined to be persons who worked full-time, year-round and had annual earnings in 1994 (either from wage and salary jobs or self-employment) of $55,312, or four times the poverty threshold for a four-person family in 1994 which was $13,828. Employment as a low earner is defined as full-time, year-round employment which yielded less than $13,828 in annual earnings in 1994.

Table 4.7 shows the incidence, or the proportion, of workers of a given characteristic who had high or low annual earnings in 1979 and 1994. The data reflect rising earnings inequality to the extent that for both men and women there are somewhat greater proportions of each group employed in high earnings and low earnings employment over this fifteen-year period.

There are a number of other interesting aspects, however, to these data. For example, among men and women, the incidence of high earnings employment rose relatively more for women than for men (even though men still have a higher incidence of high earnings employment)—from 1.3 to 4.7 percent for the women compared to an increase for men of from 15.0 to 16.0 percent. In addition, the incidence of low-wage employment increased much faster for men than it did for women (even though women still have a higher incidence of low earnings employment)—from 7.7 percent in 1979 to 12.7 percent by 1994, while the comparable figures for women were from 20.4 to 21.4 percent.

In terms of age, it is apparent that the incidence of employment in high earnings positions is much greater for older workers. The incidence of low-wage employment for young persons increased by a disturbing amount between 1979 and 1994. The increase was from 22.9 percent to 42.5 percent for persons age 18 to 24 and the incidence rose from 8.8 to 16.0 percent for those age 25 to 34 as well.

The changes in low-wage employment, of course, are correlated with those

Table 4.7

Percentage of Full-Time, Year-Round Workers with High Earnings and Low Earnings by Selected Characteristics, 1979 and 1994

Characteristics	High Earnings		Low Earnings	
	1979	1994	1979	1994
Total	10.3	11.5	12.1	16.2
Men	15.0	16.0	7.7	12.7
Women	1.3	4.7	20.4	21.4
Age, 18 to 24	0.7	0.9	22.9	42.5
Age, 25 to 34	6.4	5.6	8.8	16.0
Age, 35 to 54	15.0	15.4	9.9	11.9
Age, 55 to 64	13.7	15.6	12.0	15.5
Men, Less Than High School	4.7	3.0	15.3	30.6
Women, Less Than High School	0.3	0.4	40.1	53.0
Men, High School	8.9	6.3	7.8	14.7
Women, High School	0.5	1.5	21.1	28.3
Men, Less Than College	14.0	11.0	5.5	11.3
Women, Less Than College	1.4	2.6	15.4	19.1
Men, College or More	34.4	36.0	3.1	5.0
Women, College or More	4.2	12.3	7.2	6.2
White Men	15.9	17.1	7.2	11.7
White Women	1.3	4.9	19.8	20.6
Black Men	4.2	6.8	14.0	20.4
Black Women	0.5	3.6	24.3	25.8
Hispanic Men	5.2	4.3	13.4	28.1
Hispanic Women	1.0	2.3	32.3	35.7

Source: U.S. Bureau of the Census, Annual Demographic Survey, CPS. See also footnote 41.

Note: High earnings are defined as workers earning $55,312 (in 1994 dollars) or more; low earnings are workers earnings $13,828 (in 1994 dollars) or less.

taking place among workers with less than high school educations as well as those with just high school educations. The incidence rates almost doubled between 1979 and 1994 for men who were high school dropouts and for men who were high school graduates. While the incidence is even higher for women, the increases weren't as sharp. Even among men who were college graduates, the incidence of low-wage employment rose from 3.1 to 5.0 percent of all men with college educations or more. Reflecting the somewhat brighter earnings situation for women in this period, women with college educations or more almost tripled their incidence of high earnings employment.

Among the race and Hispanic ethnic groups there was also evidence of greater high earnings employment as well as low earnings employment. In a relative sense, however, the changes were more favorable for women than for the men. Indeed, Hispanic men saw their incidence of high earnings employment decline from 5.2 to 4.3 percent over the 1979–1994 period while their incidence of low-wage employment more than doubled from 13.4 to 28.1 percent. The incidence of low earnings employment also increased sharply for black men, from 14.0 to 20.4 percent.

These changes in the incidence of high earnings and low earnings among these groups reflect some of the fundamental changes that have taken place in the labor market in past decades and eventually had their impact upon the income distribution. As the above data have demonstrated, young men, men with poor educations (even some men with college educations), and black and Hispanic men saw their chances of ending up in low-wage employment rise considerably in the 1980s and 1990s.

A Final Comment

For the average American worker in the second half of this century, it was the best of times and then the worst of times. In the first twenty-five years, real wages were on the rise and the wage distribution was stable. Most jobs, whether they were unskilled jobs or highly skilled jobs, paid what many considered to be a decent wage. In the next twenty years or so, real wages grew much more slowly, and for some groups, they actually fell. The wage distribution grew more unequal reflecting these differential rates of wage growth. Education and skills became more important in determining those persons whose wages would rise and whose would fall. These developments, along with those taking place in the way society was changing, would play a major role in the story of growing income inequality in the United States.

5

Suggested Causes of Growing Inequality

Economists' explanations for growing inequality over the last fifteen years or so have focused on economic and social changes that have affected the demand for and supply of labor, as well as changes in certain wage-setting mechanisms in the labor market. This framework has been particularly useful for understanding growing dispersion in the earnings distribution, but less so for understanding the growth in income differences among families and households. The decision-making process within the household, which involves many other domains besides the labor market, is very complex and involves an assortment of noneconomic factors.

Unlike economists, the average American does not necessarily think in terms of demand and supply, or the process by which income or earnings inequality comes about. Rather, they think of ultimate causes. Because growing income inequality has received so much attention in the media, a large segment of the public has formed not only popular impressions about what income inequality is, but also opinions regarding its causes.

The range of this public opinion about the causes of growing income inequality is very wide. We have all heard the opinions from the extremes of this range. At one end are people who blame the greater income differences in the United States on the Scrooge-like CEOs and other corporate officials who have sacrificed the jobs of Middle America for the sake of greater profits. According to this view, our industrial leaders, in their quest for more robust balance sheets, have violated the social contract with their employees. In the process, the notion of a "lifetime" job and job security has disappeared for the average worker.

At the other end of the range are people who think the economists' research is flawed, or their data are wrong. These individuals may also believe that those who are at the bottom of the income distribution only have themselves to blame for their economic plight. According to this view, the cause of growing inequality is the pathology of social dependency that has evolved from decades of growth in government welfare programs.

In between the extremes of this range of public opinion are less accusative explanations that are nevertheless heartfelt. For example, some believe that the country has simply become too materialistic and that there must be a return to a society where there is more concern with one another—and the rich and the poor and the middle class should all live together. Others believe that the public educational system of the country has failed; it has produced a segment of society that cannot compete in today's job market. Yet others feel that the "social safety net" has become so frayed because of concern over the federal deficit and welfare reform that millions of households have slipped to the bottom of the income distribution. In short, many explanations for growing income inequality are floating about because the topic is so provocative.

The Public's View and the Economists' View

Despite this diversity of opinion, however, there is some evidence that the public believes that American business has let them down in recent years. The results of a survey in 1996 by the *Washington Post,* the Henry J. Kaiser Family Foundation, and Harvard University reflected as much.[1] Among a number of questions about the economy asked of a sample of 1,511 adults, a couple had to do with how businesses were operating and whether they were responsible for the economy's not doing better in the first half of the 1990s. One of the questions was (Is it because) "Business profits are too high?" and a second was (Is it because) "Top executives are paid too much?"

According to the survey, 46 percent of those adults surveyed felt a major reason the economy was not doing better was that business profits were too high and 36 percent believed it to be a minor reason. So a total of 82 percent of the public, to varying degrees, believed businesses were at fault. With respect to executive pay, 69 percent felt it was a major reason for the slow growth of the economy and 22 percent believed it was a minor reason. Almost the entire sample, therefore, felt businesses were the culprits to some degree. Although the questions of the survey were not specifically directed at the issue of growing income inequality, an "anti-business" sentiment was certainly expressed on the part of the public in this survey.

In addition to asking these questions, the *Post*–Kaiser–Harvard survey also asked the same questions to a sample of 250 economists randomly selected from the membership of the American Economic Association. The results of the survey of economists stood in sharp contrast to those of the public, and especially with respect to the questions relating to the behavior of businesses. Only 4 percent of the economists felt that excessive business profits were a major reason for the economy's performance and only 12 percent thought inordinate executive pay was a major reason. In other words, the survey demonstrated a "disconnect" that existed between the public's perception of the economic problems of the country and the economists' views.[2]

The disconnect that this survey identified between the public and the economists over the problems with the economy may suggest that the intermediary—the media—has either not fully explained the economists' findings (and this could very well be the case because the research is oftentimes very difficult to understand) or the media is placing its own interpretation on the economists' findings.[3] The political right in this country, of course, has often claimed that the media is liberal-biased. Certainly, there have been some prominent economists who have explicitly pointed the "finger of blame" at the business community based on their research findings and, of course, they attract the media. But attempting to prove or disprove hypotheses regarding the motivation of corporate America is statistically a difficult feat.

In the following pages, readers are provided with a flavor for some of the major research into the causes of growing income and earnings inequality that have been proposed in recent years. A thorough review is much beyond the scope of this chapter because the research is so voluminous. Most of the research on inequality has been apolitical and is not accusatory in nature, even though it does deal directly with issues that would have implications for corporate as well as household behavior. As will also become evident, most of the research has dealt with earnings and wage inequality and not income inequality.

Early Explanations

Increasing variance in the wage and earnings distributions during the 1970s and early 1980s, at the same time that real average wages and earnings were virtually stagnant, alarmed many economists, especially after the disruptive economic recessions of 1980–82. As a result, they began to examine many of the well-known changes that had been going on in the economy of the United States and its demography. What they found were a number of possible developments that might have been associated with, or indeed caused, a more unequal distribution of earnings, and ultimately, distribution of income.

Deindustrialization

For many years, economists had been observing the shift in economic activity away from the goods-producing industries to the service-producing industries. One of the consequences, of course, was the changing distribution of employment in these two broad sectors of the economy. From 1969 to 1979, for example, the proportion of total nonfarm payroll employment in the service-producing industries had risen from 65.4 percent to 70.5 percent, and by 1984, after the recessions, the proportion had risen even faster to nearly 74 percent.[4] By definition, therefore, employment was shifting away from the goods-producing industries.

As is well known, the goods-producing industries, such as manufacturing and construction, paid much higher wages than the service-producing industries. For example, in 1984, average weekly earnings for production workers in manufacturing were over twice as high as those for nonsupervisory workers in retail trade.[5] Economists could see the implications for the broad average of weekly earnings of all workers of a continued shift from high-paying goods-producing industries to lower-paying service-producing industries. And it would not be long for them to see the implications for the overall shape of the earnings distribution.

In a popular 1982 book by Barry Bluestone and Bennett Harrison, the authors argued that the loss of jobs in the goods-producing sector, specifically manufacturing, to the service-producing industries had dire implications for the middle class.[6] They attributed the loss of manufacturing jobs to what they called "deindustrialization." Stiffer import competition, technological changes, and other changes going on in corporate America were producing shifts in labor demand that were injurious to many manufacturing workers. The service-producing industries had many more jobs with low skill requirements which paid low wages, yet, like all industries, they had highly paid managers and administrators as well. Consequently, the earnings distribution in this sector of the economy was much more unequal, and as more workers flooded into this sector, cast off from the goods-producing industries, overall inequality in the earnings distribution increased.

This explanation had appeal because it was straightforward and dovetailed with the long observed change in industrial restructuring. Unfortunately, other researchers had pointed out that wage and earnings inequality had been increasing within many industries of both the goods-producing and service-producing sectors. For example, one study showed that the Gini index for all male wage and salary workers in manufacturing between 1970 and 1977 had increased from .300 to .313, and in retail trade the comparable Gini index had increased from .434 to .461 over the same period.[7] Findings such as these suggested that growing dispersion in the earnings distribution was not being induced by industrial restructuring necessarily. The cause of rising inequality was more elusive.

Other Early Explanations

Other explanations were also emerging.[8] Some of these suggested that growing earnings inequality was the result of temporary phenomena and that the situation would soon correct itself. But others involved what were believed to be structural changes that were taking place in the economy and society that had long-term implications for both the earnings and income distribution.

The Business Cycle

Business cycle fluctuations, specifically economic downturns, had immediate credibility in the early 1980s. With the slump in economic activity and the rise in unemployment, earnings inequality and income inequality increased because of its relatively greater impact on the lower end of the earnings distribution. The presumption was, of course, that once economic growth resumed, income and earnings disparities would contract. As everyone knows, this did not happen by the time the economy was in its recovery phase. Indeed, inequality continued to grow, both in terms of earnings and incomes. This explanation was quickly abandoned.

The Baby Boom

The influx of the baby boom generation into the labor market from the late 1960s to the early 1980s as an explanation also had intuitive appeal. With such a large increase in the supply of labor, downward pressure on wages was expected, which would result in increased earnings inequality. The good news, according to those who subscribed to this explanation, was that as this large cohort aged and they began ascending the age-earnings profile, inequality would shrink. The bad news, of course, was that as the full cohort of baby boomers was absorbed into the labor force and grew older during the 1980s, earnings inequality still continued to rise. So this explanation too lost credibility.

The Value of the Dollar

During the early 1980s, the value of the dollar in foreign exchange markets rose against the currencies of the United States's trading partners. Since this made our manufactured goods more expensive relative to our international competitors' goods, it was thought this development had led to reduced demand for U.S.-manufactured goods, thereby lowering the labor demand of manufacturers. It was argued that by reducing interest rates in this country and thereby reducing the foreign demand for dollars, our exporting industries could shift labor demand back to where it once was and inequality would subside. This explanation too was not sufficiently rigorous to explain the increase in earnings inequality in the 1970s and into the 1980s because the run-up in the value of the dollar occurred only during a short period in the early 1980s.

Growing International Competition

In the mid-1980s an explanation arose suggesting that growing international competition in the production of goods caused American manufacturers to reassess their employment policies. Foreign competitors could produce similar goods more cheaply primarily because their cost of labor—wages—was so much less than in the United States. In research by Tilly, Bluestone, and Harrison, a conclusion was reached that growing wage inequality was being driven by changes on the demand-side of the labor market and not by changes in the supply of labor (e.g., the baby boom influx, the entry of women into the workforce, changes in the levels of education and amounts of work experience).[9] They speculated that these demand-side changes on the part of employers were being manifested by "outsourcing" certain production activities, the introduction of "pay for performance" wage systems, the creation of more part-time jobs, and other practices of employers to lower wage costs. Elements of this explanation continue to be heard today (as will be seen below).

Household and Family Composition

Another long-term explanation, which had direct implications for the income distribution, was the change taking place in the composition of families. As had been well documented by demographers, the rise in divorce rates and marital separations, along with the upsurge in births out of wedlock, resulted in a growing proportion of single-parent families among all families. The heads of these families, primarily women, usually had low skills and poor educations and their annual incomes were at poverty or near-poverty levels. At the same time, as the proportion of married-couple families became a smaller and smaller proportion of all families, a growing proportion of married-couple families had two earners, normally the husband and wife. Many of these dual-earner families were in the upper half of the income distribution. As a consequence, some researchers suggested that this long-term change in the composition of families, along with other changes, was being reflected in growing income inequality.[10] Other changes in living arrangements, such as the growth in the proportion of persons living alone (primarily the young and the old) and the cohabitation of unrelated individuals, no doubt also led to greater variance in the income distribution. These long-term structural shifts also continue to be important today in explaining the inequality of incomes, and more will be said about them below.

It can be seen from the above when and where some of the present-day opinions about the causes of rising earnings and income inequality were born. Clearly, some of them have been refined and filtered through the work of other economists and, most importantly, the media.

One of the most provocative side issues related to deindustrialization was the erosion of middle-class jobs. Indeed, there was clear evidence that the middle of the wage distribution was thinning out for men who were employed full-time, year-round, with some of them moving up in the distribution but many moving down as well. The process could often be differentiated on the basis of workers' education and work experience. This aspect of the various explanations—growing relative wage differences—was something the average American could understand and relate to.

Relative Wage Differences

Increases in relative wage differentials during the 1980s had been observed by economists as evidence of changes taking place in the labor market. The most popular relative wage differences were by education and experience (i.e., age or work experience). The metric used in calibrating relative wages typically was the ratio of the earnings of college graduates to high school dropouts and the ratio of the earnings of older workers (usually age 45 to 54) to younger workers (usually age 25 to 34). Frequently, these ratios were further cross-classified by age and sex, for example, the ratio of the earnings of 45-to-54-year-old male high school dropouts to the earnings of 25-to-34-year-old male high school dropouts.

A crude relative wage differential by education for the 1987–1996 period can be seen in Table 5.1. It is based on the annual earnings of men and women age 25 and over who worked full-time, year-round in the year and had either a college education or more or a high school education.[11] As shown in the table, this differential for men has continuously moved up in

Table 5.1

Ratio of Median Annual Earnings of Full-Time, Year-Round Workers Age 25 and Over Who Had College Educations to Those Who Had High School Educations, by Sex, 1987–1996

Year	Men Ratio: College vs. High School	Women Ratio: College vs. High School
1987	1.49	1.55
1988	1.51	1.61
1989	1.57	1.63
1990	1.59	1.67
1991	1.62	1.69
1992	1.64	1.68
1993	1.72	1.69
1994	1.73	1.71
1995	1.68	1.70
1996	1.67	1.71

Source: U.S. Bureau of the Census, Annual Demographic Survey, CPS.
Note: Real earnings in 1996 dollars. See footnote 11 also.

the late 1980s and first half of the 1990s from about 1.50 to 1.70. This was not because the earnings of college-educated men were rising faster than those for high school–educated men; rather, it was because the earnings for the former were declining slower during the recession and recovery years of the early 1990s than the former. It is essential to point out, however, that from the 1970s and into the 1980s this relative wage differential did increase because of greater earnings growth for the college-educated men.[12]

Among the women, the relative wage differential rose much slower, especially when 1987 is excluded from the comparison (from 1.61 to 1.71). Earnings for college-educated women who worked full-time, year-round were rising gradually during most of this period, while for high school–educated women, earnings were falling slightly.

A popular graphic depiction of the effect of the growth in these educational wage differentials on the earnings distribution observed in many of the articles and professional papers of the time is shown in Figure 5.1. It shows the percent changes in the real annual wage and salary earnings of men and women who worked full-time, year-round in 1979 and 1989 at every fifth percentile of the wage and salary earnings distribution.[13] Annual earnings had dropped by 5 percent or more for men from the 50th percentile and lower—and many of these men were both young and unskilled. It wasn't until the 65th percentile and higher that real earnings for men began

Figure 5.1 **Percentage Change in Real Annual Wage and Salary Earnings of Men and Women Who Worked Full-Time, Year-Round at Selected Percentiles of Their Distributions, 1979–1989**

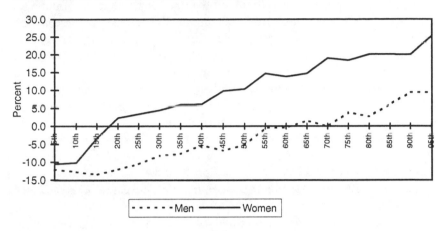

Source: Author's tabulation of the Annual Demographic Survey, CPS.
Note: Real earnings in 1992 dollars.

to increase—and at the 90th and 95th percentile earnings were up by nearly 10 percent.

For women, the earnings pattern over this period was quite different. Their real earnings also declined at the very bottom of the distribution but growth began much sooner—at the 20th percentile of their distribution. Moreover, the rate of earnings growth for women in the upper half was considerably faster than for men at comparable points in their distribution.

Demand and Supply Factors

Among the many papers and articles by economists in the late 1980s and early 1990s examining growing relative wage differences, a few are worth noting. One of the significant pieces of research into understanding the long-term changes in relative wage differences was by Kevin Murphy and Finis Welch.[14] According to these researchers, who studied the wage structure over the 1963–1989 period, the returns to schooling, or earnings differences by education, increased in the 1963–1971 period, but then declined through much of the 1970s. In the 1980s, however, education-related earnings differences rose sharply. By separating changes in labor demand and supply, they were able to show that the relative drop in earnings for unskilled men in the 1980s was related to demand shifts for their labor, while a slower growth in the supply of college-educated workers relative to the 1970s also led to growing relative earnings differences by education.

Another important article, this one by Lawrence Katz and Kevin Murphy, also focused on changes in the demand for labor as well as long-term changes in the supply.[15] They observed that the relative supply of college-educated workers slowed dramatically in the 1980s, after a surge in the 1970s, as a result of the aging of the baby boom generation. Given the constant demand for college-educated workers throughout both periods, a rise in the relative wage differential between college-educated and high school–educated workers (due to the increase in the wage premium for college-educated workers and lower demand for high school–educated workers) could have been expected. Most of this was induced by increases in labor demand within various sectors of the economy brought about by technological changes that favored highly skilled and educated workers. Other researchers would come to similar conclusions, all of which cast doubt on the deindustrialization explanation as the sole cause of the changes in the economy's wage structure.[16]

The separation of labor demand and labor supply shifts for workers of different education and experience levels was an important contribution to understanding the increase in relative wage differences. But it did not explain entirely the rise in earnings inequality. Juhn, Murphy, and Pierce showed that not only had relative wage differences widened "between" education and experience groups, but also "within" these education and experience groups (i.e., inequality of earnings within groups such as college graduates age 45 to 54)—and that the timing of the increases in both "between" and "within" group inequality differed.[17] Furthermore, and most importantly, the rise in relative wage differences only began in the decade of the 1980s after actually narrowing in the 1970s. What Juhn, Murphy, and Pierce showed was that within-group inequality had been increasing since the late 1960s and early 1970s. The reason that overall-earnings inequality did not rise much in the 1970s was that the decline in between-group inequality (i.e., the narrowing of relative wage differentials) had offset the increase in within-group inequality. In the 1980s, both between- and within-group inequality increased and the result was an acceleration in overall-earnings inequality. The identification of two separate and unique components of growing-earnings inequality was a significant development in economists' understanding of this phenomenon.

The implications of all this research for the public's understanding of growing-earnings-and-income inequality was that not only were purely demand-side explanations for growing-earnings inequality possible (which featured employers' changes in labor demand), but other explanations on the supply side as well. Earlier explanations had focused exclusively on employers' demand shifts for labor because of deindustrialization and more intensive international competition that led employers to downsize, out-source, and introduce other means of cutting labor costs.

Even the research that focused on the plummeting earnings of unskilled men (initially thought to be linked to deindustrialization) during the 1980s had pushed beyond purely demand-side explanations. In an article by Blackburn, Bloom, and Freeman that explored the economic plight of young men with low skills and education levels, changes in the supply of labor and changes in wage-setting institutions (i.e., the declining real value of the minimum wage and declining union membership) were investigated, along with shifts in demand for this type of labor.[18] The findings from their research implied that the growing wage differential between men age 25 to 34 who were college graduates and men of the same age group who were high school dropouts was "largely supply driven."[19] They also found that "deunionization" and the erosion of the real value of the minimum wage had small but nevertheless important effects on the relative earnings of unskilled young men.

Growing Inequality Within Groups

The discovery of growing inequality within specific education and experi-ence groups of workers opened up other avenues of research, as we have seen. According to Katz and Murphy (mentioned earlier), within-group inequality had increased by nearly 30 percent between the late 1960s and late 1980s and represented a long and steady rise in the demand for "skills."[20]

Unlike between-group inequality, within-group inequality is somewhat more difficult to measure. In the context of regression analysis, within-group inequality can be measured by using a regression model in which independent variables representing education levels and experience levels (as well as other covariates, such as occupation and industry) are regressed on the earnings of workers. Typically, such a model will explain only a portion of the variation in the earnings distribution and the unexplained portion is represented in the error term of the regression, or the residuals. Examining the degree of the dispersion in the residuals of the regression over time provides an indication of the amount of inequality within the education and experience groups specified in the regression, and how it has changed over time. In short, what economists were attempting to under-stand was why the distribution of earnings in a particular education-experi-ence group, such as male college graduates age 25 to 34, should grow more unequal over time.

Figure 5.2 shows the results of one estimate of the trend in within-group inequality for men who were employed full-time, year-round in the private

Figure 5.2 **Within Group Inequality as Measured by the Difference in Log Residual Earnings at the 90th and 10th Percentiles of the Distributions of Earnings Residuals for Men Who Worked Full-Time, Year-Round in the Private Sector, 1979–1993**

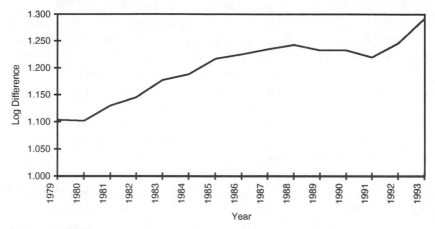

Source: Author's tabulation of the Annual Demographic Survey, CPS.

sector of the economy between 1979 and 1993.[21] The metric used is the difference in the log residual earnings at the 90th and 10th percentiles of the distributions of earnings residuals. Following the method of Katz and Murphy, the log of annual wage and salary earnings of men was regressed on a series of education and experience variables. As shown in the figure, within-group inequality in the private sector rose steadily between 1979 and 1988 and then leveled off for the next three years. After 1991, however, it began to rise again. Over the entire 1979–1993 period, within-group inequality in the private sector increased from 1.104 to 1.292 log points, or upwards of 20 percent.

Possible Explanations

Possible causes of growing within-group inequality have been mentioned by Levy and Murnane in their 1992 review of the earnings inequality literature.[22] The first involves changes that have taken place in the characteristics of workers, in other words, the labor supply. For example, worker skills may not be easily measured by standard measures of educational attainment, such as years of school completed and degrees received. Skills such as those involved with mentoring, negotiating, instructing, supervising, and so forth may be viewed by employers as more valuable in today's workplace than in earlier years, adding additional variance to the earnings of similarly educated workers.

Another cause involves growing wage differentials between industries and between companies, which then are reflected in workers' wages. These differentials may have come about as a result of different responses to greater international and domestic competition as well as new technologies. Responses may vary, for example, in how quickly they retrain workers when new technologies are introduced.

Related to these explanations for growing within-group inequality could be the greater instability that has been observed in earnings among workers of similar characteristics.[23] It is well known that the labor market is very fluid, with persons moving in and out of jobs and in and out of the labor force, resulting in fluctuations in their earnings. If these increases and decreases in earnings become larger over time, inequality in the earnings distribution measured on an annual basis would also increase.

It is clear from the foregoing that the reason or reasons for rising inequality within groups defined on the basis of education and experience in the 1970s and 1980s, and to some extent the early 1990s, are still unclear. They could be related to changes in the demand and supply of labor, as well as changes that have taken place in union membership and the real value of the minimum wage.

Trade vs. Technology

It would appear from the major research into growing-earnings inequality that outward labor demand shifts for highly skilled workers on the part of employers appear to have dominated supply-side effects as well as changes in wage-setting mechanisms. Debate still exists, however, as to how much of the outward shifts have been induced by skill-biased technological changes, increased trade competition, and other explanations such as deindustrialization. This is not to suggest that supply-side explanations and changes in wage-setting mechanisms should be dismissed.

The notion that trade is responsible for most of the increase in earnings inequality plays much better in the media than do other factors (recall the debates over NAFTA and "fast track" trade legislation). This is perhaps because the enemy—"free traders," proponents of globalization, "outsourcers"—are more visible and their policies can be attacked as inimical to the average worker, unlike those who suggest technological changes are at the root of the problem (e.g., stopping the spread of computers and other technological changes are considerably more difficult).

The trade argument is fairly intuitive. As is well known, many of our imports in recent years were manufactured goods from low-wage, less-developed countries. In effect, these were goods (e.g., athletic shoes, apparel, textiles) embodying the work of low-skilled workers. Rather than make these products in the United States where low-skilled labor is relatively more expensive than elsewhere, manufacturers looked for cheaper labor markets or decided to use that more expensive labor to produce other goods (requiring skilled workers) that would be more competitive in world markets. The consequence was an erosion of once high-paying, low-skilled jobs in this country and a reduction in the relative earnings of unskilled workers—and a growing demand for more skilled labor.

Some economists believe that the growth in imports of manufactured goods from industrializing countries is very important in explaining the rise in wage inequality of industrialized countries.[24] Others have implied a connection to varying degrees.[25] This research on trade and inequality was reviewed in the mid-1990s.[26]

In recent years, however, the predominant role of trade in explaining inequality trends has been questioned. No doubt certain production activities have been shipped overseas and outsourcing of various business activities has become more common as well. But as the economist George Johnson recently wrote, there are several problems with assigning this a major role in the overall growth in wage inequality.[27] First, the number of unskilled workers involved in foreign trade-oriented industries is too small to have caused the shifts in labor demand observed in the 1980s. Second, labor demand shifts toward more skilled and educated workers occurred in all industries of the economy, not just those manufacturing industries involved in trade. And according to Johnson and his estimates, shifts in relative demand like those in the 1980s were only a continuation of a trend observed for at least forty years.

Consequently, Johnson gives much more weight to the rise of skill-biased technological changes as a reason for growing demand for highly skilled and educated workers and he links this to the rise in computer technology throughout the economy. Research by the economist Alan Kreuger has shown that workers involved with computers tend to have higher earnings, although the flow of causation between computer usage and high earnings is still under investigation.[28]

Other economists have made similar arguments about the minor role of trade in the declining wages of our less-educated and unskilled workers.[29] They too have suggested that shifts in labor demand were brought on by technological changes such as the increased use of computers in the workplace.

From Labor Market Earnings to Household Income

The answer to the question about why inequality has grown so much in recent decades becomes even more complicated when we turn to the income distributions of households and families. Not only do a host of possible social and demographic causes emerge as possible correlates of growing income dispersion, but untangling the possible linkages between them and the labor market explanations just discussed becomes a daunting task.

The society and demography of the United States today has changed significantly since World War II, and even since the decade of the 1970s for that matter. Society has become more tolerant with respect to different lifestyles, it is more open to cultural diversity, and the attitudes toward our most revered institutions and practices, such as the government and the world of work, have changed. We have become better educated on average and our access to computers and other electronic technologies has brought forth a revolution in information creation. With respect to our population, we know that the population has aged and become more racially and ethnically diverse. Living arrangements and the nature of the family have changed. When the word "family" comes up, we no longer automatically think of the traditional four-person family composed of Dad, Mom, Dick, and Jane—and Spot the dog.

In this section some of the research into "income" inequality is presented, focusing on changes taking place not only in the labor market, but also in our society and demography. There is much less of this research in the economic literature and some of it is less rigorous than that related to earnings and wage inequality. Nevertheless, it represents a significant contribution to understanding the phenomenon of rising income inequality in the United States.

The Linchpin

Perhaps the linchpin between the trend in the income inequality of households and the trend in earnings inequality of workers is the number of earners in the household. If indeed profound changes have been occurring in the labor market, with the real earnings of some workers decreasing and others increasing over time, it would be useful to examine in what kind of households these workers live. Do they come from single-parent families where there is only one earner or do they come from married-couple households in which the possibility exists for there to be at least two adult earners?

Figure 5.3 shows married-couple households as a percentage of all households in each decile of the household income distribution in 1979 and 1994.[30] Between these two years the proportion of all households that consisted of married couples declined from about 61 percent to 54 percent, but the change across the distribution varied. The smallest declines occurred at the far ends of the distribution. Married couples as a percentage of all

Figure 5.3 **Married-Couple Households as a Percentage of All Households by Deciles of the Income Distribution, 1979 and 1994**

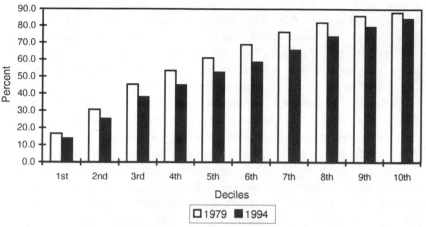

Source: Author's tabulation of Annual Demographic Survey, CPS.

households in the 1st decile fell from 17 percent to 14 percent, and in the 10th decile the reduction was from 88 to 84 percent. Percentage reductions in the middle portion of the income distribution, however, were nearly twice as large. Between the 4th and 8th deciles the declines in the proportion of married couples exceeded 8 percentage points.

The implications embodied in these data are twofold. First, with the great disparity in the proportion of married couples across the household income distribution (regardless whether it be the situation in 1979 or 1994), there is a significant force for creating income inequality because in married-couple families the potential for two breadwinners existed. And second, with the greatest reduction in the proportion of married-couple households occurring in the middle of the distribution, the potential for two breadwinner families was reduced significantly in this part of the distribution. This development accentuated the difference in the households at the bottom and top of the distribution that could possibly be two-earner households, and led to even greater income differences in 1994 than in 1979.

Social and Demographic Changes

Table 5.2 displays some of the more well-known social and demographic changes that have taken place in the United States in the second half of this century which economists have considered in their attempts to understand rising income inequality.

Table 5.2

Selected Social and Demographic Characteristics, 1950–1996

Characteristic	1950	1960	1970	1980	1990	1996
Household Composition						
Total Households (percent)	100.0	100.0	100.0	100.0	100.0	100.0
Married Couples						
(percent)	78.2	74.3	70.5	60.8	56.0	53.8
Single Parent (percent)	10.9	10.7	10.6	12.9	14.8	16.1
Female	8.3	8.4	8.7	10.8	11.7	12.6
Nonfamily Hhlds.						
(percent)	10.8	14.9	18.8	26.3	29.2	30.1
Marriage and Divorce						
Age at First Marriage						
Men	22.8	22.8	23.2	24.7	26.1	26.9
Women	20.3	20.3	20.8	22.0	23.9	24.5
Divorce Rate (per 1,000)	2.6	2.2	3.5	5.2	4.7	4.6
Births						
Total Rate (per 1,000)	24.1	23.7	18.4	15.9	16.7	15.5
Unmarried Rate (per						
1,000)	14.1	21.6	26.4	29.4	43.8	45.2
Population						
Median Age	30.2	29.5	28.0	30.0	32.8	34.0
Immigration (millions)	1.0	2.5	3.3	4.5	7.3	—
Persons 25 and Older						
with College Education						
(percent)	6.0	7.7	11.0	17.0	21.3	23.5

Source: U.S. Bureau of the Census, Annual Demographic Survey, CPS; National Center for Health Statistics; Immigration and Naturalization Service.

Note: Age at first marriage for 1996 is for 1995; divorce rate for 1996 is for 1993; total birth rate for 1996 is for 1993; birth rate for unmarried women in 1996 is for 1992; median age of population in 1996 is for 1995; immigration data are cumulative over the decade.

The first and most important involve the nation's change in living arrangements, that is, the composition of our families and households. The data show the precipitous drop in the proportion of all households in the country that were made up of married couples and the remarkable increase in single-parent families and nonfamily households. These changes, however, did not occur smoothly across the half century.

Between 1950 and 1970, the proportion of all households accounted for by married couples declined from 78 percent to 71 percent; single-parent families, on the other hand, accounted for about the same proportion of households across this twenty-year period, that is, 11 percent; and the proportion of all households composed of nonfamily households rose from 11 to 19 percent. This shifting away from family households to nonfamily house-holds during these years was no doubt in large part due to the growing propor-tion of elderly persons living alone, as well as to a rise in the divorce rate.

The decade of the 1970s witnessed a surge in living "rearrangements," again away from the traditional two-parent family to nonfamily households but also toward single-parent families. Divorce rates were continuing to move up as was the incidence of births out of wedlock. In addition, a large part of the baby boom generation was reaching adulthood and forming their own households, often by themselves or with other persons like themselves. The age at first marriage was beginning to rise for both men and women as the baby boom aged and the population grew older.

As shown in Table 5.2, the proportion of all households made up of married couples dropped sharply from 71 percent in 1970 to 61 percent by 1980 and the proportion of all households composed of nonfamilies shot up from 19 to 26 percent and single-parents grew from 11 percent to 13 per-cent. These changes, of course, were taking place in a decade when produc-tivity growth slackened, incomes and wages stagnated, and inflation soared.

One of the important social changes that was occurring during this "tran-sitional" decade was an unusually large jump in the proportion of the adult population with college educations or more—from 11 percent to 17 per-cent—an increase in ten years that was greater than what had occurred in the previous twenty years. The baby boom generation had significantly affected wage levels—and as was also discussed in the previous chapter, the relative earnings differential between college-educated workers and high school–educated workers narrowed in this decade.

In the decade of the 1980s social and demographic changes stabilized to some extent. The proportion of all households composed of married couples did not erode as rapidly—it fell from 61 to 56 percent—and the relative growth in nonfamily households slowed somewhat also—increasing only from 26 to 29 percent. The growth in the proportion of households com-posed of single families, however, was nearly as great as in the 1970s. During the 1990s, the social and demographic changes being discussed continued to change only modestly but still in the direction away from married-couple families and toward other living arrangements. While the divorce rate drifted down from the high it had reached in the 1980s, the birth rate for unmarried women continued to move up, resulting in rela-tively more single-parent families.

One last major demographic development that should be mentioned is immigration. Immigration is often viewed as injurious to the economic welfare of the native population, as the debate in France and other European countries in recent years has illustrated. The decade of the 1980s saw a relatively large increase in immigration in the United States. About 7.3 million persons entered the country in this decade, compared to only 4.5 million in the 1970s. This influx has also been associated with rising earnings inequality by some observers. Immigrants typically have low skills and do not command wage premiums and it is thought that they may have contributed to the growth in the relative wage differential between high-skilled workers and low-skilled workers. However, the bulk of the research that investigated this matter concluded that even though the immigration levels were much higher than in previous decades, they could not have contributed much to lowering wages for low-skilled workers born in this country, nor to increasing earnings inequality.[31]

Household Compositional Changes and Inequality

Frank Levy, back in the 1980s, was one of the first economists to draw attention to the relationship between changes in family and household composition and increasing income dispersion among families and households.[32] In his book he discussed the potential impact on inequality of more dual-earner married couples, more elderly households, and more families headed by women. He suggested that the first should result in more equality (about which more will be said) and the last two developments should tend to increase overall income inequality. Indeed, in a statistical exercise he performed with CPS income data for 1984 and earlier years, he showed that the U.S. income distributions moved toward greater equality until the early 1970s and then grew more unequal after that, primarily because of the increase in "female-headed families."[33]

Some of the demographic and social changes, like the influx into the labor market of the baby boom generation, the growing participation of women in the labor market, and immigration, had been considered as potential explanations of rising income inequality in the 1980s. And as has been shown, many of them were dismissed as major players in expanding income differences. A few, however, lingered and continued to be examined by economists.

The shifting composition of households, and specifically the growing proportion of single-parent families, has received much attention from the media (especially to the political right) and those who did not believe the "deindustrialization" explanation for rising inequality. This was because the "composition of households" explanation was basically a supply-side argument and not much could be done about it in a policy sense. Deindustrialization involved the demand-side (i.e., employers) and industrial policies could be changed if indeed this was the source of the problem. During this time, of course, the debate over the declining middle class was raging and the search for explanations was in high gear.

One study by Ryscavage, Green, and Welniak that appeared in the early 1990s lent support to the idea that the income distribution and income growth had been affected by social and demographic changes in living arrangements.[34] Using CPS income data, household income distributions in 1969, 1979, and 1989 were compared for the effects of certain economic, social, and demographic changes over the twenty-year period. A standardization technique was used in which certain questions were asked. For example, if the composition of households had not changed between 1969 and 1989, how fast would have median household income grown and what would have been the impact on the household income distribution? Other social, economic, and demographic factors were examined, such as the industries in which householders worked, their race, age, and education, how much they worked, and whether or not the wife (if one was present) worked. In other words, this exercise attempted to find out the effects of these various factors on the income distribution over the 1969–1989 period.

The findings of this study were illuminating with respect to shifts in the composition of households. The standardization exercise showed that real median household income in 1989 would have been $32,132 (in 1989 dollars) instead of the actual median of $28,906, or over $3,200 more, in the absence of the shifts between 1969 and 1989. In other words, the shifts in household composition away from married-couple families to nonfamily households and single-parent families over these years represented a "drag" on income growth. This was understandable given the much lower incomes of single-parent and nonfamily households.

The impact of these household compositional changes on income inequality was also revealing. The Gini index for the household income distribution in 1969 was .391 and by 1989 it had reached .429—an increase of almost 10 percent. Had the nature of households not changed as they had in the twenty-year period, the Gini index would have only been .411—an increase of only about 5 percent. The results of the analysis also showed, however, that changes in the industry in which the head of the household worked also depressed real median household income and increased inequality more than it would have been had not the changes occurred.

As the Ryscavage et al. study pointed out, standardization exercises are only first approximations of effects on broad income measures. This is because they are not sufficiently sensitive to the interactions of the various characteristics and, in the case of this exercise, they did not take into account other changes that had taken place in the economy, such as employment in trade-sensitive industries and the greater utilization of computers in the workplace.

Dual-Earner Families and Inequality

Another change that has taken place in conjunction with the overall rise in female labor force participation has been the emergence of dual-earner families and their influence on the income distribution. This topic is not necessarily new, but has been revisited in recent years as a result of the growth in income inequality. Past studies of the effect of working wives on the family income distribution have shown that it has tended to produce an "equalizing" effect.[35] In other words, had wives not entered the workplace, income inequality would have been even greater.

The reason for this was that traditionally the wives who entered the work force came from families in which the husband had relatively low earnings and the earnings of wives exhibited little variance relative to their husbands. So, even if the same proportion of wives worked across all income classes, if the variance in wives' earnings was very small it would be almost like adding a constant amount of earnings to their husbands' earnings, thereby making the family income distribution more equal (because the relative effect of the wives' earnings would be so much larger to husbands with low earnings).

More recent studies into the effect of dual-earner families on the income distribution of families have come to similar conclusions, but they also imply that the equalizing effect may have changed in recent years because of household compositional shifts.[36] Although working wives are more common in married-couple families than ever before (62 percent in 1996 compared to 39 percent in 1970), married couples as a percent of all households have declined sharply (from 71 percent in 1970 to 54 percent in 1996).

Indeed, some economists investigating the linkages between growing earnings inequality and household income inequality have suggested that the equalizing effect of working wives on the income distribution has waned. Karoly and Burtless demonstrated that there is more to the growth in income inequality in the 1980s than simply the growing dispersion in men's earnings.[37] They found that changes in family composition, like those depicted in Figure 5.3 showing the drop in married-couple households as a proportion of all households, especially from the middle- and lower-income ranks, have deprived many households of a second earner. In addition, earnings increases among wives in the 1980s, especially from upper income families, were becoming more highly correlated with their family incomes, also contributing to growing income inequality. Consequently, these economists viewed the rise in income inequality in recent years as a combination of events taking place in the labor market and in the household.

While the influences of social and demographic changes on growing income inequality have not been investigated to the same extent as labor market changes, it is clear they play a role. Indeed, this has been acknowledged by some of our leading researchers in this area.[38] But considerably more research needs to be done before a complete understanding of the linkages between the growing earnings inequality of workers and the growing income inequality of households is reached.

No Simple Explanations

So what can average Americans conclude from this review of some of the major explanations offered by economists for the growth in inequality? Are these the same explanations Americans have read about in the newspapers and seen on television? Judging from the *Washington Post*–Kaiser–Harvard poll cited earlier, they aren't. Some of these explanations have never really made it into the mainstream of the public debate on the topic.

One thing is clear: Income inequality has increased in recent years, but agreement over the definitive cause or causes of this phenomenon has yet to be decided despite what much of the media reports. As Sheldon Danziger and Peter Gottschalk wrote in the introduction to their 1990 book of research findings by various economists: "There are no simple explanations. No single factor accounts for the many complex changes in the distribution of income."[39]

6

Inequality Before 1950

Important perspective on income inequality today can be obtained from reviewing the trend in income inequality in the first half of the century. We are often swept away by current events and forget that the country has passed through other economic eras that have also changed the shape of the nation's income distribution.

The principal problems involved in analyzing the trend in income inequality in the first half of the twentieth century are the data—and the lack of them. No single database covering the entire period exists, as does the Annual Demographic Survey of the CPS for the 1947–1996 period. Some data sources do exist which cover portions of the period, but these partial databases often contain problems. Comparability issues exist as do issues of data quality because of the way the data were collected and assembled.

We can, however, rely on the work of economic historians and others interested in the way the economy worked in years gone by. They have scoured the libraries, government records, data repositories of private institutions, and other sources for information on the incomes and wages of Americans living generations ago. It is from the work of these economists that it is possible to obtain some idea as to the level and trend in income inequality between 1900 and 1950.

Statisticians and economists of those years should not be faulted for their job of keeping track of such matters as income inequality. They did collect data on the wages and earnings of workers in important occupations and industries and there were estimates made of the size distribution of income. Furthermore, there was interest in the matter of inequality, as the political rhetoric of the Great Depression years attests. The problem was simply a matter of the adequacy of the existing data for interpretation. Simon Kuznets, the economist who studied the U.S. income distribution in great detail in the first half of the century, referred to measures of income distribution as "preliminary informed guesses."[1]

In this chapter, an attempt will be made to profile the trend in earnings

Figure 6.1 **Real Gross National Product Per Capita, 1900–1970**

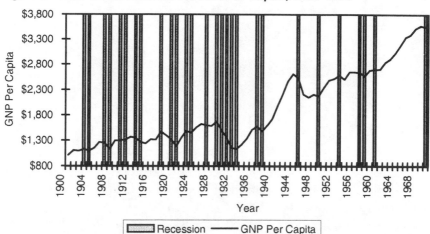

Source: U.S. Bureau of Economic Analysis (published in U.S. Bureau of the Census, *Historical Statistics of the United States: Colonial Times to 1970,* Part 1, Series F4, p. 224) and the National Bureau of Economic Research (NBER).
Note: Real gross national product per capita in 1958 dollars.
Shaded areas represent periods of economic recession according to the NBER.

and income inequality in the 1900–1950 period based on the major research that has been carried out for those years. Background about the performance of the U.S. economy in the first half of the century will be first presented. While most people are familiar in a general way with such events as the stock market crash of 1929 and the Great Depression of the 1930s, they may not be as familiar with such things as economic growth rates, productivity trends, and other aspects of the economy's performance over these years. Trends in earnings and wage inequality will then be presented. Although the data are fragmentary, they probably are very reflective of the trends in income inequality because the income derived from the labor market represented the only source of income for most households. It was only with the advent of the New Deal in the 1930s and particularly the Great Society of the 1960s that cash transfer programs began to play an important role in distinguishing the income distribution from the earnings distribution. The discussion will then turn to income inequality. Trends in income inequality will be examined from a couple of different statistical series that were developed for this period. A concluding section will summarize what can be said about income inequality and its trend since the turn of the century and up to and including World War II.

Table 6.1

Real Gross National Product, Population, and Real Gross National Product Per Capita, 1900, 1940, 1946, and 1970

Year	Real GNP (in billions)	Population (in thousands)	Real GNP Per Capita
1900	$ 76.9	76,063	$1,011
1940	227.2	132,093	1,720
1946	312.6	141,384	2,211
1970	722.5	203,235	3,555
Average Annual Percentage Change			
1900–1940	2.7	1.4	1.3
1946–1970	3.5	1.5	2.0

Source: U.S. Bureau of Economic Analysis (published in U.S. Bureau of the Census, *Historical Statistics of the United States: Colonial Times to 1970,* Part 1, Series F 1–5, p. 224).

Note: Real GNP and real GNP per capita in 1958 dollars.

Some Economic History

A flavor for the economic times of the pre-WWII era in relation to the post-WWII era (or at least twenty-five years of it) can be obtained by looking at Figure 6.1. The figure shows the nation's gross national product (GNP) on a per capita basis in constant 1959 dollars from 1900 to 1970, as well as the years in which the economy was officially in recessionary periods according the National Bureau of Economic Research (NBER).[2] While this per capita series is not an income series like those previously analyzed here, it does provide one of the few consistent, long-term views of the relationship between the growth in national output and growth in population.

A couple of facts stand out clearly in the figure. First, putting aside the years of WWII, real GNP per capita grew much more slowly in the pre-WWII era than it did in the twenty-five years after the post-WWII era. And second, the periods of economic contraction appear to be more numerous and frequent in the first half of the century than in the 1950–1970 period.

Further insight into the figure can be seen in Table 6.1. This table shows that the faster rate of growth in real GNP per capita in the 1946–1970 period compared to the pre-WWII period (2.0 percent a year vs. 1.3 per-

Table 6.2

Selected Indicators of Economic Change, 1900–1949

Indicator	1900	1909	1919	1929	1939	1949
Private Gross Domestic Product by Origin of Sector (billions of 1929$)	$35.8	$52.9	$68.7	$99.3	$103.0	$159.8
Farm (percent)	23.5	17.4	14.1	10.8	11.2	7.9
Nonfarm (percent)	76.5	82.6	85.9	89.2	88.8	92.1
Percent Change in Output Per Man-hour	N.A.	18.1	20.4	26.6	17.1	30.1
Patents Issued (thousands)	24.6	36.6	36.8	45.3	43.1	35.1
High School Graduates as Percent of Those Age 17 and Over	6.3	8.0	16.0	27.5	49.0	57.4
Immigration (thousands)	3,694	8,202.0	6,347.0	4,296	699	857
Gainful Workers (millions)	29.1	38.2	41.6	48.8	49.6	60.2
Men (percent)	81.7	78.8	79.5	78.0	75.6	72.6
Women (percent)	18.3	21.2	20.5	22.0	24.4	27.4
Occupational Distribution (percent)	100.0	100.0	100.0	100.0	100.0	100.0
White Collar (percent)	17.6	21.4	24.9	29.4	31.1	36.6
Manual (percent)	35.8	38.2	40.2	39.6	39.8	41.1
Service (percent)	9.0	9.6	7.8	9.8	11.7	10.5
Farm (percent)	37.5	30.9	27.0	21.2	17.4	11.8
Industrial Distribution (percent)	100.0	100.0	100.0	100.0	100.0	100.0
Agriculture (percent)	36.8	30.9	26.7	21.5	16.9	na
Goods-Producing Industries (percent)	30.9	32.2	35.0	31.6	31.3	na
Service-Producing Industries and Other Industries Not Identified (percent)	32.3	36.9	38.3	46.9	51.8	na

Source: The secondary source for all the data presented is U.S. Bureau of the Census, *Historical Statistics of the United States: Colonial Times to 1970,* Origination of Pvt. GDP, Series F 126-128; Output/Man-hour, Series D 683; Patents Issued, Series W 99; High School Graduates, Series H 599; Immigration, Series C 89; Gainful Workers, Series D 26; Occupational Dist., Series D 182; Industrial Dist., D 152. Primary sources are, in order of presentation, John W. Kendrick, *Productivity Trends in the United States,* National Bureau of Economic Research, New York, 1961; U.S. Bureau of Economic Analysis; U.S. Patent Office; U.S. Bureau of the Census; U.S. Immigration and Naturalization Service; *Population Redistribution and Economic Growth* (Philadelphia: American Philosophical Society, 1957), Table L-4; U.S. Bureau of the Census; Solomon Fabricant, "The Changing Industrial Distribution of Gainful Workers," *Studies in Income and Wealth,* vol. 11 (New York: National Bureau of Economic Research, 1949), p. 42.

Table 6.2 *(continued)*

Note: Private GDP data for 1900 and 1909 actually relate to 1897–1901 and 1907–1911, respectively; high school graduates in 1939 and 1949 are actually for 1940 and 1950, respectively; Immigration data are cumulative totals between years and the data for 1900 reflect the 1890 to 1899 period; occupational and industrial distributions are as of the decennial census year.

N.A.—Not applicable.

na—Not available.

---

cent) was due primarily to the faster growth in total GNP and not because of a slowdown in population growth. Between 1900 and 1940, real GNP was growing at an annual rate of 2.7 percent a year and in the approximately twenty-five years after WWII economic growth was 3.5 percent a year. (Much has been made about the economy's slower rate of economic growth in the 1990s and, indeed, since the early 1970s. Between 1970 and 1995, real gross domestic product increased by 2.8 percent a year. Looking at the long-term trend in economic growth over the century, therefore, suggests that the period from 1946 to 1970 was atypical.)

From Agriculture to Industrial Giant

In the decades before the nation's entrance into the twentieth century, the economy had been expanding rapidly. The first large corporations appeared in the railroad, telephone and telegraph, oil, steel, and other industries. Despite the periodic interruptions of economic slumps and the clamor of the "muckrakers" and other business and political reformers, the industrialization process continued into the new century unabated. Indeed, two historians wrote, "The most significant events of the period between the Civil War and World War I occurred not in diplomacy or in the halls of Congress, but in the economic sphere."[3]

The shift from an agriculturally based economy to an industrially based one, of course, did not take place overnight, but it is apparent that the process was going on much more rapidly in the decades surrounding the turn of the century than in later decades. In the period of 1869 to 1878, the percentage of the nation's gross private domestic product originating in the farm sector stood at 37.6 percent.[4] As shown in Table 6.2, by around 1909 the comparable proportion had fallen to 17.4 percent. In only forty years, the share of the national output of the country derived through agriculture had plummeted by twenty percentage points.

As is well known, this is also the period when great American fortunes were being created. The now familiar names of Rockefeller, Carnegie, Armour, Ford, Vanderbilt, Morgan, DuPont, Astor, and Eastman were mentioned in a 1918 listing in *Forbes* magazine as among the thirty richest men in America.[5] And most of these men's fortunes involved the processing, producing, and transporting of physical things. At the same time as this acceleration in the economic transformation of the economy was taking place and the fortunes of these "captains of industry" were being amassed, significant changes were also taking place in the labor market.

The First Two Decades

At the start of the century, almost 40 percent of the nation's 29 million "gainful" workers were involved in farming occupations, as shown in Table 6.2.[6] But this proportion was soon to decline rapidly. Industrially, about the same proportion was involved in agriculture, while the remaining workers were almost evenly divided between the goods-producing industries (forestry and fisheries, mining, construction, manufacturing) and the service-producing industries (transportation, communication, public utilities; trade; finance, insurance, and real estate; professional services; government; and so on).

With the large influx of immigrants during the first decade of the new century, the work force expanded by almost ten million workers (from 29.1 million to 38.2 million) in less than ten years. As shown in Table 6.2, immigration in the last decade (1890 to 1899) of the nineteenth century amounted to 3.7 million persons, but in the first decade of the twentieth century it more than doubled, surpassing eight million. As the story goes, it was the men from this surge in immigration that provided the labor for Carnegie's steel mills and the other blossoming industries of America.

Despite the mild economic slowdowns in the first ten to fifteen years of the new century and the growing threats of antitrust prosecutions, the industrialization process continued.[7] Productivity or output per man-hour moved up by 20 percent between 1909 and 1919, after rising by 18 percent in the first decade (see Table 6.2). The number of patents issued rose from an annual level of 25,000 in 1900 to 37,000 by 1919. And the leaders of industry introduced new and improved methods of production, such as Henry Ford's innovative assembly-line method of automobile production.

These were also years in which unionism began to spread industrially. Trade unions had been common around the turn of the century and they were organized under the American Federation of Labor (AFL). But in the mining and clothing industry, the United Mine Workers and the International Ladies' Garment Workers' Union grew more powerful. Leaders of industry resisted labor's demands in many instances and often circumvented them by adopting unique anti-union policies. A classic example was Henry Ford's announcement in 1914 that he would double the daily wage rate for his factory workers, thereby quieting the demands of union organizers.

Economic activity rose even faster with the advent of WWI as the federal government became industry's most important customer. A War Industries Board was established and war production was coordinated. For the first time in the century, the reins of private industry had been handed over to the government. While the American labor movement cooperated with industry in the war effort, there were demands for wage increases. And these were generally agreed to by the government for the sake of staving off labor strikes.

The size of the nation's economy had nearly doubled between the start of the century and the end of WWII (see Table 6.2). The role of the agricultural sector had diminished further with only 14 percent of gross private domestic product originating in that sector. Farmers and farm workers now accounted for only a little more than one out of every four gainful workers. Blue-collar, or manual, workers represented four of every ten gainful workers, and white-collar workers had increased their share of all workers to one out of every four. Indeed, the managing class in America had been born. Between 1900 and 1920, the number of managers, officials, and proprietors in manufacturing had increased from 174,000 to 406,000, or an increase of 133 percent.[8]

Another significant change that occurred in the first two decades of the twentieth century was in the area of education (Table 6.2). In 1900, only 6 percent of all persons age 17 and over had graduated from high school. While this percentage changed very little in the next decade (rising only to 8 percent by 1909), it doubled in the next ten years and stood at 16 percent in 1919. The great American investment in education had begun.

The nation's economy stumbled into a couple of economic slumps after WWI, most likely the result of the rapid war demobilization. Thousands of returning veterans began looking for work along with the workers who had lost jobs in those industries involved in war production. But soon the country found its economic footing as wartime savings began to be spent for goods that had been hard to buy during the war and an expanding export trade provided jobs for the unemployed.

The Roaring Twenties

With the return to political power of the Republicans in the 1920s, the sentiment toward business improved. Union strength had waned to some extent since the end of the war and, as a result of the economic recessions, businesses had an ample supply of labor from which to expand their operations. In addition, it appeared that many workers were improving their economic lives without unions, and the growth in union membership slowed appreciably in the 1920s. Another factor working in the favor of business was the continued growth in immigration. Certainly the flow of immigrants was not as heavy as in the first and second decades of the century, but for the ten-year period from 1919 to 1929 4.3 million persons entered the country and the number of gainful workers increased from 42 million to 49 million.

The industrialization process in the United States moved into second gear in the 1920s, with the growth in the automobile business leading the way. The production of passenger cars surpassed the 2.0 million mark a year for the first time in 1922 and by 1929 4.5 million automobiles rolled off the assembly lines.[9] But other industries were flourishing as well. Electric power was becoming more greatly utilized in the factory and at home, and utility companies were becoming organized into larger and larger holding companies. Chemical companies, led by DuPont, which received a boost due to the military needs of WWI, continued to grow in the 1920s as new products for industrial and household use were developed. The decade was also one of industrial consolidation. Mergers and holding companies became more common than ever before in manufacturing, mining, public utilities, and banking.

The prosperity of the 1920s was real. Private gross domestic product (in real terms) rose by 45 percent, from $68.7 billion in 1919 (in 1929 dollars) to $99.3 billion by 1929. The increase dwarfed the 30 percent real growth experienced in the 1909–1919 period. As the data in Figure 6.1 reveal, real private GNP per person rose strongly throughout most of the decade and the real incomes of families and the real wages of workers rose. Propelling much of this prosperity was the improvement in machinery and production methods, which increased the productivity of American workers. Between 1919 and 1929 output per man-hour, or labor productivity, increased by 27 percent, the largest decade increase of the century.

The Crash and Great Depression

The collapse of the stock market in 1929 has become one of the most significant economic events of this century because it signaled the start of the Great Depression. Its causes have been the subject of countless books, articles, and Ph.D. dissertations. According to some historians, the causes can be found in the rampant stock market and real estate speculation, the overextension of credit, the abuses in the banking system, the declining value of U.S. exports, the fall-off in commodities prices, and the very narrow base upon which the prosperity rested, or, in other words, the very unequal distribution of family income (a subject to which we shall return).[10]

The decade of the thirties represented a major slowdown in the industrialization process, although it could be argued that the process was nearing completion by the end of the 1920s. But the data in Table 6.2 do reflect a slowing in many of the economic characteristics that have been presented to represent the industrialization process. Real private GNP between 1929 and 1939 rose by a meager 3.7 percent, barely climbing over the $100 billion mark at decade's end. Moreover, the share of output accounted for by the farming sector actually changed very little in this ten-year period—it remained at around 11 percent. Productivity growth fell off to only about a 17 percent gain and the number of patents issued in 1939 was smaller than in 1929. The occupational structure of gainful workers displayed only modest changes and, interestingly, the proportion of women who were gainful workers inched up to 24 percent after remaining at a little over 20 percent since 1909. This development undoubtedly reflected the high unemployment rates among men. According to the Bureau of Labor Statistics (BLS), the civilian unemployment rate for all workers rose from 3.2 percent in 1929 to 24.9 percent by 1933 and stayed above the 20 percent level until 1936 and did not return to single-digit levels until 1941.[11] On the brighter side, the educational attainment of the population continued to increase. By the end of the 1930s, almost half of the population age 17 and over had graduated from high school, an increase of more than twenty percentage points since the end of the previous decade.

With the inauguration of President Franklin D. Roosevelt in 1933 and the start of his administration, major federal intervention into the economic lives of both industry and households got under way. The approach of the New Deal, according to the new administration, would be cooperation between business and government. Numerous federal programs were begun, with initials that are remembered to this day, such as the WPA, or Works Progress Administration. Social Security and Aid to Families with Dependent Children were introduced, and federal unemployment taxes were levied upon employers. A modest economic recovery did occur by the mid-1930s, but by 1937 the economy had weakened.

Unionism revived during the 1930s. With the flow of immigrants slowing to a trickle relative to earlier decades, workers were no longer willing to work under the conditions of their earlier immigrant relatives. Job security and higher wages were demanded and industrial unionism in the form of the Congress of Industrial Organization (CIO) was established.

WWII and Demobilization

With the entry of the United States into WWII, the economic tempo of the country changed radically. Despite the economy's erratic performance in the 1930s, by the start of the 1940s it was an industrial giant whose power had yet to be fully realized. Mobilization for war, a feat that had been required a generation earlier, was once more the task at hand. A War Production Board was established and by the early months of 1942 all production for civilian use of automobiles, radios, refrigerators, vacuum cleaners, washing machines, and most electrical appliances was halted.[12] Planes, tanks, ships, bullets, and the other necessities of war were now the products of much of American industry.

Women were drawn into the workforce in large numbers, a turning point in women's role in the workforce. Even after WWII and the return of many women to the home to raise families, the proportion of women who were gainful workers continued to rise.

Because of the war effort the economy was soon operating at full employment. With the limitations imposed on the production of consumer goods, upward pressure on consumer prices was growing. Price controls were introduced in the war years and rationing was begun. Although the price controls helped retard inflation more effectively than during WWI, prices did increase, squeezing the cost of living at home and encouraging unions to strike. And some work stoppages did occur, although in general unions adhered to a "no-strike" pledge.

As shown in Figure 6.1, real GNP per person skyrocketed during the war years as the economy's output mushroomed. The greatest industrial war machine ever created had reached full capacity by the mid-1940s and this ultimately would be the deciding factor in the war against the Axis nations.

The demobilization process led to a recession after the war. Labor unions were now stronger than ever and, as the economy demobilized, fears arose that wages would fall leading to reductions in family incomes. The removal of wage and price controls soon after the war's end resulted in an increase in consumer prices, further adding to workers' concerns about the rising cost of living. Strikes did result in the auto, steel, and mining industries.

Shifts in political power further complicated the demobilization process. On the one hand, there was a growing feeling among economists that it was government's responsibility to maintain full employment and to intervene in the private economy when economic slowdowns occurred. On the other, concern was rising about the power of unions to virtually paralyze the economy. In both instances, federal legislation was passed that attempted to respond to these concerns; in the first, in the form of the Maximum Employment Act of 1946, and in the second, in the form of the Taft-Hartley Act of 1947.

As the nation reached the half-century mark and the bumpy transition from a wartime to peacetime economy had been completed, the economy was prepared for one of its longest periods of rapid economic growth in the twentieth century. Consumer demand, pent up for nearly two decades because of the Great Depression and WWII, was unleashed and American industry responded.

Earnings and Wage Inequality

Reliable data on wages and earnings in the pre-WWII period are fragmentary at best. Indeed, simply trying to arrive at an overall average wage or earnings level for the period, not to mention a distribution, is difficult. Very frequently, average wage and earnings series have been created by extrapolating backwards wage or earnings series that were begun in the late 1930s, based on data obtained through federal government programs such as the State Unemployment Insurance program of the Department of Labor. Another method involved interpolating wage or earnings data obtained from decennial censuses.

Trends in Real Wages

To provide some sense for what the trend in the average real wage level was during the first half of the twentieth century, the real average weekly earnings for production workers in manufacturing, as collected by the Bureau of Labor Statistics, are presented in Figure 6.2. The data for the period beginning in 1932 are based on an actual mail survey of manufacturing establishments which provided information on the number of production or nonsupervisory workers who received pay for any part of the payroll period including the twelfth of the month, the amount of the payroll before deductions, and the total man-hours paid for these employees. (This survey is still in existence but now covers all production and nonsupervisory workers in the nonfarm sector of the economy.) The estimates for the 1909–1931 period are based on periodic wage and hour surveys of certain manufacturing industries. Consequently, it is felt that the real average weekly earnings data presented in Figure 6.2 are a fairly reliable indicator of wage trends over the period. The average weekly earnings were adjusted for inflation by the BLS's CPI (1967 =100) and then indexed so that the 1909 real average weekly earnings for production workers in manufacturing is equal to 100.0.

Figure 6.2 **Trend in Real Average Weekly Earnings of Production Workers in Manufacturing, 1909–1950** (1909 = 100)

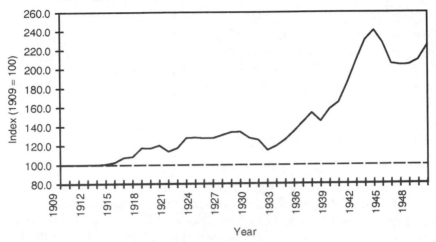

Year

Source: U.S. Bureau of Labor Statistics (as published in U.S. Bureau of the Census, *Historical Statistics of the United States: Colonial Times to 1970,* Part 1, Series D804, pp. 169–170).
Note: Average weekly earnings were adjusted for inflation by the CPI and were in terms of 1967 dollars before indexing.
Data for 1910–1913 were not available.

(In nominal dollars, the factory worker in 1909 averaged a little less than $10 a week, which in 1967 dollars would be equal to about $36.)

The trend in factory workers' real average weekly earnings was very flat between 1909 and 1914 or 1915, rising by as little as 2 percent over the entire period. While it is difficult to know whether this was a continuation of a trend from the turn of the century or simply a slowdown in real wage growth because of economic downturns, there is some evidence that the latter may indeed be the case. An index of average full-time weekly earnings in manufacturing between 1899 and 1907 developed by the U.S. Department of Commerce and Labor shows that nominal weekly earnings had increased by almost 21 percent. Considering that consumer prices had risen by an estimated 12 percent over this period, that would mean there had been some real wage growth in the first decade of the new century.[13] Furthermore, there had been mild recessions at the beginning of the second decade which could have affected real wage growth in that period.

The real weekly earnings of factory workers began to increase sharply with the involvement of the country in WWI, but then slumped with the economic downturns after the war. Earnings growth resumed with the return of prosperity in the 1920s. Between 1909 and 1929, the real weekly earnings of factory workers had increased by an impressive 34 percent.

In the decade of the 1930s, factory workers' real earnings plummeted. The collapse of real wage growth for factory workers in the early 1930s, along with the joblessness of millions of factory workers, had a staggering effect on the economic well-being of millions of families across the land. Real wages, however, made a comeback as the decade was coming to an end, but these gains had come as a result of falling consumer prices. Between 1929 and 1939, nominal average weekly earnings for factory workers had actually declined from $24.76 to $23.64, or about 5 percent, but consumer prices had dropped by almost 20 percent.

WWII, of course, had a profound effect on the course of real earnings growth in the nation. The problem, of course, was despite the tremendous improvement in the size of paychecks, there weren't many consumer goods available to purchase. Demobilization and the removal of wage and price controls resulted in an inflationary surge in the 1945–1948 period. As a consequence, real wages of factory workers plummeted following the war and changed very little toward the end of the decade.

As useful as these BLS data have been in representing the trend in workers' earnings over the first half of the century, they are of no help in telling us how the distribution of earnings may have changed. This is because of the way the data were collected and derived, that is, from the payrolls of manufacturing establishments that fall into the BLS sample rather than from a sample of individual workers. To answer questions about what happened to the distributions of wages and earnings in these years, economists have had to turn elsewhere.

Detecting the Trend in Earnings Inequality

Because of the lack of distributional data on wages and earnings in the early years of the country's history, economists have had to use various techniques for making inferences about the trends in wage and earnings inequality. One of the standard practices over the years has been to examine occupational wage differentials. This is very similar to the examination of relative wage differentials on the basis of education and experience (i.e., age or work experience) that were discussed in the previous chapters, except that in this case, occupations known to require different skill levels are used.

Typically, one would calculate the pay ratio between the average earnings of skilled workers, for example, craftsmen, to the average earnings of unskilled workers, for example, laborers. The movement of the ratio would then be used to infer whether the distribution of earnings was becoming more unequal or more equal. Obviously, these are inferences at best since these two classes of workers represent only a part of the labor force, blue-collar workers, and don't provide any direct evidence of relative wage changes taking place among white-collar, service, or farm workers.

Occupational Skill Differentials

The available statistical evidence on the pay ratio between skilled workers and unskilled workers in the first half of the twentieth century, derived from periodic industry surveys of the BLS, suggests that the ratio slowly narrowed or declined. According to one major study by the BLS, in the manufacturing industry in 1907 the median earnings of skilled workers was slightly more than twice as great as that for unskilled workers. By the end of WWI, the pay ratio between skilled and unskilled workers had slipped to 1.75 but remained near that level as the decade of the 1930s opened when it averaged 1.80. By the end of the 1930s, however, this ratio dropped to 1.65 and in the years immediately after WWII it averaged only 1.55.[14]

Later data from the BLS for the 1952–1953 period and 1955–1956 period suggest that this ratio may have dropped even further to roughly the 1.37–1.38 range.[15] But some economists have cautioned that these ratios are not exactly comparable to those derived from the earlier studies.[16]

The long-term reduction of this occupational-pay differential received considerable attention in the economic literature of the 1950s. For example, the economist Lloyd Reynolds pointed out that the sharpest reductions in the differential were associated with the two world wars.[17] He suggested that these reductions were probably caused by the rapid inflation and full employment situations during those periods which resulted in labor shortages that raised wage rates for unskilled workers faster than wage rates for the skilled.

As might be suspected, other data relating to the skilled-to-unskilled worker pay ratio portray a somewhat different trend. Data relating to the average hourly earnings of men employed in skilled and semi-skilled jobs in manufacturing as well as unskilled jobs in the same industry were collected by the National Industrial Conference Board between the years of 1914 and 1948.[18] The nominal hourly earnings for skilled and semi-skilled male workers and male unskilled workers and the pay ratio appear in Table 6.3. Figure 6.3 presents the pay ratio graphically.

These data indicate that the pay differential may not have been as large in the early part of the century as the BLS pay ratio indicated. (Of course, this may simply reflect the combination of earnings of both skilled and semi-skilled workers.) In any event, the ratio, according to these data, stood at 1.433 in 1914 and then dropped to 1.300 by 1920, which is consistent with the BLS data. Thereafter, the ratio rebounded, moving up to 1.406 by

Table 6.3

Average Hourly Earnings of Skilled and Semi-Skilled Male Workers, Average Hourly Earning of Unskilled Male Workers, and the Pay Ratio, 1914–1948

Year	Skilled and Semi-Skilled	Unskilled	Pay Ratio (Skilled and Semi-Skilled/ Unskilled)
1914	0.291	0.203	1.433
1920	0.687	0.529	1.300
1921	0.599	0.437	1.371
1922	0.566	0.402	1.408
1923	0.619	0.443	1.397
1924	0.644	0.458	1.406
1925	0.644	0.455	1.415
1926	0.652	0.461	1.414
1927	0.656	0.471	1.393
1928	0.659	0.474	1.390
1929	0.668	0.486	1.374
1930	0.663	0.478	1.387
1931	0.634	0.460	1.378
1932	0.559	0.400	1.398
1933	0.550	0.401	1.372
1934	0.643	0.479	1.342
1935	0.665	0.495	1.343
1936	0.689	0.501	1.375
1937	0.777	0.570	1.363
1938	0.802	0.586	1.369
1939	0.808	0.594	1.360
1940	0.827	0.611	1.354
1941	0.914	0.682	1.340
1942	1.043	0.773	1.349
1943	1.164	0.854	1.363
1944	1.227	0.892	1.376
1945	1.248	0.917	1.361
1946	1.320	1.015	1.300
1947	1.478	1.147	1.289
1948	1.567	1.227	1.277

Source: The Economic Almanac for 1950, The Conference Board Inc. 1950, pp. 336–344 (published in U.S. Bureau of the Census, *Historical Statistics of the United States: Colonial Times to 1970, Part 1,* Series D 839 842 p. 172).

Note: Average hourly earnings in nominal dollars.

Figure 6.3 **Pay Ratio of Average Hourly Earnings of Skilled and Semi-Skilled Male Workers to the Average Hourly Earnings of Unskilled Male Workers, 1914–1948**

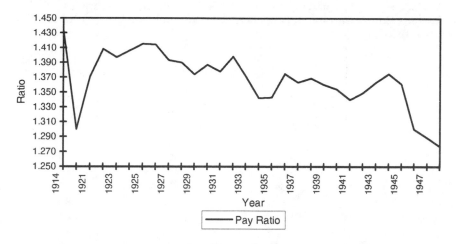

Source: Hourly earnings are from *The Economic Almanac for 1950,* The Conference Board, Inc., 1950, pp. 336–344 (published in U.S. Bureau of the Census, *Historical Statistics of the United States: Colonial Times to 1970,* Part 1, Series D 839, 842, p. 172).

1924, which would be indicative of growing inequality in the earnings and wage distributions. Toward the end of that decade the ratio began to slip downward and by the eve of WWII it had fallen to 1.354. During the war the pay ratio moved up somewhat but after the war it dropped substantially and by 1948 was only 1.277. Like the BLS data, these data also indicate that major movements in the pay differential were associated with the world wars and the immediate periods thereafter.

Recent Research

One of the most recent pieces of research focusing on trends in earnings and wage inequality in the first half of the century was conducted by Claudia Goldin and Robert A. Margo.[19] Although they concentrated on the decade of the 1940s in which, according to their research, an extraordinary amount of equalization of the wage distribution occurred, they also attempted to detect what had happened to wage inequality trends in the decades previous to the 1940s. To do so they relied on the occupational pay differentials mentioned above as well as others and concluded that the wage distribution had indeed narrowed before 1940 and that the narrowing accelerated in the 1940s. But their contribution to understanding trends in earnings inequality in these early years goes much beyond that.

They pointed out that the skilled-to-unskilled pay ratios in manufacturing relate only to what was happening to blue-collar workers. They extended their analysis to cover white-collar occupations so as to examine trends in the returns to education and the relative earnings differential by education. According to Goldin and Margo, when pay ratios between specific white-collar occupations and unskilled blue-collar occupations are calculated for the 1920s and 1930s, the more educated workers gained relative to less educated workers in the early years of the Great Depression. That is, the earnings of educated workers were rising faster than those less educated workers probably because of the greater cyclical impact on workers employed in goods production such as manufacturing. As the depression wore on, however, this differential declined because of the passage of the minimum wage law which, in a relative sense, lifted the wages of the unskilled. So by the end of the 1930s, the earnings differential by education was about the same as it was at the end of the 1920s. As an example, Goldin and Margo show that the pay ratio between railroad clerks and railroad laborers (based on hourly earnings) had risen from 1.68 in 1929 to 1.82 by 1935 and then fell back to 1.71 by 1939.

Using data from the Census Bureau's public use microdata samples for 1940, 1950, and 1960 (derived from the decennial censuses), they went on further to describe how the wage distribution between 1940 and 1950 became considerably more equal, or "compressed," for men who were wage and salary earners. Not only was there strong evidence of wage compression "between" groups by education, experience, and occupation, but also "within" these groups. Overall (between and within group inequality combined), the difference in the log of weekly wages between men at the 90th percentile and the log of weekly wages for men at the 10th percentile had fallen from 1.447 in 1940 to 1.181 in 1950, or more than a 25 percent reduction in wage inequality.

As they remarked in their conclusion, the acceleration in the trend toward wage "equality" in the 1940s was the result of the coming together of certain short-run events affecting the demand for labor and institutional changes brought on by the war. This reflected the rising minimum wage which continued to push the bottom of the wage distribution upward, the constant pressure for higher wages on the part of organized labor, and the

Table 6.4

Percentage of Aggregate Wage and Salary Income Received by Each Quintile of Male Wage and Salary Recipients, 1939 and 1949

Quintile	1939	1949
Total	100	100
Lowest	3.5	3.6
2nd	9.0	12.3
3rd	15.5	19.2
4th	23.3	24.8
Highest	48.7	40.1

Source: Herman P. Miller, *Income Distribution in the United States* (A 1960 Census Monograph), Washington, DC: USGPO, 1966, Table III-2, p. 77.

growing supply of educated labor which served to hold wages down for those in the upper end of the wage distribution.

The Wage and Salary Distribution: 1939 vs. 1949

By way of summarizing the great wage compression that occurred in the 1940s, it is possible to examine the basic wage distribution for men in 1939 and 1949 as tabulated by the Census Bureau.[20] Although there are some comparability issues with these distributions, they have been referenced in the literature before.[21] It should be remembered that the nominal median annual wage and salary earnings for these men in 1939 was $939 and in 1949 the comparable median was $2,476. This represented an increase of about 164 percent over a period of time when the Consumer Price Index had increased by about 72 percent.[22] Table 6.4 displays the shares of aggregate wage and salary income received by each fifth of male wage and salary workers in 1939 and 1949. The shifts in the shares are dramatic.

The most profound change was that which occurred in the top quintile of the distribution. The earnings share for these workers fell from almost 50 percent of total aggregate wage and salary income down to 40 percent in just ten years. And the gainers were not necessarily at the bottom of the distribution, but rather in the middle. The middle three quintiles received about 48 percent of the aggregate in 1939, but 56 percent by 1949. Consequently, this is another reason why the decade of the 1940s can be referred to as the decade of great wage compression.

To say the least, our knowledge of changes in the nation's wage structure during the first half of the century is not as precise as it is for the second half. However, based on the long-term trends in occupational pay differentials it appears that earnings and wage distributions had grown somewhat more unequal after WWI and into the 1920s, but then grew more equal during the 1930s and especially during the 1940s.

Income Inequality

The pattern of the trend in wage and earnings inequality during the first fifty years of this century, as difficult as it has been to detect, does provide some help in discerning the trend in income inequality. Income statistics for the period, of course, are incomplete. The decennial census of 1940 was the first census to include questions on income. With the exception of periodic federal government inquiries around the turn of the century into personal consumption expenditures and a few other small studies, size distributions of income were virtually nonexistent. The first income-size distribution was for 1929 and had been "developed" only years later by income statisticians of the federal government by integrating income tax return information with survey data, and then adjusting them for comparability problems with later income statistics. It was with the advent of the federal income tax in 1913, however, that the first income data became available on a regular basis by which serious inquiries into income "concentration" could be carried out. Therefore, it is necessary to refer to several statistical series to obtain some sense of average income trends and the trends in income inequality in the first half of the century.

Measuring the Trend in Real Income

Some very rough idea about the pattern of real income growth for Americans between 1900 and 1950 has already been observed in Figure 6.1. Real GNP per capita growth was modest at best in the first three decades, dropped in the fourth, and then soared (because of WWII). Such a thumbnail sketch using this statistical series is lacking in an "economic well-being" sense, however, because it doesn't really measure the "command" over goods and services that a family or household actually possessed over time.

As mentioned above, income distributions and distributional measures had been created by income statisticians and economists from the Office of

Table 6.5

Real Income Growth in Average Family Personal Income, 1901–1950

Year	Real Income	Average Annual Rate of Change
1901	$2,359	NA
1929	4,250	2.1
1936	3,740	−1.8
1941	4,650	4.4
1944	5,910	8.0
1946	5,760	−1.3
1947	5,450	−5.4
1948	5,430	−0.4
1949	5,250	−3.3
1950	5,520	5.1

Source: Herman P. Miller, *Income Distribution in the United States* (A 1960 Census Monograph) (Washington, DC: USGPO, 1966), Table I-3, p. 9.

Note: The estimate for 1901 was taken from a consumer expenditure survey of the Bureau of Labor in 1901 and has been adjusted to 1962 dollars. The other real income estimates are in 1962 dollars. See footnote 24 for further explanation, and text.

NA — Not applicable.

Business Economics (OBE, now the Bureau of Economic Analysis) and private organizations by mid-century. These distributions related to the pre-WWII years. They combined data from tax returns and periodic incomes surveys of the mid-1930s, and then further adjusted the data so as to become comparable with annual post-WWII survey data (the CPS) and the income concepts of the OBE. The result was a fairly consistent income-distribution series beginning in 1929 referred to as "family personal income."[23] Unlike the money income concept used in the CPS, family personal income includes not only money or cash income (e.g., wages, interest, dividends, and rent), but also nonmonetary income items such as in-kind payments for work, the value of food and fuel consumed on farms, and the net imputed value of owner-occupied homes.

Table 6.5 displays the real mean family personal income (in 1962 dollars) from these distributions in 1929, 1935–1936, and various years during the 1940s, as well as for 1950, and the average annual percent change between each of the periods. In addition, a crude real income estimate for 1901 from a consumption expenditure survey of the Bureau of Labor is included and the average annual percent change in income between 1901 and 1929.[24]

As the table shows, the long-term growth trend in real mean family incomes between 1901 and 1929 was about 2.1 percent a year. This estimate is no doubt biased for several reasons: the sources of the estimates are quite different, the income deflators are different (the family personal income series uses the implicit price deflator for personal consumption expenditures while the mean family income estimate is adjusted for inflation by the CPI), and income concepts are different (indeed, the 1901 estimate is based on a survey in which families with wage and salary incomes above $1,200 a year were excluded). Nevertheless, even if the bias on the growth rate amounts to upwards of plus or minus 25 percent, the estimate of real income growth in the 1901–1929 period would range roughly from 1.6 to 2.6 percent a year.

In the period following the stock market crash and up until 1936, real average family personal income declined from $4,250 to $3,740, or 1.8 percent a year. Real income growth rose sharply in the second half of the 1930s by about 4.4 percent a year, thanks in good measure to preparatory measures in connection with the start of WWII. Real incomes continued to soar during the war and between 1941 and 1944 they were growing at an almost unbelievable rate of 8.0 percent a year. In 1944, real family personal income reached its high-water mark for the decade at $5,910. According to these income statistics, real incomes drifted downward after the war but then moved upward in 1950. By 1950, real family personal income averaged $5,520. (In nominal dollars, average family personal income was $4,440 compared to an average family income, as measured by the CPS, of $3,815, the difference, in part, reflecting the much broader income concept of the OBE than the income concept used in the Census Bureau's CPS.)

This review of real income trends of families in the first half of the twentieth century suggests that between 1901 and 1950 American families saw their incomes more than double, or on an annual basis grow by 1.7 percent a year. Using a more consistent but somewhat different income series (from the Census Bureau's CPS), real mean family incomes between 1950 and 1996 also more than doubled. Indeed, they increased from $22,846 to $53,676 (in 1996 dollars), or by about 1.9 percent a year. The somewhat faster growth in the second half of the century, as compared to the first, no doubt reflects the surge in the nation's economic growth rate in the twenty-five years or so following WWII.

Income Inequality Trends

It is through the work of Simon Kuznets that modern-day economists have their best glimpse at one aspect of income inequality through most of the 1900–1950 period. Kuznets, working at mid-century, used data from federal income tax returns to examine how much of aggregate income was received by the top 1 percent and top 5 percent of the population between 1913 and

Figure 6.4 **Shares of Aggregate Income (in percent) Received by Top 1 Percent and Top 5 Percent of the Population, 1913–1948**

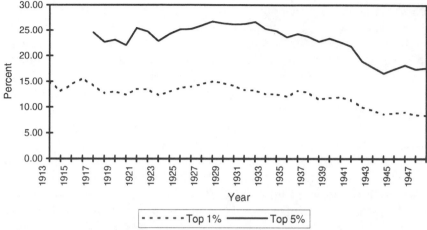

Source: Simon Kuznets, *Shares of Upper Income Groups in Income and Savings,* New York, National Bureau of Economic Research, 1953.
Note: Data for the top 5 percent of the population for the years 1913–1916 were not available.

1948.[25] While this gives us only a look at one part of the income distribution, it is an important part. It is to these income recipients that much of the media and the public often turn, even today, when the topic of rising income inequality is raised.

His methodology involved working with the net incomes of persons from federal income tax returns and the population represented by these returns as reported in tabulations of the government's tax collecting agency (today's Internal Revenue Service). Basically he calculated the per capita net income by the income classes of the tabulations and then arrayed them in descending order. As with a Lorenz curve, it then became possible to find out what percentage of the population, ranked by net income, received what percentage of the aggregate net income. Net income is made up of wages and salaries, self-employment income, interest, dividends, rents and royalties, and excludes capital gains. The population consisted of the number of persons on each tax return (including dependents) that the net income referred to. By arraying the data in this way, Kuznets was able to find out the share of aggregate net income that was received by the top 1 percent and top 5 percent of income recipients. His data for 1913 to 1948 are charted in Figure 6.4.

The data for the highest income receivers—the top 1 percent—tend to initially bounce around between 1913 and WWI. That is, between 1913 and 1914 there is a significant decline from nearly 15 percent to 13 percent, but the percentage moves back up to almost 16 percent (15.6 percent) on the eve of the country's entrance into WWI in 1916. Toward the end of that decade, the percentage of aggregate net income going to the top 1 percent dropped back to the 1914 level or so. It didn't begin to move up again until 1924 and by 1928 had almost reached 15 percent again (14.94 percent). Thereafter, this group's share of aggregate net income drifted downward through the years of the depression, with a slight pause toward the end of the 1930s, and then further downward to below 10 percent during WWII and ending at 8.4 percent in 1948—the lowest share level for the entire period.

The trend for the top 5 percent of income recipients, according to the Kuznets data, is quite similar, with two exceptions. First, this group's share of income tended to begin rising in the mid-1920s and reached a sustained high level of approximately 26 percent between 1928 and 1933. In other words, these income recipients had reached their high-water mark somewhat later than the top 1 percent. The second difference is that the decline in the net income share of the top 5 percent appears to be much faster after reaching its peak level. By 1940, it had dropped to 23 percent (22.7 percent) and by 1944 it was down to just under 17 percent (16.6 percent).

The work of Kuznets was very important in providing the first serious, long-run view of income concentration during the last stages of the nation's transformation from an agricultural to an industrial economy. Such evidence corroborated the beliefs of other economists at mid-century that the changes in the distribution of incomes of the 1930s and 1940s represented "one of the great social revolutions of history."[26] Indeed, the trends in these income shares of the richest segments of the taxpaying population (along with the trends in certain occupational pay differentials) have been used in the 1980 work of the economic historians Jeffrey Williamson and Peter Lindert.[27] As a part of their more extensive review of inequality in America, they also concluded that inequality had been on a high "uneven plateau" between the end of the Civil War and 1929, after which there had been a dramatic reduction.[28]

The great reduction in income inequality between the late 1920s and late 1940s implied by Kuznets's data on income concentration was also reflected in the family personal income distributions of the OBE, referred to earlier. These data, shown in Table 6.6, bring us deeper into the income distribution, and its changes over the period from the late 1920s and up to 1950. The data here show the share of aggregate "family personal income" going to the top 5 percent of families in the income distribution on a steady downward course from 30 percent in 1929 to 21 percent by 1950. This represented an enormous "redistribution" of income in roughly twenty years, or about a generation. (Kuznets's data showed a drop from 26 to 18 percent between 1929 and 1948.)

Within the highest quintile, the share of income had fallen from 54 percent

Table 6.6

Shares of Aggregate Family Personal Income by Quintiles of the Income Distribution, 1929–1950

Quintile	1929	1935–36	1941	1944	1950
Total	100.0	100.0	100.0	100.0	100.0
Lowest	3.5	4.1	4.1	4.9	4.8
2nd	9.0	9.2	9.5	10.9	10.9
3rd	13.8	14.1	15.3	16.2	16.1
4th	19.3	20.9	22.3	22.2	22.1
Highest	54.4	51.7	48.8	45.8	46.1
Top 5%	30.0	26.5	24.0	20.7	21.4
Gini Index	0.49	0.47	0.44	0.39	0.40

Source: Edward C. Budd, Introduction in *Inequality and Poverty,* ed. Edward C. Budd, New York: W.W. Norton & Company, 1967, Table 1, p. xiii.

to 46 percent, while the third and fourth quintile gained five percentage points and the first and second quintiles gained about three additional percentage points of aggregate income at the expense of the richest income recipients. Gini indexes were computed to summarize the changes in the income distribution between 1929 and mid-century. The trend in the Gini index is unmistakably downward, from .49 in 1929 to .40 by 1950. It is also of interest to note that, according to the OBE estimates, the "great income redistribution" had been completed by 1944, since the income shares, as well as the Gini index, were not much changed in the 1944–1950 period.

According to the CPS data, the Gini index for families in 1950 was .379 and the share of income received by the richest 5 percent of families was 17 percent. These differences are understandable given the CPS's much narrower income concept, but in another sense are remarkably similar, given the differences in the way the two databases were created.

Selma Goldsmith, a staff economist at OBE who pioneered the development of these income distributions of family personal income, compared the OBE data and Kuznets's data in the mid-1950s.[29] She reviewed the many limitations in both data sets, but found them to be suggesting essentially the same pattern of reduction in relative income differences in the post-1929 period.

Discussion

This review of inequality trends in the first half of the century obviously lacks precision when compared to the analysis of trends in the second half of the century presented in Chapter 3. Furthermore, it raises certain questions. For example, how large were income differences between the top and the bottom of the income distribution at the turn of the century? Was inequality really higher in the first half than in the second half? When did income inequality actually begin to fall in the first half of the century?

These questions have troubled economists for some time and because of the lack of good data can only be approximated. Regarding the first question, income differences might conceivably have been the largest they ever had been at the beginning of the century. The rationale for such a guess is this was the period of mass immigration from Europe, the vast majority who were from the lowest skill and income stratums of their originating countries. At the same time, the industrialization process had produced great fortunes for many men, not only in the steel and oil industries (e.g., Carnegie and Rockefeller), but also in the banking and finance industries (e.g., Morgan). In the process of amassing these fortunes, no doubt, the incomes of thousands of others were swept upward as well. Consequently, it is possible that income differences between the unskilled laborer-immigrants and the managers in the upper echelons of America's blossoming corporations were larger than income differences in the late 1920s and early 1930s.

Williamson and Lindert reached a somewhat different conclusion. They suggest that inequality had plateaued at a very high level between the Civil War and the 1929 stock market crash, but with some deviations. One of these deviations was at around the turn of the century when they believe inequality may have dipped somewhat as a result of the decline in the income gap between the farm and nonfarm sectors and the absence of a trend toward inequality in the farm sector.[30]

Regarding the question of the level of inequality in the first half of the century versus the second half, the evidence is considerably more robust. The data of Simon Kuznets and the OBE show that income concentration and income inequality were higher (especially in the late 1920s and early 1930s) than they are today, when income inequality is at its highest in the post-WWII period. In 1996, the share of aggregate money income received by the richest 5 percent of households was 21 percent compared to the highest estimate of Kuznets of almost 27 percent in 1928 and 1932 and the 30 percent estimate of OBE for 1929. Furthermore, the Gini index in 1929 according to OBE stood at .490 compared to the 1996 index for all households of .455. Obviously, there are many conceptual and empirical differences in the derivation of these estimates, but considering that they are generally attempting to measure the same thing—the income distribution and changes in it—these comparisons are compelling.

Other economists who have examined the issue of inequality across most of

Figure 6.5 **Estimated Gini Index for Families Between 1913 and 1947 (according to Smolensky and Plotnick) and the Actual Gini Indexes for Families and Households Between 1947 and 1996 (according to the Census Bureau)**

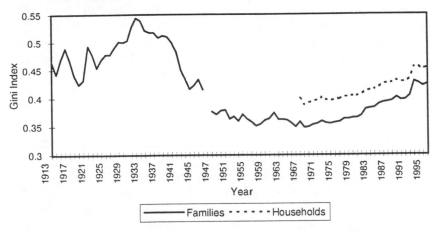

Source: Eugene Smolensky and Robert Plotnick, "Inequality and Poverty in the United States: 1900 to 1990," University of California, Berkeley, July 1992 (unpublished paper) and U.S. Bureau of the Census, Annual Demographic Survey, CPS.

the twentieth century have reached a similar conclusion on this question. Smolensky and Plotnick, for example, concluded, "Despite the uncertainty surrounding the data prior to 1947, we think it is safe to say that inequality was greater in the first three or four decades than any period since."[31] Indeed, Smolensky and Plotnick estimated the Gini index for households and families back to 1913, and their estimates are presented in Figure 6.5.[32] To these Gini indexes for the 1913–1947 period have been added the Gini indexes for families and households from the Census Bureau's March CPS for the 1947–1996 period. If the Smolensky-Plotnick estimates are just fairly accurate, one would have to conclude that the U.S. income distribution in the first half of the century was considerably more unequal than in the second half.

With respect to the last question regarding when income inequality began to decline, the Smolensky-Plotnick Gini index estimates are also helpful. They show that income inequality reached its high point in 1932 at .544 after rising steadily from 1923 when it was .454. During most of the Great Depression it receded gradually downward to .510 by 1939 and then plunged to .416 by 1944. According to their data, therefore, the beginning of the great income redistribution began in the 1932–1933 period and continued into the late 1940s.

7

International Comparisons

An obvious question after examining income and earnings inequality in the United States is, "What has been happening in other countries?" Many countries with large economies, of course, also function in a relatively free market environment. The United Kingdom, Germany, Japan, France, Italy, and others have experienced economic changes (some very dramatic) in the post-WWII era, much as we have.

From time to time there have been references in the media to comparisons of the United States's economic performance with other countries and the implications for inequality. One of the most popular has involved our economy's job creating ability versus that of the economies of Europe, in particular those of France, Germany, and Sweden. In the parlance of the economists, this has often been referred to as the flexible vs. inflexible wage structure debate.

The debate has generally followed these lines. The U.S. economy has generated millions of jobs in the 1980s and 1990s. This has been accomplished while the nation's rate of unemployment has remained relatively low (except for during the 1990–91 recession). During this same period, however, the U.S. wage structure has become more dispersed (i.e., flexible). In Europe, on the other hand, job creation has been anemic at best and unemployment rates have remained stubbornly high, often above the 10 percent mark. However, European wage distributions have not become as unequal (i.e., they are inflexible) as in the United States and their job benefits and, in general, their social welfare benefits, are much greater than in the United States. The question that this raises, then, is, Which model is best?

This debate was joined as a result of the work of economists in the late 1980s and early 1990s who were exploring the income and earnings distributions of other countries. The majority of these studies found that of all the industrialized nations of the world, the United States's income and earnings distributions were the most unequal. Furthermore, while inequality had increased to some extent in other countries in recent years, the increase in the

United States was the sharpest. Reports of these studies have also found their way into the popular press.

The Emerging World Economy

To the extent that the largest industrialized nations of the world are linked together through trade, commerce, and other forms of international contacts, and since they are all part of a larger world economy, it is useful to take a brief look at how this world economy has changed in recent years. Certainly words such as "globalization," "integration," and "openness" have been frequently associated with media stories concerning the world economy. (As will be recalled from Chapter 5, our trading practices and international business activities have often been mentioned as a cause of growing wage and income inequality in the United States.)

In the Council of Economic Advisers (CEA) 1997 *Economic Report of the President,* three events were singled out that have shaped the emerging world economy.[1] These were the end of the Cold War, the industrialization of developing countries, and globalization. According to the CEA's report, the end of the cold war in the late 1980s signaled the victory of the free market system over its major competitor, communism and its central planning approach. A powerful message had been sent to the world that capitalism, with all its deficiencies, was a superior system to communism for social and economic organization.

The second sweeping change was the continued industrialization of developing countries in several parts of the world. The CEA pointed out that between 1960 and 1993, eight of the world's ten fastest-growing economies were in East and Southeast Asia. Although some of these countries' economies faltered in 1997 (e.g., South Korea, Indonesia, Thailand), it was clear that many had reached new levels in terms of industrialization. The CEA also pointed to the revival of economic growth in Latin America during the 1990s and took special note of the recent economic expansion of Chile.

A third factor that was shaping the world economy according to the CEA was globalization. In a general sense, globalization simply means the greater ease in doing business around the world. Tariffs today are comparatively lower than what they once were and technological barriers have fallen. Technological developments, like those involved with computers and telecommunications, now flow relatively easier from country to country. The CEA listed the enormous changes in certain transportation and communication costs over the past decades as examples of the greater ease with which companies can do business around the world. In 1920, for example, the average ocean freight charge per short ton was $95 (in 1990 dollars) but seventy years later this same cost had dropped to $29 per short ton; and a three-minute phone call from New York to London that cost $245 in 1930 (in 1990 dollars) cost $3.32 in 1995.[2]

In sum, the capitalistic incentive to make or produce products or services as cheaply as possible and to sell them anywhere at their highest possible price has become a worldwide reality. Without doubt, the world market is a much different place to operate in at the close of the twentieth century than it was at the close of the nineteenth century.

But these changes also have implications for how incomes and earnings are distributed in the major nations of the world (and the United States), or so some think. Economists such as Lester Thurow believe globalization is at the heart of the problem of growing wage inequality and of growing income differences.[3] Millions of low-wage workers around the world now produce goods that are sent to the United States and other high-wage countries, further eroding the jobs and paychecks of many low-skilled, high-wage workers in our country and others. Because capital has become so mobile and transportation and communication technologies are ever improving, companies can locate their operations anywhere it is cost advantageous, and certainly those countries with relatively low wage labor markets are prime candidates. But other economists, such as Paul Krugman, disagree.[4] The problem, he contends, is that businesses, because of more intense competition, have placed a premium on highly skilled workers, increasing the wages of such workers, while the wages of the less skilled stagnate or fall. The labor demand of employers has shifted because of the skill-biased technological changes that have improved production processes. Krugman concedes that some of the increase in inequality could be due to globalization, but suggests that in time wage levels will equalize as productivity rises and countries realize their comparative advantages in world markets.

In any event, the opening of the world's market and its greater accessibility to the industrialized nations of the world in recent years has not only had implications for inequality trends in the United States (the degree of which is still open to debate), but most likely abroad as well.[5] But to this possible cause of growing income and earnings inequality must be added the other prime suspects mentioned in the context of the U.S. experience in Chapter 5. On the demand side, there are the possible shifts in demand for workers between industries (i.e., deindustrialization), the impact of technological changes, and the effects of the business cycle; on the supply side, there are the influences of migration patterns (both within and between countries), the changing age and education composition of the work force, and the role of worker attitudes toward work. And last are the effects of the wage-setting processes in different countries, that is, the extent to which the work force is unionized and the impact of laws governing minimum wages.

Consequently, the task of understanding growing inequality "across" countries is an even more challenging task than confining the examination to the United States. As a result, causes will be discussed only briefly and greater emphasis will be placed upon quantifying the extent of income and earnings inequality in other industrialized countries. This is a difficult task in itself because of the many social, demographic, and economic differences to be considered. On a very practical note, for example, it has taken researchers much effort to not only assemble the necessary data to be examined, but also to understand the many differences that exist across nations in terms of income and earnings concepts, data collection, and other empirical matters.

Measuring Inequality Across Nations

It has only been within the last ten years or so that economists (primarily in the United States and now to a large extent in other countries) have turned their attention to what has happened to the income and earnings distributions of other industrialized nations. To do this, they have had to seek out the necessary data sources—a formidable task in many instances because of language barriers and unfamiliarity with the statistical systems of foreign countries. In this section, three aspects of measuring income inequality across countries are discussed: accessing data, data comparability, and data quality.

Accessing the Data

Researchers have taken two approaches in conducting international comparative studies of income and earnings distributions and the trends in inequality. The first approach has been to consult the country's statistical agency that produces the relevant statistics. This may be a simple matter in countries that have one statistical agency responsible for all the nation's statistics, such as Canada. The relevant agency there is Statistics Canada (although it might take some time finding the appropriate income or earnings data within that agency). Other countries, like the United States, have no single statistical agency, but rather many that are responsible for particular aspects of economic and social life in America. As we know, the U.S. Census Bureau is the relevant statistical agency to contact for income distribution information, not the Bureau of Labor Statistics nor the Bureau of Economic Analysis. Consequently, simply knowing where to go for the relevant income statistics for a nation can be problematic.

The second approach that many researchers have taken is to consult organizations that have already assembled data sets that can be used for cross-national comparisons of earnings and income distributions. One of the major organizations of this type is the Luxembourg Income Study (LIS) project located in Luxembourg, but headed primarily by U.S. academicians. This project was started in 1983 under the joint sponsorship of the government of Luxembourg and the Center for Population, Poverty, and Policy Studies. The primary objective of LIS has been to assemble, from the different household surveys of foreign countries, a consistent database containing social and economic data from which policy-relevant research can be conducted.

Since its inception, the LIS project has grown into a cooperative research project with other countries from Europe, North America, as well as Asia and Australia. The LIS obtains the data files from individual countries that have been produced by their statistical agencies and then applies consistent concepts and measures to create a more uniform and consistent database. The goal is to maximize comparability without distorting the basic data.

The result is a LIS microdatabase of economic, social, and demographic information for more than twenty-five countries for one year or more in the 1960–1989 period. Additional data for other countries have been added in the 1990s so as to represent the situation in this decade as well.[6] The LIS database has been used extensively for international comparative research in a number of social policy areas and in recent years has been used in studies of cross-national comparisons of income and earnings inequality.

A second major source of data and information on inequality is the Organization for Economic cooperation and Development (OECD). This organization has assembled information primarily on earnings and wage inequality from national statistical agencies, and to a lesser extent on income inequality.[7] The earnings and wage data are taken directly from individual countries' statistical reports and from individuals with access to the survey data of a specific country. Although microdata are not available, in 1996 the OECD published distributional measures of the earnings distributions by sex in nineteen of their member countries for the 1979–1995 period.[8] Similar data were published in 1993.[9] These data, along with their analyses, provide useful insights into the trends in wage structures in the major industrialized nations of the world.

A third data set used to analyze inequality on a cross-national basis is the International Social Survey Programme (ISSP).[10] The ISSP is a program that had its inception in 1983. It was created so that a common set of questions about social attitudes and values could be asked in almost a dozen countries. These questions form a "module" which is attached to a specific country's social survey. While the questions focus primarily on social attitudes, and sample sizes can be problematic, this data source also provides insights into inequality.

One last source of inequality information is available from the World Bank.[11] Their information on inequality relates to developing nations as well as developed nations and their primary distributional metric is the Gini index.

Data Comparability

Comparability issues abound in cross-national comparisons of income and earnings distributions, as might be expected. This is why the LIS database is so useful in research of this kind because its purpose is to standardize the data from the different countries as much as possible. However, even the LIS database cannot deal with all the issues involved with comparability, such as how questions about income are worded in the surveys of various countries. The following are two of the major reasons data comparability problems exist.

Data Source

Several nations, like the United States, have specific income and consumer expenditure surveys that are the primary source of income distribution data. For example, Canada collects annual earnings and income data through its Survey of Consumer Finances, and Australia has collected income data through its periodic Income Surveys. But other countries' earnings data come from administrative records such as social security data (Austria) or tax registers (Denmark). Still other countries, such as Sweden, use a combination of data from their Income Distribution Survey and from administrative records to measure their income distribution. And the Italian income and earnings information is obtained from the Bank of Italy, which conducts a survey called the Survey of Household Income and Wealth.

The very fact that the sources of income and earnings data vary among countries creates numerous comparability issues. For example, some of the most elementary problems involve the statistical testing of hypotheses. Comparing statistical characteristics of income distributions obtained from scientifically designed samples of households to statistical characteristics of income distributions derived from administrative records can create formidable challenges for the income statistician. Another problem inherent in comparisons of income distributions derived through household surveys is accounting for the effects of wording differences in survey questionnaires.

Income and Earnings Concept

Comparability problems also arise from the various definitions of income and earnings that are used among countries. The concept of labor market earnings, for example, can vary as to whether only full-time workers are covered, whether gross or net earnings are being measured, whether self-employment income is included, whether certain transfer payments (such as unemployment insurance) are included, and so on.

In the United States, with the CPS data, it is possible to focus on the gross earnings of all workers employed full-time, year-round in wage and salary jobs, but in other countries the earnings measures can be different. For example, in the OECD reports covering Japan, the earnings data relate to the monthly "scheduled" earnings of full-time workers, excluding those employed in the government sector, public enterprises, agriculture, forestry and fisheries, private household services, and all establishments with less than ten regular workers.[12] In Italy, however, the earnings data studied by the OECD relate to the monthly "net" earnings of wage and salary earners.[13]

According to economists who have examined the income and earnings distributions of many countries, even greater diversity exists in what is included in the income definitions of various countries.[14] Differences exist on the basis of whether the income concept relates only to money income or includes nonmoney income items as well, whether incomes are before or after taxes, and how the income recipient unit is defined. For example, in Italy, Belgium, and Luxembourg, only after-tax income is included, but in Sweden, Finland, and Norway taxes actually paid are included in the distributions. With respect to income recipients, the household concept tends to predominate in most nations included in the LIS database, but in Canada the recipient unit is all related persons living together, and in Sweden related persons are defined on the basis of tax regulations.[15]

Obviously, the task of grappling with the vast number of comparability problems is of Herculean proportions for researchers. Again, this is why the work of the LIS project is so important. Those responsible for the LIS project realize that complete comparability among income and earnings distributions in the LIS data set will never be achieved, but they also believe that they can increase the level of comparability.[16]

Data Quality

Because of the different amount of resources that nations allocate to the development and maintenance of their statistical systems, qualitative differences exist in many countries' income and earnings databases. For those countries in which surveys are used to collect data, data quality differences reflect different degrees of total survey nonresponse, specific income-item nonresponse, and incorrect response to income and earnings questions.

The LIS project has made an exhaustive analysis of how reported income data from surveys for many of the member countries of the OECD compare to aggregate income amounts reported through countries' national income accounts and other external sources.[17] The assumption is if the survey has accounted for all of total aggregate income or all of the aggregate of a specific income item according to the national income accounts or some other independent benchmark, then the survey data are of high quality. (Obviously, this can be misleading because of respondent "overreporting" of certain income items, and LIS points out that these comparisons must often be supplemented with other qualitative comparisons.)

According to the LIS comparisons, survey income aggregates for the United States, Canada, Finland, Italy, United Kingdom, and the Netherlands were about 90 percent of national benchmark totals and in Australia and Germany the survey aggregates were around the 80 percent level. Of course, this masks much larger variations by specific income items. For example, wages and salaries are usually well reported in income surveys (over 90 percent of benchmark levels) but property income is generally poorly reported (as low as 40 or 50 percent in some countries). Government transfer income is another item that is only moderately well reported.

In summary, qualitative differences in earnings data, specifically wage and salary earnings, are less problematic than those for total income and other specific income items such as property income across some of the OECD nations. Nevertheless, concerns over qualitative differences in earning and income data across nations should always be of paramount concern in cross-national studies of inequality.

Cross-National Studies of Inequality

Only toward the end of the 1980s and early 1990s did economists in this country turn their attention to the income and earnings distributions of foreign countries, specifically those of Western Europe and Japan. Since then a growing literature has appeared on international inequality comparisons, a review of which was recently conducted by Peter Gottschalk and Timothy Smeeding in 1997.[18] According to these two economists, some of the major "stylized facts" that have emerged from this research are the following:

- Wide differences in earnings inequality exist among modern countries. Less inequality in earnings distributions is found in countries with centralized wage bargaining (e.g., Sweden, Germany) than in countries where wage bargaining is not as centralized (e.g., the United States, Canada).

- Differences also exist in the trends of earnings inequality, with the largest increases occurring in the United States and the United Kingdom and the least in the Nordic countries.
- Almost all industrial economies experienced growing earnings inequality among prime-aged males during the 1980s.
- With respect to income inequality among OECD countries, the United States has the most unequal distribution, with the Nordic countries and northern European countries the most equal.
- Income inequality increased in most, but not all, OECD countries during the 1980s and early 1990s. Growing earnings inequality among men was probably the most important reason for the growth in income inequality.

As with studies focusing on inequality in the United States, most of the work has been concerned with the earnings distribution. Consequently, the following discussion focuses on a recent analysis of earnings inequality trends by the OECD conducted in 1995–1996 for some of their member countries. A subsequent section will examine the factors that have been thought responsible for these trends.

Earnings Inequality Trends: OECD Findings

The OECD, in their *Employment Outlook* for 1996, discussed trends in earnings inequality in almost twenty of their member countries.[19] The discussion covers the trends in most of the major industrial countries not only over the 1979–1989 period, but also into the 1990s. The data in Table 7.1 are taken from that report and show the trends in earnings dispersion for men using ratios of the upper earnings limits of the 1st, 5th, and 9th deciles of earnings distributions. The 9th-to-the-5th decile (the median) ratio tracks what has been happening in the upper half of the distribution while the 5th-to-1st decile ratio tracks the situation in the lower half of the earnings distributions (the upper earnings limit of the 9th decile is equivalent to the 90th percentile, and so on).

Because earnings inequality had accelerated in the United States during the 1980s and then moderated in the early 1990s when the last recession

Table 7.1

Trends in Earnings Inequality for Men in Selected OECD Countries

	Ratios			Ratios			Ratios	
Country	9th to 5th	5th to 1st	Country	9th to 5th	5th to 1st	Country	9th to 5th	5th to 1st
Australia			**Italy**			**United States**		
1979	1.69	1.62	1979	1.46	1.57	1979	1.73	1.84
1989	1.68	1.67	1989	1.56	1.39	1989	1.97	2.05
1995	1.75	1.68	1993	1.65	1.60	1995	2.04	2.13
Austria			**Japan**					
1980	1.39	1.63	1979	1.63	1.59			
1989	1.43	1.65	1989	1.73	1.65			
1994	1.44	1.67	1994	1.73	1.60			
Belgium			**New Zealand**					
1985	1.38	1.40	1984	1.66	1.64			
1989	1.37	1.41	1988	1.64	1.74			
1993	1.37	1.38	1994	1.79	1.77			
Canada			**Portugal**					
1981	1.67	2.07	1985	2.13	1.56			
1988	1.71	2.23	1989	2.24	1.72			
1994	1.73	2.18	1993	2.40	1.72			
Finland			**Sweden**					
1980	1.67	1.46	1980	1.61	1.31			
1989	1.73	1.51	1989	1.60	1.35			
1994	1.73	1.46	1993	1.62	1.36			
France			**Switzerland**					
1979	2.04	1.66						
1989	2.14	1.63	1991	1.68	1.45			
1994	2.13	1.61	1995	1.68	1.51			
Germany			**United Kingdom**					
1983	1.63	1.46	1979	1.58	1.55			
1989	1.65	1.39	1989	1.80	1.71			
1993	1.64	1.37	1995	1.86	1.78			

Source: Organization of Economic Co-operation and Development, *The 1996 OECD Employment Outlook,* Table 3.1 pp. 61–62.

Note: These ratios represent the ratios of the upper earnings limits of the 1st, 5th, and 9th deciles. For Austria and Belgium the 9th-to–5th ratios are actually the 8th-to-5th ratios.

occurred, the decade of the 1980s is focused on first. According to the OECD data, in about half of the countries, greater earnings dispersion was registered in both the upper and lower half of their distributions during the 1980s—Austria, Canada, Finland, Japan, Portugal, the United Kingdom, and the United States—with the largest changes taking place in the United Kingdom and the United States. In the United Kingdom, dispersion had increased by 14 percent in the upper half of the distribution and by 10 percent in the lower half; in the United States, the comparable increases in dispersion between 1979 and 1989 were 14 percent and 11 percent, respectively.

In some of the other countries, dispersion increased in either the top half or bottom half of their distributions during the 1980s. Earnings dispersion increased in only the bottom half of the men's distribution in Australia, New Zealand, and Sweden during this period, and in the top half only in France and Italy. And in Belgium and Germany there was little discernible change in the amount of dispersion in either half of the distribution.

Obviously, the trends in earnings inequality among men for these countries were not uniform, but there was somewhat of a tendency for distributions to become more dispersed rather than compressed. The trends for women (the data are not shown in Table 7.1) in the United States, the United Kingdom, Sweden, New Zealand, and Australia indicated greater dispersion in both halves of these countries' distributions.

As these countries moved into the 1990s, earnings inequality for men in the United Kingdom and United States continued to grow but perhaps at a more modest pace, especially in the upper halves of the distributions. In the other countries in which inequality was growing at both ends of the distribution—Austria, Canada, Finland, Japan, and Portugal—trends moderated considerably, perhaps with the exception of Portugal where inequality continued to grow in the upper half of the men's distribution. Despite the slowdown among countries where inequality had been increasing, inequality appeared to accelerate in the 1990s in Italy and New Zealand and also in the upper half of Australia's earnings distribution for men. In the European countries of France, Germany, Belgium, and Sweden, earnings distributions for men appeared relatively stable or tended to compress slightly in the 1990s.

The OECD data do suggest that earnings inequality has increased most rapidly in the United States and the United Kingdom in the 1980s and 1990s—and, in addition, that the level of earnings inequality is greatest in these countries compared to the other major industrial nations, such as Canada, Japan, Italy, Germany, and Sweden. According to the OECD figures, men's earnings at the 90th percentile in the United States and United Kingdom were 1.9 to 2.0 times as large as those at the median. In Japan, Italy, and Canada, the comparable figure was around 1.7 and in Germany and Sweden, 1.6. (The ratio in France according to the OECD data was 2.1, but France's earnings data, like the U.S. data, include annual bonuses which most likely affected the top-end of the earnings distribution.)

As might be expected, however, the ranking of countries with respect to the most unequal earnings distribution is sensitive to the nature of the earnings being measured, the measure, the time period of the comparison, and other factors. Based on data for men from the LIS project and using the ratio of the 90th to the 10th earnings percentiles, Gottschalk and Smeeding presented a different ranking.[20] The United States still had the most unequal distribution when the distribution for full-time, year-round workers is considered, but instead of the United Kingdom coming in second place, Canada was in second place. Sweden was in third place, then only followed by men from the United Kingdom. Their comparisons were based on somewhat earlier years than the comparisons based on the OECD data.

Low-Wage Employment

The OECD also analyzed the incidence and distribution of low-paid employment among member countries.[21] "Low pay" was defined as earnings that were less than two-thirds of the median earnings (from the annual, monthly, weekly, or daily earnings distributions) for full-time employees. The incidence of low pay is a natural concern flowing from analyses of wage inequality that have shown the lower halves of the wage structures of many countries collapsing in the 1980s as labor demand shifted toward the higher skilled and better educated workers.

But as the OECD points out, measuring low-wage employment can be problematic. They mention that the definition can be an absolute or relative one (OECD selected a relative definition) and the choice depends on the issues being addressed. Concerns about the risk of "social exclusion or a sense of deprivation," according to the OECD, argue for a relative definition. Presumably, they believe that when one's earnings are a certain distance away from the median earnings of a distribution, a sense of exclusion and deprivation occurs. They also say that the low-pay definition is sensitive to whether or not earnings are measured on a gross or net basis.

Along with these concerns, however, are other conceptual issues in identifying low-paid employment. For example, a couple of these are the differences in persons' backgrounds (i.e., age, sex, educational level, household income, urban-rural residence) and the different opinions regarding what is a low-wage or low-paid employment. For example, a Wall Street lawyer might consider $20 an hour as low (which certainly would be above the median in today's hourly wage distribution), while a

Table 7.2

Incidence of Low-Paid Employment in Selected OECD Countries

Country	Percentage of Workers Who Are Low Paid
Australia, 1995	13.8
Austria, 1993	13.2
Belgium, 1993	7.2
Canada, 1994	23.7
Finland, 1994	5.9
France, 1995	13.3
Germany, 1994	13.3
Italy, 1993	12.5
Japan, 1994	15.7
Netherlands, 1994	11.9
New Zealand, 1994/95	16.9
Sweden, 1993	5.2
Switzerland, 1995	13.0
United Kingdom, 1995	19.6
United States, 1994	25.0

Source: Organization of Economic Co-operation and Development, *The 1996 OECD Employment Outlook,* Table 3.2, p. 72.

Note: "Low paid" is defined as earnings that are less than two-thirds of the median earnings for full-time workers.

high school student might be delighted to find a full-time job paying $6 an hour (which is probably below two-thirds of the median hourly earnings in the United States).

In any event, the OECD estimates of low-paid employment are of interest because they mirror their decile dispersion measure (i.e., the ratio of earnings at the upper limit of the 5th decile to those at the upper limit of the 1st decile) and provide further insights into the lower end of the wage distributions. The data in Table 7.2 show the incidence of low-wage employment across fifteen OECD nations in the 1993–1995 period. The United States ranks first with a rate of low-wage employment of 25.0 percent, followed by Canada at 23.7 percent, the United Kingdom at 19.6 percent, and New Zealand at 16.9 percent. The lowest incidences of low-paid employment were found in the Nordic countries of Finland (5.9 percent) and Sweden (5.2 percent). The incidence of low-wage employment among other major industrial countries was as follows: Japan, 15.7 percent,

Australia, 13.8 percent, Germany, 13.3 percent, France, 13.3 percent, and Italy, 12.5 percent.

Explaining Earnings Inequality Trends Across Countries

As we know, wage inequality rose only modestly in the United States in the 1970s, and then accelerated in the 1980s. Relative wage differentials by education and experience widened significantly in the 1980s as did earnings inequality within education and experience groups. Relatively slower growth in the supply of college-educated workers in the face of a stronger relative demand for highly skilled workers explained much of the increase in the skill premium. The degree to which skill-biased technological changes, international trading practices, and the erosion of the minimum wage and declining influence of unions have created greater wage inequality is still a matter of dispute. Many economists, however, now consider technological changes as accounting for most of the greater earnings dispersion.

Several studies by academic economists focusing on international comparisons of earnings inequality have been conducted. Typically, the situation in the United States is the point of comparison. In one of the very early analyses (1992) by Peter Gottschalk and Mary Joyce, earnings distributions for men age 25 to 55 were accessed through the LIS project for Australia, Canada, France, the Netherlands, Sweden, the United Kingdom, and the United States for different time periods between the late 1970s and 1980s.[22]

Gottschalk and Joyce found that not only had inequality in these countries' wage distributions increased, but that inequality had increased both between and within groups of men classified by education and experience. They also found that the situation occurring in the United States was not unique. They concluded that shifts in the industrial structures of these countries (from the manufacturing sector to the service sector) had little to do with the increases in inequality.

In another study by Katz, Loveman, and Blanchflower published in 1993, the wage structures of men and women in France, the United Kingdom, Japan, and the United States were compared over a twenty-year period.[23] These economists accessed earnings data directly from the individual countries.[24] Their comparisons were instructive in pointing to the similarities and dissimilarities of the changes that took place in each of these country's wage structures.

According to the research of Katz, Loveman, and Blanchflower, in Britain and Japan skill and educational wage differentials increased in the 1980s, as was the case in the United States. The slowdown in the relative supply of college-educated workers, at the same time that the relative demand for more skilled labor was rising, explained much of the increase in educational wage differentials in these countries. However, the somewhat greater increase in skill differentials in the United States and the United Kingdom relative to Japan, they believed, reflected the former two countries' greater industrial shift from goods to service-producing activities as well as within sector skill upgrading. They also concluded that relative skill demands were probably growing in France also during the 1980s, but the impact on France's wage structure was muted by the presence of their relatively high minimum wage and the ability of French unions to stave off market forces.

One of the more interesting differences Katz, Loveman, and Blanchflower found between the United States and other countries was the role of wage-setting institutions—unions and minimum wage laws—in understanding differential growth rates in wage inequality across countries (Richard Freeman and Lawrence Katz had also observed such differences).[25] In many European countries, unions negotiate wages in a more centralized fashion than in the United States, that is, the wage bargaining process can involve a whole industry, not just a single company. Germany, Italy, the Nordic countries, and to some extent France have these relatively more centralized wage bargaining systems. In other words, the existence of strong unions bargaining across large sectors of the economy can mitigate the market forces of supply and demand.

Similarly, the existence of more beneficent minimum wage laws in some European countries helped to prop up the lower half of their earnings distributions. An example was the effect of the French minimum wage law, or the SMIC *(salarie minimum interprofessional de croissance),* on France's wage structure. The much higher relative value of the SMIC compared to the United States's minimum wage in the 1980s is one reason cited for why real wages at the low end of France's wage distribution did not erode to the same extent they did in the United States's wage distribution.[26]

The fact that earnings inequality has grown much faster in the United States than in other countries in recent years has left this country with an earnings distribution that is much different than many of our foreign friends. To demonstrate how the United States's distribution differs from that of other nations, Gottschalk and Smeeding, using LIS data for these various countries, compared the monetary differences (in percentage terms) of workers at various points in their countries' earnings distributions relative to their country's median earnings.[27]

According to Gottschalk and Smeeding, the earnings of U.S. men age 25 to 54 who worked full-time, year-round in 1991 at the 10th percentile of their earnings distribution were only about 34 percent as large as those of men of the same age group with earnings at the median. In Sweden, however, in 1992, the earnings of men at the 10th percentile of their distribution were 48 percent as large as their co-workers at their median. On the other hand, at the other end of the distribution—the 90th percentile—U.S. men's earnings were 193 percent larger than the median while Swedish men's earnings at their 90th percentile were only 166 percent as high as their respective median.

Interpreting statistics like these, however, requires some care. As the authors point out, the medians in the United States and Sweden are different, with the median earnings being higher in the United States. To overcome this problem, Gottschalk and Smeeding converted the Swedish earnings (and the earnings of workers from other countries) into U.S. dollars (using purchasing power parities) so as to achieve a greater degree of comparability.[28] The results, however, still showed that Swedish men at the low end of their distribution were better off than American men at the same point in their distribution (41 percent vs. 34 percent), and American men at the 90th percentile were still better off than Swedish men at the comparable point in their distribution (193 vs. 140 percent).

So, if one believes these statistics after all of the efforts to arrive at comparable distributions, then one can conclude that success in the job market is more greatly rewarded in the United States than in Sweden, while failure (or the inability to move out of the low end of the earnings distribution) is treated more harshly.

Income Inequality Trends: OECD Findings

The most exhaustive analysis of cross-national comparisons of income distributions was conducted by the OECD, and this study was based largely on the LIS data as obtained from individual countries.[29] As was pointed out earlier, the LIS database of individual countries' income distributions was created for the purpose of achieving as much comparability across distributions as possible. Adjustments to individual country distributions were made in the LIS project, for example, for uniformity in the income concept, unit of analysis, and differences in household size.

The LIS definition of income used in the OECD analysis was disposable income. It was derived from several components as follows: To wages and salaries were added self-employment income, certain property income (i.e., interest, dividends), and various public and private transfer income items

Table 7.3

Gini Indexes and Shares of Disposable Income Received by the Top 20 Percent and Bottom 10 Percent of Households in Selected OECD Countries, Selected Years

	Gini Index	Top 20 Percent	Bottom 10 Percent
Australia			
1981	0.287	36.3	2.8
1985	0.295	37.0	2.9
Belgium			
1985	0.228	33.1	4.2
1988	0.235	33.6	4.2
Canada			
1981	0.286	36.3	2.7
1987	0.289	36.7	2.8
Finland			
1987	0.207	31.4	4.5
1990	0.215	31.9	4.3
France			
1979	0.297	38.4	3.1
1984	0.296	38.4	3.0
Norway			
1979	0.222	32.8	4.1
1986	0.234	33.3	3.9
Sweden			
1981	0.199	30.8	4.0
1987	0.220	31.8	3.3
United Kingdom			
1979	0.270	35.6	3.5
1988	0.304	38.2	2.5
United States			
1979	0.309	37.3	2.1
1986	0.341	39.8	1.9

Source: Organization for Economic Co-operation and Development, *Income Distribution in OECD Countries,* Social Policy Studies No. 18, 1995, Tables 4.7 and 4.8, p. 49 (Luxembourg Income Study).

(e.g., social security benefits and private pensions), which resulted in a total income figure; from this figure, personal income taxes and contributions for social security were deducted, resulting in disposable income. The household was selected as the basic unit of analysis since it was the most common in the countries under investigation, even though there are some exceptions, such as in Italy where the family is the basic unit. All household disposable incomes were adjusted for household size differences so as to account for presumed differences in need. A consistent equivalence scale was used across all nations in the LIS data.

Table 7.3 shows the trends in the Gini index for nine OECD countries' disposable household income distributions over different time periods covering the late 1970s to the early 1990s. It also shows the shares of aggregate disposable income received by the top 20 percent of households in the distribution and the bottom 10 percent.

According to the Gini indexes calculated on the LIS data sets for these countries, all countries experienced increases in inequality during the 1980s except France. The amounts of the increase varied (and really aren't comparable because of the different time periods), but the increases appeared to be the sharpest in the United States, United Kingdom, and Sweden.

The United States had the most unequal distribution of income of all the nine OECD countries studied. The Gini index in 1986 was .341 up from .309 in 1979—an increase of 10.4 percent (it should be remembered that these Gini indexes are based on after-tax household incomes that were adjusted for household size differences). The share of income going to the top 20 percent rose from 37 percent to almost 40 percent while the share going to the lowest 10 percent of households moved down from just above the two-percentage-point mark to just below it.

The Gini index for the United Kingdom was the next highest of the nine OECD countries and it had increased by 12.6 percent over the 1979–1986 period. Disposable income also became more concentrated at the top and the share received by the bottom 10 percent of households fell sharply.

Sweden also experienced a significant increase in inequality, with its Gini index rising from .199 to .220 between 1981 and 1987 (a 10.6 percent increase). The share of income going to the top 20 percent of households edged up to almost 32 percent (a full percentage point increase) and the share received by the lowest 10 percent of households fell from 4.0 to 3.3 percent.

More modest changes in income inequality were recorded in Norway, Finland, Belgium, Australia, and Canada. All of these countries experienced small increases in the share of income received by the top 20 percent of households, and in Norway and Finland small declines were observed in the share received by the bottom 10 percent.

Income Inequality Trends: Special Studies

In Gottschalk's and Smeeding's review article of cross-national comparative studies of income inequality, they also reviewed research that was based on data from individual countries that had not undergone the comparability procedures of the LIS project.[30] According to their review of these studies, a somewhat similar pattern of inequality increases emerged. Disposable income inequality had increased most rapidly in the United Kingdom, the United States, and Sweden between the early 1980s and early 1990s—over 16 percent as measured by the Gini index. In Canada, Norway, Belgium, and Australia increases were more modest—in the 5 to 10 percent range—while in Finland there was little perceptible change.

Their review also contained information on some other countries of interest, such as Japan, Germany, France, and Italy. In Japan, the Gini index increased by between 5 to 10 percent in the 1981–1990 period, but there was little change in inequality in France and West Germany through most of the 1980s and early 1990s. And in Italy the Gini index actually fell.

In summary, it is very apparent that household incomes in many major industrial nations of the world have become more dispersed in recent years. However, the degree to which their distributions have grown more unequal varies substantially.

As was true with the analysis of earnings inequality, because the income distribution in the United States has become so much more dispersed in recent years relative to other countries, households with incomes at the low end of the distribution (e.g., the 10th percentile) and with incomes at the high end (e.g., the 90th percentile) are much further away from the households with incomes at the median. This fact is also true when foreign incomes are converted into dollars and the comparison has been adjusted for differences in purchasing power. According to the LIS income data presented in the Gottschalk-Smeeding review article, U.S. households at the 10th percentile of the income distribution are worse off (i.e., in terms of living standards) than households from thirteen other OECD countries with incomes at the 10th percentiles of their income distributions.[31] But on the other hand, for the lucky households at the 90th percentile of the U.S. income distribution, incomes are much greater than their counterparts in these countries.

Why Income Distributions Are Changing

It comes as no surprise that economists who have studied the rise in household income inequality in specific countries have linked it to rising earnings inequality; in other words to changes taking place in the labor market of the economy. However, other factors have been considered also, such as changes in social and demographic factors across countries. Furthermore, because these analyses involve foreign countries, many of which have different and more extensive social welfare systems than ours, changes to these systems have been examined as well.

One of the early international analyses of changing income inequality was by McKinley L. Blackburn and David E. Bloom.[32] They examined income distributions for various years from the late 1970s to the early 1990s of married-couple families in the United States, Canada, Australia, France, the Netherlands, Sweden, and the United Kingdom (the data for the last four countries were obtained from the LIS). They found that earnings inequality had increased for husbands in all the countries to varying degrees (with an especially large increase in the United Kingdom), except in the Netherlands where it fell slightly. They also found that the correlation between the earnings of the husband and wife was very important in explaining the overall rise in income inequality in the United States and Canada and that this correlation had also increased in Sweden and the United Kingdom; it had not increased, however, in Australia, France, and the Netherlands. Therefore, not only were changes in the men's wage structure affecting income inequality trends across countries, but so too were changes in family labor supply decisions.

Of course, analyses such as these only beg the question. Is the greater dispersion in earnings caused by relative demand-supply shifts brought about by technological changes, new trade patterns, or institutional changes in the country? As was discussed earlier, some economists suggest that trade with developing nations has depressed the earnings of unskilled labor in advanced nations because of the nature of the labor content in the imported goods. Or is the greater dispersion traceable to the international migration of technological changes in the production of goods and services? Whatever the ultimate cause, however, it is clear that changes in earnings inequality are of primary importance in explaining income inequality because market earnings represent such a large part of household incomes on average.

Economists have found that social and demographic changes have played some role in the rise in inequality as well. For example, single-parent families have become a larger proportion of all families and households in the United Kingdom, Germany, Belgium, and the Netherlands, and births out of wedlock rose in these countries as well.[33] This factor, of course, has been thought to be connected to growing income inequality in the United States as well, although disagreement exists as to its relative importance.

Gottschalk and Smeeding also point to changes in the social welfare systems of many countries as having an impact on their levels of inequality.[34] They point out that the Nordic and northern European countries, which have the lowest levels of income inequality and the smallest increases, were also countries in which relatively large amounts were spent on the "safety net," or social protection. Indeed, spending on social welfare systems is inversely correlated with changes in income inequality, according to these two economists.

Closing Remarks

The analysis of income and earnings inequality reaches another level of complexity when cross-national comparisons of income and earnings distributions are attempted. Many of the empirical difficulties have been enumerated. As much as economists and others attempt to "standardize" income and earnings distributions across nations, comparability problems and issues will remain. Indeed, comparability issues even plague analyses within a country, as we saw in the chapter dealing with U.S. trends in inequality before 1950. Consequently, the ranking of countries as to whose distribution is the most unequal or least unequal must be viewed with caution (as was shown, the ranking can differ simply on the basis of the type of earnings being measured).

But there are other difficulties inherent in these comparisons which have not been mentioned. These can be summarized simply as cultural differences. These differences can range from the different consumption patterns of households at similar points in their income distributions to the different tastes (or tolerances) societies have for economic differences. In the first instance, households at the 25th percentile of one country's income distribution may have an entirely different view about women in the labor force as compared to households at the 25th percentile of a second country's income distribution. In other words, cultural differences with respect to the world of work may also create differences in income distributions across countries. In the second instance, some societies simply have different attitudes, ideas, or notions about what the role of the government should be in one's life. These differences may lead to different patterns of social behavior which ultimately are reflected in the income and earnings distributions of countries.

This is all by way of saying that comparing and contrasting income and earnings distributions across nations is inherently a complex undertaking. Judgments about whose form of government or whose socio-economic system is preferable, based upon comparative analyses of economic inequality, must be made with a thorough understanding of the countries involved. The distributions of earnings and income, as we learned at the outset, are the result of a complex array of interrelated factors.

8

The Future

So, where do we go from here? The century is coming to end and, in terms of the trend in income inequality across this span of time, it might be likened to a "roller coaster ride."[1] From reaching the apex of the ride in the first part of the century, to hurtling down the slope during the decades of the mid-century, only to begin to climb again in the last quarter of the century, the ride, like any other roller coaster ride, has been memorable. Will income inequality in the years ahead continue upward, level off, or even decline?

As an economist who worked in two of the federal government's "number mills" for almost thirty-five years, I am reminded that in that capacity speculation about the future was unheard of. While the opportunities to speculate about the future trends in family incomes, wages, unemployment, income inequality, and other federal statistics were ever present, thanks to the inquiring media, the unwritten rule was, "Don't!" Consequently, there remains for this author a built-in, institutionally based reluctance to look into the future.

In addition, attempting to plumb the future is full of many unknowns, as we all know, and especially in the case of income inequality. It would be one thing if the assignment was to predict, for example, the course of computer chip production for the next five or ten years (I suspect it is up), but income inequality is, as has been shown, such a complicated affair. While most economists believe that skill-biased technological changes in the workplace are most important in explaining the growth in income inequality in the last twenty-five years, a number of other candidates, such as trade, declining unionism, and changes in household composition, are thought to be important as well. As the economists would say, "If we don't know what goes on the right side of our equation, how good is it going to predict what we have on the left side?" Until the research community has a better idea as to how to apportion the relative importance of the various causes of growing income inequality (and how they interact), predictions based on the standard methodologies of economists (econometric modeling) will continue to be problematic. Nevertheless, we've all heard of educated guesses, informed conjectures, hunches, and even opinions. Persons involved in such activities bring different amounts of background information and informed views to their predictions—some hardly anything, others years of study and experience. It is in this spirit that the following discussion about the future course of income inequality in America is presented.

In this final chapter, the first point of discussion will be, How much more income inequality can our society expect? This very blunt but reasonable question, no doubt, lurks in the recesses of many Americans' minds. A second question concerns the future course of income inequality: Can the trend level off? As was shown, trends in inequality, like trends in most everything else, do eventually change. The recent slowdown in the growth of income inequality in the 1990s will be examined in this context. The last section summarizes what has been learned about the trends in income inequality in recent years. Hopefully, it provides an improved perspective on the topic of income inequality in the United States at the end of the twentieth century.

How Much More Inequality?

The flurry of good economic news in the mid-1990s has seemed never-ending. Unemployment, inflation, and interest rates are all at their lowest levels in years; gross domestic product, or GDP, continues to rise along with the earnings of most corporations and their stock prices. Nevertheless, uneasiness about the economic problems confronting the middle class and the degree of income inequality in society continues to make the news.

A case in point was the Census Bureau's release of its income and poverty report for 1996 released in September 1997. In general, the news was good. Median household incomes between 1995 and 1996 had increased for the second consecutive year, income inequality was unchanged for the third consecutive year, and the poverty level and rate appeared to stabilize at its lowest level since the 1990–91 recession.[2] There was also some "not-so-good" news: Average family incomes in the lowest quintile dropped, the number of families considered to be "very poor" increased, and the earnings of men working full-time, year-round fell.

The New York Times, in its lead editorial, accentuated the negative and made no apologies for it.[3] Their headline read: "The Tide Is Not Lifting Everyone." The editorial pointed out that despite the fact that the Census Bureau set "the White House aglow" with its report on rising incomes and so forth, the gap between the rich and poor had not closed and the poor at the bottom of the distribution were not faring well at all, and, indeed, were losing ground.

This continuing concern about income inequality raises a question about how much more inequality we can expect. Or, in the language of the economists, how much further can some of our measures of inequality, like the Gini index, rise?

Judging from the inequality levels in the late 1920s and early 1930s, today's level is far below what existed back then. Recalling the discussion of Chapter 6, the Gini index for the famiiy income distribution in the early 1930s, according to some economists, reached almost .550. This compares to the Census Bureau's 1996 estimate for households of .455. Other estimates of income concentration showed that around that same time the top 5 percent of income recipients received almost 27 percent of the country's aggregate income. In 1996, the Census Bureau's estimate for the top 5 percent of households was just over 21 percent. Clearly, income inequality was more severe in the early 1930s—and the overall health of the economy was much more precarious also.

This is not to deny that many middle-income and low-income families in present-day America face labor market problems and other economic difficulties. Rather it is to place them in the context of where the country has been with respect to income differences in the past. So there is no question that if income differences begin to widen again in the next few years (especially from the upper part of the income distribution), it is not like our society has never experienced such disparities before—and survived.

The uneasiness over inequality, whether or not it continues to level off or begins to grow again, can be tolerated for two additional reasons. First, despite the seeming unresponsiveness of the politicians in Washington, D.C., some changes affecting the economic situations of Americans have been forthcoming in recent years. The raising of the federal minimum wage and the Earned Income Tax Credit, the passage of the balanced budget and tax cut acts of 1997, and the other legislative efforts, while meaningless to many Americans, do mean for others that someone is listening in Washington. As long as gestures such as these are evident, income differences will be accepted.

Second, as long as the nation's economy continues to perform as it has in the mid-1990s, concern over inequality will be held in check. Even if many of the jobs that are created in the economy pay low wages, there are many that pay high wages, offering an incentive for those with the ambition to pursue them. As we have seen mentioned in the press and in the literature, for many Americans, working longer hours, even at the same wage rates, is one way to raise incomes. Inflation has been kept at bay and interest rates have remained low, permitting even those in the lower part of the income distribution to purchase cars, homes, and other consumer durables.

Our society, therefore, can sustain further growth in income and earnings inequality in the years ahead. If another recession were to occur in the next few years, however, the uneasiness over growing income inequality will only intensify. As was shown, even though income inequality during the 1990–91 recession remained unchanged, the loss of jobs and income during this period, particularly in the higher ranks of the income distribution, awakened America to the sizable income gap that had occurred between the rich, the middle class, and the poor over the previous decades. Income differences were on the minds of many and the fairness issue, thanks to the media, had come center-stage. When another recession occurs like the one of the early 1990s, regardless of what happens to inequality, it is very likely that the issue of inequality in the nation will again become "big news" in the media.

But before we hunker down, waiting for the worst to happen, we should ask another question about the future course of inequality. After all, it is possible that the upward trend could level off, despite what some economists have predicted.[4] This is because there has been some leveling off in the income inequality trend in recent years. Admittedly, the trend during the late 1980s and early 1990s is difficult to interpret because of methodological changes that occurred in the Census Bureau's CPS, but developments in inequality in this most recent period are worth closer scrutiny.

Can the Trend Level Off?

As all economists know, trends in any economic time series do change. Determining when a trend has changed or is changing, however, is challenging. The change in the trend in real median family incomes which took place in the early 1970s (see Figure 3.1) looks like it was a rather easy event to call, looking back at it twenty-five years later. But for the economists back then, let's say in 1977 or 1978, looking at how this statistical measure was tracking up until then, the assessment might have been different. Clearly, they would have noted the slower growth, but they didn't know that this development was turning into a long-term trend. In many respects, this is the position we find ourselves in with respect to the trend in income inequality in the mid-1990s.

Some economists would argue that this isn't important anyway. Inequality is a phenomenon that should only be considered in a long-term context. The forces that go into shaping and propelling these trends usually take a long time in developing. For these economists, therefore, the important point is the fact that a growing income gap has been observed over a long period of time, and for the sake of public policy, it is best to understand why.

This is certainly true to a point. However, it can also be argued that we

Table 8.1

Selected Measures of Income Inequality, 1979 and 1987–1996

Year	Gini Index	Top 5 Percent	Top 20 Percent	Bottom 20 Percent	95th/ 20th	80th/ 50th	50th/ 20th
1979	0.404	16.4	44.0	4.2	6.77	1.77	2.35
1987	0.426	18.2	46.2	3.8	7.49	1.86	2.41
1988	0.427	18.3	46.3	3.8	7.52	1.86	2.39
1989	0.431	18.9	46.8	3.8	7.59	1.86	2.39
1990	0.428	18.6	46.6	3.9	7.58	1.84	2.40
1991	0.428	18.1	46.5	3.8	7.66	1.88	2.39
1992	0.434	18.6	46.9	3.8	7.86	1.89	2.43
1993	0.454	21.0	48.9	3.6	8.07	1.93	2.41
1994	0.456	21.2	49.1	3.6	8.18	1.95	2.40
1995	0.450	21.0	48.7	3.7	7.85	1.91	2.37
1996	0.455	21.4	49.0	3.7	8.09	1.92	2.40

Source: U.S. Bureau of the Census, Annual Demographic Survey, CPS.

should have some idea as to what is happening to the trend in the short run from the standpoint of public policy as well. Establishing certain policies to halt the continued rise in wage inequality, for example, may be overkill if indeed the trend had been misread and was in the process of leveling off anyway. We know from examining the long-term trend in income inequality that there have been periods when inequality stabilized, for example, from the end of the 1940s until the early 1970s. Shouldn't we be on the watch for developments of trends like this as well? In this section, the trend in income inequality from the late 1980s to the mid-1990s is given a closer look.

The Numbers

Various inequality measures used in this book on the household income data obtained in the Census Bureau's March CPS are displayed in Table 8.1. They relate to each of the years over the 1987–1996 period and to 1979. They should be examined in three stages: First, the 1979–1987 period, second, the 1987–1992 period, and third, the 1993–1996 period. The last two periods do not overlap because this was when the March CPS underwent methodological changes that make data comparisons between 1992 and 1993 problematic. Consequently, for the purposes of this exercise, these two years are not compared.

What one sees over the 1979–1987 period, of course, is a relatively strong indication of growing inequality in each measure, whether it be the summary measure of inequality, the Gini index, the aggregate income share measure of the top 5 percent of households or the top and bottom 20 percent of households, or the three ratios of income percentiles. In the next period, 1987 to 1992, most of these measures exhibit little change, especially up to 1991. In the 1991–1992 period, the Gini index, the 95th-to-20th income percentile ratio, the 50th-to-20th income percentile ratio, and the shares of income going to the highest 5 and 20 percent of households, all exhibited some upward movement. In the last period, 1993–1996, all the measures with the exception of the shares measure for the bottom 20 percent of households and the 50th-to-20th income percentile ratio, appeared to have jumped to another level or plateau, no doubt due in part to the changes in the CPS. But once again, for the four years making up this period, all of the inequality measures display remarkable stability—much like most of them did between 1987 and 1991.

As was indicated in Chapter 3, there is no doubt a significant increase in income inequality occurred between 1992 and 1993 when the recession was over and the economic recovery was beginning.[5] Signs of an increase in inequality were appearing between 1991 and 1992. Were it not for the methodological changes in the CPS, it would have been possible to obtain a fairly accurate reading of this increase. The interesting fact is that this increase in inequality occurred as the recovery was getting under way, but thereafter inequality changed very little, as the data for 1993 to 1996 indicate. The experience of the 1980–82 recessions was much different. Income inequality rose during the recessions—and continued rising after the recession was over and the recovery was under way.

An Explanation for the Difference

Central to the explanation for the increase in income inequality in the 1991–1993 period and then the leveling off, compared to the increase in income inequality between 1979 and 1982 and then the continued rise, is the nature of the recessions in these periods and the economic times in which they occurred. In the 1979–1982 period, the employment cutbacks were particularly severe in the goods-producing industries (especially manufacturing) relative to the service-producing industries. Blue-collar workers were hit hard. The era of downsizing and paring back worker payrolls so as to cut costs and increase efficiency got off to a roaring start in this period.

The 1990–91 recession was much milder but the proportion of white-collar workers affected by the economic slump relative to blue-collar workers was much greater than in past recessions. This meant that the effect of the recession was felt much further up in the earnings distribution than in the 1980–82 recessions. As was shown in Chapter 3, incomes fell across the distribution. In addition, manufacturing employment growth, which had been weak in the 1980s anyway, had already been scaled back before the start of the 1990–91 recession.[6]

Consequently, in the years of the 1980s, earnings inequality began to accelerate as more high-paying, low-skilled jobs were eliminated while the white-collar work force remained largely unaffected. The blue-collar workers who lost jobs over this period ended up for the most part finding lower-paying jobs, oftentimes in the service-producing industries, further exacerbating earnings and income inequality. Toward the end of that decade, however, the forces responsible for the acceleration in inequality apparently moderated or began offsetting one another.

In the years following the 1990–91 recession, many white-collar workers who had been caught in the downsizings of the late 1980s and early 1990s returned to the workforce. While many returned for much smaller paychecks, others returned to new career paths and opportunities because of their skills and educational backgrounds and ended up doing better than before. This caused the unquantifiable "spurt" in inequality in the 1992–1993 period, discussed in Chapter 3.

The fact that overall income inequality has changed very little in the 1993–1996 period—even though income differences are the largest they have been in this half of the twentieth century—suggests that the forces that were driving income inequality up in most of the 1980s had subsided or were offsetting one another in the mid-1990s.

Making the Case for Leveling Off

Despite the "learned" opinions of the pundits and academics, one could argue that inequality has reached a new plateau in recent years. Clearly, with the exception of the early 1990s, the upward trend in income inequality appeared to stabilize in the 1987–1996 period relative to the earlier years. The problem for "trend watchers" is trying to understand why and whether or not this will turn into a long-run development.

The gist of the problem is that while economists have uncovered a number of possible reasons for growing income inequality, with perhaps skill-biased technological changes leading the list, they are unsure of their relative importance. That is, they are unsure of how to apportion, or weight, all of these various causes of growing earnings and income inequality. Furthermore, they have as yet to untangle the potential interactions among the causes—an even more challenging task.

To illustrate the problem—as well as explain why the trend in inequality could be leveling off—some of the possible causes of growing income inequality are listed below. This ranking is not intended to reflect anyone's particular view on the matter.[7]

Cause	Relative Weight
Immigration	?
Deindustrialization	?
Skill-biased, technological change	?
Declining unionization	?
Trade	?
Household compositional changes	?
Minimum wage erosion	?
All others	?
	100%

Few economists today would suggest that growing income inequality has been the result of one specific cause. Even if one cause is more important than the others, such as technological change or foreign trade, it can be easily seen how a multi-causal paradigm could lead to a leveling off in income inequality. As the forces generating growing income differences ebb and flow over time, it could very well be the case that the shifting influence of the causes reduces the overall tendency for the income distribution to grow more unequal. For example, it is possible that increases in the real value of the minimum wage as well as the appearance of more aggressive unionism reduced the influence of these causes relative to the others. Or that over the 1987–1996 period, the process of deindustrialization has lost its influence along with the role of technological changes. All of this, of course, is purely speculation, but the point should be clear: Given what is known about the causes of growing income inequality, it is very possible that the ultimate strength of the forces causing the income distribution to grow more dispersed could very well change as a consequence of the shifting importance of the many causes.

Needless to say, the changing importance of the causes producing growing income inequality is further complicated by the interaction of the causes, and their shifting importance. Many of these interactions are very obvious; for example, the influence of the higher minimum wage for single parents with low skill levels and poor educations. However, others are not well understood, such as the relationship between technological changes and employment in trade-sensitive industries. Nevertheless, the strength and influence of these interactions—which also have an influence on the inequality trend—can change.

Only time will tell whether or not the apparent stabilization of the trend in income inequality in recent years is turning into a more permanent leveling off. Considering the recent developments in the trend in the 1990s, it is as much a possibility as the further increases that are predicted by others.

An Improved Perspective on Inequality

By now the reader should have developed an improved perspective on the topic of growing income inequality. The popular impressions of inequality in America discussed at the outset in Chapter 1—the haves and have nots, the rich get richer and the poor get poorer, the declining middle class—should now be seen in the light of other significant facts surrounding this issue.

Some of the more important ones are the following:

1. Household and family income determination is not only a function of one's present life circumstances, but also the past decisions made with respect to education, living arrangements, and, more generally, one's view of their role in society.
2. The measurement of income and earnings inequality requires careful examination of the measuring device as well as the source of the data being measured.
3. The upward trend in income inequality since the early 1970s has not been a steady, monotonic progression. Indeed, income inequality rose moderately in the 1970s, accelerated in the 1980s, and then slowed down or stablilized by the mid-1990s.
4. Growing earnings inequality explains much of the increase in income inequality. Widening relative wage differentials on the basis of education and experience in the 1980s, along with a continuation of growing inequality within specific education-experience groups, resulted in a more unequal earnings distribution.
5. Growing income inequality is thought to have many causes. Paramount among them, perhaps, are technological changes that raise the labor demand for the highly skilled and educated but lower it for unskilled workers. Foreign trade and other international business practices also have been mentioned as the cause of job loss for millions of low-skilled workers. But other causes of growing income inequality have been suggested, including changes in the composition of households and the break-up of families, declining union membership, and the erosion of the real value of the minimum wage. The problem is that economists have not agreed on the relative importance of all the causes that have been proposed.

6. Although the evidence is sketchy, inequality in both the income and earnings distributions was believed to be at its highest levels in the early decades of this century. From these heights at the end of the 1920s and early 1930s, income and wage differences became more compressed by the end of the 1940s. Income inequality thereafter fluctuated (slightly downward) within a narrow range, reaching its century-low point in the late 1960s. The growth in income inequality in the second half of this century never reached the peaks experienced in the early decades of the century.

7. Other industrialized nations, like the United Kingdom, Japan, Canada, and Australia, have also experienced increases in income and earnings inequality in recent years. However, the increases have been the greatest in the United States and the United Kingdom.

Another aspect of this improved perspective on income inequality is a more general one. It concerns the meaning of inequality. As was indicated in Chapter 1 and elsewhere, our responses to inequality involve social judgments. In recent years, the concern has been over the economic problems of the middle class. These have been manifested in a variety of forms: the fear of downsizing and the loss of health insurance and other benefits, the employment in low-wage, dead-end jobs, the stagnant wage growth that makes workers put in longer hours just to stay in place economically, and so forth. In the 1960s, the concern over inequality was directed at the poor and disadvantaged. Even though measured income inequality was at its lowest point in the entire century, the fact that large pockets of poverty existed in many urban centers and rural areas resulted in a massive effort on the part of the federal government to wipe out poverty. And, of course, during the 1930s, the concern over inequality was manifested in simply resuscitating a collapsed economy and improving the economic lot of both the lower- and middle-income classes. In all these instances, of course, an overriding concern has been "fairness" and its perception on the part of society. The perception as to what is fair is formed by the economic situation confronting society and the events shaping that situation which is then recorded and reported on (accurately, one hopes) by government authorities and eventually the media.

A discussion of the public policies required to confront income inequality and its manifestations at the close of this century, or if they are required at all, is well beyond the scope of this book. Indeed, some legislation recently enacted has been referred to (e.g., the new minimum wage law, the balanced budget and tax cut acts of 1997) as a response to growing income inequality. But rather than speculate on whether or not more remedies are needed, and if so, of what kind, it is better to leave that to those who have made their social judgment about the level of income inequality in the United States today.

Instead, as this book comes to a close, it is preferable to leave the reader with another thought about the relationship between income inequality and society. This thought has not been fleshed out with hard facts and statistics. Nor has the thought been subject to rigorous debate or scrutiny by fellow economists. Rather, it is the result of working with the subject of income and earnings inequality for many years, and it too may provide additional perspective on the topic.

The thought concerns the "new socio-economic dynamic." As was mentioned in the first chapter, the income distribution can be thought of as the result of a complex assortment of choices made by members of society and its institutions. These choices interact dynamically, and it is this dynamic interaction of social, demographic, and economic factors that produces the "static" distribution of income that we have been examining.

Social, demographic, and economic changes in the last twenty-five years have come fast and furious, as they have at other times during the century. Many of these changes have been alluded to earlier. The new socio-economic dynamic at the end of this century is much different than the one existing in the 1950s, which in turn was much different than the one existing in the 1920s and 1930s. Simply consider the changes that have occurred down through the years to the traditional American family. The traditional family has dissolved into a variety of living arrangements in which some traditional family roles have blurred. So much change has gone on that popular journalists now even question the meaningfulness of some of our statistical barometers of economic well-being, like the "median household income."[8] Consequently, as a nation's socio-economic dynamic changes, it is most likely that its distribution of income will change as well.

Has income inequality in the United States gotten out of hand? While this book has not answered that question, maybe it has improved the reader's understanding of it.

Appendix A

Inequality Measures

The mathematical construction of four of the more complicated inequality measures referred to in this book are presented below. They are presented as if they were being used to derive measures of household income inequality based on a distribution of annual household incomes. Obviously, they could also be used on distributions of earnings as well as on income and earnings distributions reflecting monthly, weekly, or other periods of time in which income or earnings were received.

The Variance of the Natural Logarithm of Income (Var ln Y)

This measure is found frequently in the literature relating to earnings inequality. It is written as

$$\text{Var } \ln Y = \frac{\sum_{i=1}^{n} (\ln y_i - \ln \bar{y})^2}{n}$$

where $\ln y_i$ is the natural logarithm of household i's annual income, $\ln \bar{y}$ is the logarithm of the mean annual household income, and n is the number of households with income.

The Gini Index (G)

The Gini index, or the index of income concentration, as it is sometimes called, is perhaps one of the more traditional summary measures of inequality. When used on income distributions composed of grouped data, it is written as

$$G = 1.0 - \sum_{i=1}^{n} f_i (p_i + p_{i-1})$$

where f_i is the proportion of households in interval i and p_i is the proportion of total income received by recipients in interval i and all lower intervals.

Theil's Index of Inequality (T)

The Theil index of inequality can be written as

$$T = (1/n) \sum_{i=1}^{n} (y_i/\bar{y}) \log (y_i/\bar{y})$$

where y_i is the annual household income of the i th households, $\bar{y}$ the mean annual household income, and n the number of households in the distribution.

Atkinson's Index of Inequality (A)

The family of Atkinson indexes are constructed as follows:

$$A = 1 - [(1/n) \sum_{i=1}^{n} (y_i/\bar{y})^{1-\varepsilon}]^{\frac{1}{1-\varepsilon}}$$

with the identical notation as found in the other measures, except for the ε, or epsilon. Although this is a very helpful analytical measure, it has not been used extensively in the inequality literature.

Appendix B

Changes in the Current Population Survey (CPS)

Over the long history of the CPS, many changes have taken place in its design and methodology. The following is a brief description of the more significant changes that are relevant to the study of the United States's income distribution and the level and trend in income inequality.

1. In March 1996 (income year 1995) there was a 7,000-household sample reduction in the CPS, dropping its sample size to about 50,000 eligible households. For other changes in the CPS sample size in recent years, see the Census Bureau's 1996 report on *Money Income in the United States.*[1]

2. As was mentioned in the text, one of the most recent significant changes occurred in January 1994 when computer-assisted survey information collection (CASIC) was introduced into the basic CPS for collecting information on the nation's monthly employment and unemployment situation. The CASIC technology replaced the traditional paper-and-pencil interviewing procedure in that all CPS questions are administered from a computer, either a laptop at the site of the interview or from a centralized telephoning facility. This procedure was adopted in the March 1994 Annual Demographic Survey (income year 1993) as well, the source of the income and work experience information for the previous calendar year.

In addition to this change, two other technical changes were introduced that could affect the measurement of income inequality in the CPS. The first was the reweighting of survey results with estimates of the civilian noninstitutional population derived from the 1990 decennial census. Consequently, the CPS income data for 1993 (and later years) reflect new weights, and the data also were adjusted for the census undercount of the population. (The introduction of decennial census-based population controls and census-based sample redesigns are typically introduced around the time of the decennial censuses. See the Bureau's 1996 report on *Money Income in the United States* for more information.[2]) A second change occurring with the March 1994 CPS and the income data for 1993 was the introduction of new top codes in the income questions. The most important top code that was increased concerned earnings from a worker's longest job or business. With the beginning of the March 1994 CPS, this top code was increased from $299,999 to $999,999 a year. The impact of these changes on the CPS income data have been analyzed.[3]

2. Significant procedural changes were introduced with the March 1989 CPS (income year 1988) and, to allow for comparisons over time, these changes were applied to the income data collected in the March 1988 CPS (income year 1987). These changes involved a new processing system reflecting changes in the CPS questionnaire, specifically the expanded detail of income sources. Income imputation procedures were also revised to allow individual income items to be imputed separately as well as to impute entire sets of income information from the same interviewed person.

3. In March 1986 (income year 1985) certain income top codes were adjusted upward. The top code for earnings from the longest job was increased from $99,999 to $299,999.

4. In March 1980 (income year 1979) the income questionnaire was expanded to include income from fifty-one possible sources.

5. In March 1975 (income year 1974), a new March CPS processing system was introduced and the income questionnaire was expanded to eleven income questions.

6. In March 1968 (income year 1967) a new March CPS processing system was introduced; in March 1967 (income year 1966) the questionnaire was expanded to eight income questions; in March 1966 (income year 1965) new procedures were introduced to impute only missing income data because in March 1962 the imputation procedures involved imputing all income data even if only one income item was missing.

7. Income data for 1949 were based on expanded income questions to show details for wage and salary income, self-employment income (both farm and nonfarm), and all other nonearned income.

Appendix C

Statistics

The data in the following tables, obtained through the March Annual Demographic Survey of the Current Population Survey, relate to the household income distribution in the 1967–1996 period.

Table C-1

Households by Money Income Classes (in 1996 dollars), 1967–1996

Year	Households (thousands)	Households (percent)	Less than $5,000	$5,000 to $14,999	$15,000 to $34,999
1996	101,018	100	3.4	17.0	29.1
1995	99,627	100	3.5	16.8	29.5
1994	98,990	100	3.8	17.5	29.9
1993	97,107	100	4.0	17.5	30.1
1992	96,426	100	3.9	17.7	29.8
1991	95,669	100	3.6	17.2	30.0
1990	94,312	100	3.6	16.3	29.1
1989	93,347	100	3.2	16.0	29.0
1988	92,830	100	3.4	16.5	28.8
1987	91,124	100	3.6	16.5	29.0
1986	89,479	100	3.8	16.7	28.9
1985	88,458	100	3.7	17.3	29.8
1984	86,789	100	3.7	17.4	30.6
1983	85,290	100	3.9	17.5	31.5
1982	83,918	100	3.9	18.1	31.4
1981	83,527	100	3.6	18.0	31.3
1980	82,368	100	3.3	17.8	30.7
1979	80,776	100	3.2	17.2	30.0
1978	77,330	100	3.1	17.3	30.1
1977	76,030	100	3.2	18.2	30.5
1976	74,142	100	3.1	18.1	31.1
1975	72,867	100	3.3	18.5	31.8
1974	71,163	100	3.2	17.3	31.7
1973	69,859	100	3.8	16.9	30.2
1972	68,251	100	4.1	16.9	30.1
1971	66,676	100	4.7	17.1	31.9
1970	64,778	100	4.9	16.5	32.0
1969	63,401	100	5.0	16.2	31.8
1968	62,214	100	5.4	16.6	33.6
1967	60,813	100	6.0	17.2	35.3

Source: U.S. Bureau of the Census, Annual Demographic Survey, CPS.
Note: Household incomes in 1996 dollars.

$35,000 to $49,999	$50,000 to $74,999	$75,000 to $99,999	$100,000 or more	Median
16.3	18.0	8.2	8.2	$35,492
16.9	17.4	8.0	7.7	35,082
16.3	16.9	7.8	7.7	34,158
16.3	16.9	7.8	7.2	33,922
16.5	17.8	7.5	6.8	34,261
16.9	17.5	7.9	6.8	34,705
17.8	17.9	8.0	7.2	35,945
17.2	18.4	8.6	7.7	36,575
17.2	18.5	8.3	7.3	36,108
17.3	18.3	8.4	6.9	35,994
17.3	18.6	7.9	6.8	35,642
17.8	17.8	7.7	5.8	34,439
17.9	17.6	7.4	5.5	33,849
17.8	17.2	6.9	5.0	33,110
18.2	17.0	6.7	4.8	33,105
18.3	17.7	6.8	4.3	33,215
19.1	17.9	6.8	4.4	33,763
18.8	18.9	7.0	4.9	34,902
19.0	18.8	7.1	4.6	35,015
19.3	18.3	6.3	4.1	33,694
19.5	18.2	6.1	3.8	33,509
19.4	17.8	5.7	3.5	32,943
19.8	18.0	6.3	3.8	33,850
20.0	18.6	6.4	4.2	34,943
20.5	18.3	6.0	4.0	34,267
20.9	17.1	5.1	3.2	32,865
21.3	16.8	5.3	3.2	33,181
21.7	17.0	5.1	3.1	33,407
21.7	16.0	4.2	2.6	32,225
20.7	14.3	3.9	2.6	30,874

Table C-2

Shares of Aggregate Money Income Received by Household Income Quintiles and Top 5 Percent of Households, 1967–1996

Year	Total	Lowest	2nd Quin.	3rd Quin.	4th Quin.
1996	100	3.7	9.0	15.1	23.3
1995	100	3.7	9.1	15.2	23.3
1994	100	3.6	8.9	15.0	23.4
1993	100	3.6	9.0	15.1	23.5
1992	100	3.8	9.4	15.8	24.2
1991	100	3.8	9.6	15.9	24.2
1990	100	3.9	9.6	15.9	24.0
1989	100	3.8	9.5	15.8	24.0
1988	100	3.8	9.6	16.0	24.3
1987	100	3.8	9.6	16.1	24.3
1986	100	3.9	9.7	16.2	24.5
1985	100	4.0	9.7	16.3	24.6
1984	100	4.1	9.9	16.4	24.7
1983	100	4.1	10.0	16.5	24.7
1982	100	4.1	10.1	16.6	24.7
1981	100	4.2	10.2	16.8	25.0
1980	100	4.3	10.3	16.9	24.9
1979	100	4.2	10.3	16.9	24.7
1978	100	4.3	10.3	16.9	24.8
1977	100	4.4	10.3	17.0	24.8
1976	100	4.4	10.4	17.1	24.8
1975	100	4.4	10.5	17.1	24.8
1974	100	4.4	10.6	17.1	24.7
1973	100	4.2	10.5	17.1	24.6
1972	100	4.1	10.5	17.1	24.5
1971	100	4.1	10.6	17.3	24.5
1970	100	4.1	10.8	17.4	24.5
1969	100	4.1	10.9	17.5	24.5
1968	100	4.2	11.1	17.5	24.4
1967	100	4.0	10.8	17.3	24.2

Source: U.S. Bureau of the Census, Annual Demographic Survey, CPS.
Note: Household incomes in 1996 dollars.

Highest	Top 5%	Mean	Gini Index
49.0	21.4	$47,123	0.455
48.7	21.0	46,265	0.450
49.1	21.2	45,665	0.456
48.9	21.0	44,983	0.454
46.9	18.6	43,435	0.434
46.5	18.1	43,685	0.428
46.6	18.6	44,901	0.428
46.8	18.9	46,210	0.431
46.3	18.3	45,116	0.427
46.2	18.2	44,763	0.426
45.7	17.5	44,034	0.425
45.3	17.0	42,383	0.419
44.9	16.5	41,474	0.415
44.7	16.4	40,014	0.414
44.5	16.2	39,896	0.412
43.8	15.6	39,681	0.406
43.7	15.8	40,155	0.403
44.0	16.4	41,460	0.404
43.7	16.2	41,212	0.402
43.6	16.1	39,970	0.402
43.3	16.0	39,415	0.398
43.2	15.9	38,468	0.397
43.1	15.9	39,585	0.395
43.6	16.6	40,412	0.397
43.9	17.0	39,882	0.401
43.5	16.7	37,798	0.396
43.3	16.6	37,994	0.394
43.0	16.6	38,006	0.391
42.8	16.6	36,457	0.388
43.8	17.5	34,531	0.399

Table C-3

Household Income at Selected Percentiles of the Household Income Distribution, 1967–1996

Year	Percentiles				
	20th	40th	60th	80th	95th
1996	$14,768	$27,760	$44,006	$68,015	$119,540
1995	14,825	27,709	43,242	67,047	116,337
1994	14,214	26,679	42,454	66,530	116,268
1993	140,80	26,797	42,122	65,475	113,618
1992	14,091	26,996	42,384	64,870	110,736
1991	14,501	27,648	42,704	65,386	111,051
1990	15,006	28,405	43,457	66,271	113,741
1989	15,305	29,102	44,729	67,960	116,093
1988	15,096	28,515	44,439	67,101	113,583
1987	14,917	28,314	44,197	66,797	111,775
1986	14,828	28,321	43,742	66,024	111,986
1985	14,582	27,490	42,319	63,881	106,830
1984	14,497	27,037	41,537	62,820	105,088
1983	14,178	26,423	40,514	61,276	101,764
1982	13,983	26,276	40,308	60,183	100,290
1981	14,210	26,180	40,742	60,252	98,041
1980	14,405	26,881	41,198	60,434	98,182
1979	14,861	27,638	42,458	61,693	100,639
1978	14,839	27,893	42,179	61,423	98,956
1977	14,431	27,060	41,040	59,831	96,724
1976	14,472	26,765	40,739	58,618	93,459
1975	14,029	26,383	39,772	57,221	91,239
1974	14,883	27,492	40,510	58,809	93,974
1973	14,686	27,900	41,386	59,785	94,768
1972	14,312	27,564	40,745	58,307	93,857
1971	13,833	26,371	38,806	55,334	87,871
1970	14,007	26,836	39,039	55,698	88,054
1969	14,233	27,318	39,504	55,353	86,813
1968	13,830	26,219	37,581	52,805	82,612
1967	12,967	25,286	35,901	51,181	82,124

Source: U.S. Bureau of the Census, Annual Demographic Survey, CPS.
Note: Household incomes in 1996 dollars.

Notes

Chapter 1. The Income Distribution: Incomes as Outcomes

1. For example, see Steven Greenhouse, "Corporate Greed, Meet the Maximum Wage," *New York Times,* June 16, 1996, sec. 4, p. 6.

2. For example, see Pete DuPont, "Economic Fate That Awaits Us?" *Washington Times,* October 8, 1996, p. A17.

3. Radio Address by the President to the Nation, The White House, Office of the Press Secretary, October 7, 1995.

4. Interestingly, while the federal government has official measures of unemployment, inflation, and poverty, it does not have an official measure of income inequality, although the U.S. Bureau of the Census each year does produce a few statistical measures of inequality from its annual surveys of household incomes.

5. For example, see Peter Henle and Paul Ryscavage, "The Distribution of Earned Income Among Men and Women," *Monthly Labor Review* (April 1980): 3–10.

6. Barry Bluestone and Bennett Harrison, *The Deindustrialization of America* (New York: Basic Books, 1982).

7. For example, see Robert Kuttner, "The Declining Middle," *The Atlantic* (July 1983): 60–72.

8. Frank Levy, *Dollars and Dreams: The Changing American Income Distribution* (New York: Russell Sage Foundation, 1987).

9. For example, see Louis Uchitelle et al., "The Downsizing of America," *New York Times,* March 3–9, 1996.

10. The statistics discussed in the following sections have been taken from the following Census Bureau publication: *Money Income in the United States: 1996* (P60-197), U.S. Bureau of the Census, HHES Division (Washington, DC: USGPO, September 1997). It is important to distinguish between income, earnings, and wealth, although more will be said about them in Chapter 2. For purposes of this chapter, income represents the sum of all money received by a household (single-person or multiple-person households). Earnings represent only money received from work. Wealth represents the money value of assets held by persons or households, such as houses, stocks, bonds, certificates of deposit, jewelry, and so on.

11. It is important to note that we have been referring to middle income classes and quintiles, not necessarily the middle class. This is not semantics, but rather an important distinction.

12. All nominal incomes from the CPS in this book are adjusted for inflation in the same manner as the Census Bureau adjusts its income data. The Census Bureau uses the experimental Consumer Price Index (CPI-U-X1), provided by the Bureau of Labor Statistics (BLS), for 1967 through 1982 and the CPI-U for 1983 through 1996. All real

incomes are expressed in terms of 1996 dollars unless otherwise stated. (The experimental index was constructed to account for the overstatement of the inflation rate in the 1970s due to the way housing costs were calculated prior to 1983. The CPI-U-X1 incorporates a rental equivalence approach for measuring homeownership costs and is consistent with the methodology of the CPI-U.) The CPI-U-X1 was extended back to 1947 by applying the CPI-U-X1-to-CPI-U ratio for 1967 to the CPI-U for the 1947-to-1966 period.

The accuracy of the CPI-U has been questioned in recent years and in the mid-1990s a congressional commission, the Advisory Commission to Study the Consumer Price Index, was established to look into it. The Advisory Commission found that the CPI-U overstated inflation by 1.1 percent a year, which means that the growth in real incomes mentioned above would have been greater.

13. Blinder's comment was made in an interview on the weekly television program, *Wall Street Week.*

14. *Webster's New World Dictionary of the American Language,* 2d College Ed. (New York: Simon and Schuster, 1980), p. 899.

15. The foregoing analyses must be qualified with an important acknowledgment: no adjustments have been made for households of different sizes and the presumed economies of scale that are achieved. Economists who focus directly on the economic welfare implications of growing income inequality typically adjust the income data for household size differences. In addition, it is well known that average household size has declined in recent decades. The adjustment procedures—and the debate about their usage—will be discussed more fully in Chapter 2.

16. Kenneth J. Arrow, "Conference Comments," in *The Changing Distribution of Income in an Open Economy,* J. H. Bergstrand, T. F. Cosimano, J. W. Houk, and R. G. Sheehan, eds. (Amsterdam: North Holland, 1994), pp. 345–347.

17. One cannot ignore the simple matter of "luck" in the income determination process either.

18. The age-earnings profile for men rises from the late teens and early 20s, when many are preparing for jobs and careers, and does not peak until the ages of 55 to 64 as retirement approaches. Thereafter, it begins to fall.

19. Economists usually classify these factors as being either exogenous or endogenous variables when involved in explaining certain economic behavior. The former are variables that cannot be affected by individual or family/household behavior, while the latter can be affected. For example, one's race would be an exogenous variable but one's occupation would be an endogenous variable.

20. In 1995, wages and salaries, fringe benefits, and proprietors' incomes accounted for 70.9 percent of personal income, according to the National Income and Product Accounts of the U.S. Bureau of Economic Analysis. See the *Economic Report of the President, 1996* (Washington, DC: USGPO, 1997), Table B-27, p. 330.

21. Greg J. Duncan, Timothy Smeeding, and William Rodgers, "W(h)ither the Middle Class? A Dynamic View," in *Poverty and Prosperity in the USA in the Late Twentieth Century,* Dimitri B. Papadimitriou and Edward N. Wolff, eds. (London: Macmillan Press, 1993), pp. 240–271.

22. Wilfred Masumura, *Dynamics of Economic Well-Being: Income, 1992 to 1993, Moving Up and Down the Income Ladder* (P70-56), U.S. Bureau of the Census, HHES Division, July 1996.

23. Lester C. Thurow, *The Future of Capitalism* (New York: William Morrow, 1996), p. 8.

24. In 1992, the Committee on National Statistics of the National Academy of Science (NAS) began evaluating alternative definitions of poverty; their report was

released in the spring of 1995 (Constance F. Citro and Robert T. Michael, *Measuring Poverty: A New Approach* [Washington, DC: National Academy Press, 1995]). The Census Bureau is continuing its research program on income and poverty measurement and will be publishing research papers on various aspects of the committee's report.

25. Leatha Lamison-White, *Poverty in the United States: 1996* (P60-198), U.S. Bureau of the Census, HHES Division (Washington, DC: USGPO, September 1997), pp. A-2–A-4.

26. See, for example, McKinley L. Blackburn, David E. Bloom, and Richard B. Freeman, "The Declining Economic Position of Less Skilled American Men," in *A Future of Lousy Jobs,* Gary Burtless, ed. (Washington, DC: Brookings Institution, 1990), pp. 31–67.

27. John McNeil, *Workers with Low Earnings: 1964 to 1990* (P60-178), U.S. Bureau of the Census, HHES Division (Washington, DC: USGPO, 1992).

28. Leatha Lamison-White, *Poverty in the United States: 1996,* Table C-3, p. C-8. Actually, these percentages relate to March of the following year; for 1996, this means March of 1997.

29. *Money Income in the United States: 1996* (P60-197), U.S. Bureau of the Census, Table 1, p. 1.

30. Ibid., Table 4, p. 13, and *Money Income of Families and Persons in the United States: 1979* (P60-129), U.S. Bureau of the Census (Washington, DC: USGPO, November 1981), Table 21, p. 81.

31. Jacob Mincer, *Schooling, Experience, and Earnings* (New York: National Bureau of Economic Research, 1974).

32. For example, see Paul Ryscavage, "Working Wives and Growing 'Household' Income Inequality," paper presented at the Western Economic Association International 67th Annual Conference, San Francisco, CA, July 12, 1992.

33. Lynn A. Karoly and Gary Burtless, "Demographic Change, Rising Earnings Inequality, and the Distribution of Personal Well-Being, 1959–1989," *Demography* (August 1995): 379–405.

34. For example, see Jennifer Reingold, "Executive Pay," *Business Week* (April 21, 1997): 58–66.

35. *Economic Report of the President, 1996* (Washington, DC: USGPO, 1997), Chapter 5, p. 166.

Chapter 2. Concepts and Methods of Inequality Analysis

1. These two probably represent the major governmental sources of income statistics that the public thinks of. Other agencies, such as the Department of Agriculture, Department of Health and Human Services, and Department of Labor, however, also collect income data in order to carry out various programs that they administer.

2. *Money Income in the United States: 1996* (P60-197), U.S. Bureau of the Census, HHES Division (Washington, DC: USGPO, September 1997), pp. xii–xvi.

3. Ibid., p. 48, Table 12. Actually, this particular experimental distribution also excludes the Federal Earned Income Tax Credit and includes capital gains.

4. Related to this notion, of course, is the permanent income hypothesis of the famous economist, Milton Friedman. It states that there are really two kinds of income, permanent and transitory. The former is the amount of income consumers expect to receive over a long period of time, while transitory income is the amount of income consumers receive unexpectedly. His hypothesis helped explain the relationship of savings to income.

5. For example, see Edgar Browning, "Inequality and Poverty," *Southern Economic Journal* (April 1989): 819–830.

6. Comprehensive definitions of household and family can be found in *Money Income in the United States: 1996* (P60-197), U.S. Bureau of the Census, p. A-1.

7. These poverty lines are actually the weighted average thresholds, weighted by the actual number of related children under age 18. See Leatha Lamison-White, *Poverty in the United States: 1996* (P60-198), U.S. Bureau of the Census, HHES Division (Washington, DC: USGPO, September 1997), p. A-4.

8. Stephen P. Jenkins and Peter J. Lambert, "Ranking Income Distributions When Needs Differ," paper presented at the 22nd General Conference of the International Association for Research on Income and Wealth, Flims, Switzerland, August 31 to September 5, 1992.

9. Robert A. Pollack and Terence J. Wales, "Welfare Comparisons and Equivalence Scales," *Papers and Proceedings of the Eighty-Fourth Annual Meeting of the American Economic Association* (May 1979): 216–221.

10. The data in this table are from a paper by the author. See Paul Ryscavage, "Has Growing Income Inequality Come to an End?" a paper presented at the 68th Annual Conference of the Western Economic Association, Lake Tahoe, NV, June 23, 1993.

11. Related to this measure are relative income classes. These classes are typically devised in relation to the median income of the income distribution. For example, one might define the middle-income class to range from 50 percent to 150 percent of the median and so on.

12. As an example of the effective use of this measurement technique, see Lynn Karoly, "The Trend in Inequality Among Families, Individuals, and Workers in the United States: A Twenty-Five-Year Perspective," in *Uneven Tides: Rising Inequality in America,* Sheldon Danziger and Peter Gottschalk, eds. (New York: Russell Sage Foundation, 1992), pp. 19–97.

13. This is because in each formula, the income data are being weighted somewhat differently (see Appendix A). It is assumed these formulas are being applied to micro, or individual, data rather than grouped data (incomes grouped into income intervals).

14. This principle is usually associated with Hugh Dalton. See Hugh Dalton, "The Measurement of the Inequality of Incomes," *Economic Journal* (September 1920): 348–361.

15. There are other measures of inequality—both simple and complex—that have been used by researchers. For example, a very simple measure is the relationship between the median and mean income of the distribution. In an income distribution, the mean is usually higher than the median and will be pulled to the right more than the median when income inequality is rising because of an increase in very high incomes. Another complex measure of inequality is the mean log-deviation of income which is the natural logarithm of the mean of income minus the mean of the natural logarithm of income.

16. Gertrude Bancroft, *The American Labor Force* (New York: John Wiley, 1958), p. 183.

17. *Money Income of Households, Families, and Persons in the United States: 1992* (P60-184), U.S. Bureau of the Census, HHES Division (Washington, DC: USGPO, 1993), Table C-1, p. C-12.

Chapter 3. Inequality in the Post–World War II Era

1. The author was employed by the Bureau of the Census from 1983 to 1996 where he was involved primarily with the analysis of income and labor force statistics from the Current Population Survey and other surveys.

2. All average annual rates of change in this book have been calculated by the following formula:

$$r = \ln\left(\frac{P_1}{P_0}\right) \div N \times 100$$

where ln is the natural logarithm of the ratio; P_1 is income at the end of some time interval; P_0 is income at the beginning of the interval; N is the number of years in the interval; and r is the average annual rate of percent change.

3. Alan S. Blinder, "The Level and Distribution of Economic Well-Being," in *The American Economy in Transition,* Martin Feldstein, ed. (Chicago: University of Chicago Press, 1980), p. 416.

4. Simon Kuznets, "Economic Growth and Income Inequality," *American Economic Review* (March 1955): 1–28.

5. Rebecca M. Blank and Alan S. Blinder, "Macroeconomics, Income Distribution, and Poverty," in *Fighting Poverty: What Works and What Doesn't,* Sheldon H. Danziger and Daniel H. Weinberg, eds. (Cambridge: Harvard University Press, 1986).

6. Rebecca M. Blank and David Card, "Poverty, Income Distribution, and Growth: Are They Still Connected?" *Brookings Papers on Economic Activity* (2:1993): 285–339.

7. See, for example, Alfred L. Malabre, Jr., "A Good Statistic Tells of Good Times," *Wall Street Journal,* September 8, 1986, p. 1.

8. Frank S. Levy and Richard C. Michel, "An Economic Bust for the Baby Boom," *Challenge* (March–April 1986), pp. 33–39.

9. Ibid., p. 36.

10. Because these data have been obtained from a scientifically designed sample of families and households around the country, they are subject to sampling variability. Each statistic from the survey, therefore, contains a confidence interval which permits one to test hypotheses regarding the reliability of the statistic in question. These confidence intervals can be calculated based on certain statistical parameters relating to the survey; these parameters are found in the Census Bureau publications containing the income data.

11. It is important to point out that one reason for the erratic movement in the Gini index in this period is that up until the early 1960s, the Gini index was calculated from "grouped" income data as opposed to individual or "micro" income data. The former practice requires an assumption to be made about the distribution of incomes in the groups or income intervals (usually the assumption is that incomes are distributed uniformly). The latter practice involving micro-data does not require this assumption because the actual income data are used. It was only with the advent of modern-day computers that Gini indexes could be easily derived from the actual income estimates of individual family and household micro-records.

12. Rebecca M. Blank and Alan S. Blinder, "Macroeconomics, Income Distribution, and Poverty," in Danziger and Weinberg, eds., *Fighting Poverty: What Works and What Doesn't.*

13. Eugene Smolensky and Robert Plotnick, "Inequality and Poverty in the United States: 1900 to 1990," Graduate School of Public Policy, University of California, Berkeley, July 1992 (unpublished paper).

14. See, for example, Michael Harrington, *The Other America* (New York: Macmillan, 1962). He pointed to the poverty situation of the aged and uneducated and inspired President Kennedy's concern. President Johnson's War on Poverty began with planning carried out in President Kennedy's administration.

15. Discussions about poverty and welfare, however, were popular topics in those years, as they still are to a certain extent today.

16. Some economists believe that signs of growing wage inequality were evident in the 1960s.

17. The average annual growth rates in real incomes for "families" between 1973 and 1979 at these percentiles are only slightly more sanguine. The comparable rates, beginning at the 20th percentile, were 0.6 percent, 0.5 percent, 0.8 percent, 0.8 percent, and 1.3 percent at the 95th percentile. The fact that the household income data include unrelated persons living alone or with other unrelated individuals, many who are either very young or old, probably explains why the family income data are somewhat brighter. Nevertheless, what is evident is the same stepwise progression in growth rates as was true among households, which is symptomatic of growing inequality.

18. According to the National Bureau of Economic Research Inc. (NBER), which determines the troughs and peaks of the business cycle, the country experienced two recessions in the 1980–1982 period. The first occurred between January 1980 and July 1980 and the second took place between July 1981 and November 1982.

19. Rebecca M. Blank and David Card, "Poverty, Income Distribution, and Growth: Are They Still Connected?" *Brookings Papers on Economic Activity.*

20. The changes were quite similar for families, although perhaps somewhat stronger. Families in the top quintile did experience a significant increase in their share of aggregate income from 41.4 to 44.6 percent over the period, while the shares received by the other quintiles declined. The declines, however, were relatively greater in the lowest, second, and third quintiles of families as compared to the situation for households. In each case the declines approached a percentage point. The Gini index for the family income distribution increased from .365 in 1979 to .401, or 9.9 percent, faster than for households.

21. See Joseph Meisenheimer II, Earl Mellor, and Leo Rydzewski, "Job Market Slid in Early 1991, Then Struggled to Find Footing," *Monthly Labor Review* (February 1992): 3–17; and Jennifer M. Gardner, "The 1990–91 Recession: How Bad Was the Labor Market?" *Monthly Labor Review* (June 1994): 3–11.

22. The official peak and trough of this business cycle, according to the NBER, was July 1990 and March 1991, respectively.

23. Paul Ryscavage, "A Surge in Growing Income Inequality?" *Monthly Labor Review* (August 1995): 51–61.

24. Daniel H. Weinberg, "A Brief Look at Postwar U.S. Income Inequality," *Current Population Reports* (P60-191), U.S. Bureau of the Census, HHES Division (Washington, DC: USGPO, June 1996), p. 1, footnote 3.

25. Paul Ryscavage, "A Surge in Growing Income Inequality," *Monthly Labor Review,* Table 2, p. 55.

26. Ibid., pp. 57–59.

27. The author conjectured about this development some years ago based on income data that extended only to 1991. See Paul Ryscavage, "Has Growing Income Inequality Come to an End?" paper presented at the Western Economic Association International 68th Annual Conference, Lake Tahoe, CA, June 23, 1993.

28. For a discussion of income-to-poverty ratios, see *Money Income of Households, Families, and Persons in the United States: 1991* (P60-180), U.S. Bureau of the Census, HHES Division (Washington, DC: USGPO, August 1992), pp. xvi-xvii.

29. See *Money Income in the United States: 1996* (P60-197), U.S. Bureau of the Census, HHES Division (Washington, DC: USGPO, September 1997), pp. xii-xvi, and Table 12, pp. 48–53.

30. For a discussion of the estimating techniques and procedures used to estimate

taxes and value noncash benefits, see *Income, Poverty, and the Valuation of Noncash Benefits: 1994* (P60–189), U.S. Bureau of the Census, HHES Division (Washington DC: USGPO, April 1996).

31. "Means-tested" refers to whether or not a cash or noncash transfer program has an income (or asset) amount below which a family's or household's income (or assets) must be to qualify for participation in the program.

32. *Money Income in the United States: 1996* (P60-197), U.S. Bureau of the Census, HHES Division, p. xv.

33. Daniel H. Weinberg, "A Brief Look at Postwar U.S. Income Inequality" (P60-191), U.S. Bureau of the Census, p. 3.

34. The CPS surveys were conducted in January of 1984, 1986, 1988, 1990, 1992, and February of 1994 and 1996. Because each survey is retrospective over the preceding five years, the seven surveys cover the years 1979 to 1995.

35. Diane E. Herz, "Worker Displacement Still Common in the Late 1980s," *Monthly Labor Review* (May 1991): 3–9.

36. Wilfred Masumura and Paul Ryscavage, *Dynamics of Economic Well-Being: Labor Force and Income, 1990 to 1992* (P70-40), U.S. Bureau of the Census, HHES Division (Washington, DC: USGPO, November 1994), p. 6.

37. Indeed, the poverty rate would even be lower if the poverty thresholds used by the Census Bureau were updated over time by the CPI-U-X1 instead of the CPI-U. For example, in 1996 the rate would have been 12.2 percent instead of 13.7 percent. See footnote 12 in Chapter 1 for more explanation regarding the use of the CPI by the Census Bureau.

38. See Gordon Fisher, "Estimates of the Poverty Population Under the Current Official Definition for Years Before 1959," U.S. Department of Health and Human Services, 1986 (mimeo) and Eugene Smolensky and Robert Plotnick, "Inequality and Poverty in the United States: 1900 to 1990," Graduate School of Public Policy, University of California, Berkeley, July 1992 (unpublished paper).

Chapter 4. Trends in Earnings and Earnings Inequality

1. Frank Levy and Richard J. Murnane, "U.S. Earnings Levels and Earnings Inequality: A Review of Recent Trends and Explanations," *Journal of Economic Literature* (September 1992): 1341–1342.

2. Peter Henle, "Exploring the Distribution of Earned Income," *Monthly Labor Review* (December 1972): 16–27. At the time, Henle was the chief economist of the Bureau of Labor Statistics and would eventually become a deputy assistant secretary of labor in President Carter's administration.

3. *New York Times,* December 27, 1973, p. 1.

4. The terms "earnings" and "wage(s)" will be used interchangeably in this chapter, unless reference is being made to a specific set of data or study. Wages are sometimes considered to be a subset of earnings. Earnings are the combination of money earned through self-employment (or self-employment income) and money earned from a job provided by an employer (or wage and salary income).

5. The data on labor force participation discussed in this section are taken from various publications of the Bureau of Labor Statistics (BLS), which monitors the nation's labor force with the monthly Current Population Survey (CPS).

6. The data relating to the educational level of the labor force are from the BLS and derived from the monthly CPS.

7. *Statistical Abstract of the United States: 1995,* 115th ed. (Washington, DC: U.S. Bureau of the Census, 1995), pp. 190–191.

8. Ibid., p. 430.

9. Ibid., p. 451.

10. More formally, the service-producing industries are composed of transportation, communications, and public utilities; wholesale and retail trade; finance, insurance, and real estate; services (e.g., hotels and motels, beauty shops, computer programming services); and government. The goods-producing industries consist of mining, construction, and manufacturing. Agriculture, of course, would also be included as a goods-producing industry, but usually when these terms are used, it is in the context of the BLS nonfarm payroll employment series which is based on a count of jobs in the nonfarm sector of the economy obtained from their Current Employment Survey (CES).

11. *Statistical Abstract of the United States: 1995,* p. 451.

12. Barry Bluestone and Bennett Harrison, *The Deindustrialization of America* (New York: Basic Books, 1982).

13. Maury Gittleman, "Earnings in the 1980s: An Occupational Perspective," *Monthly Labor Review* (July 1994): 16–27.

14. *Statistical Abstract of the United States: 1995,* p. 437.

15. Henry S. Farber, "Are Lifetime Jobs Disappearing? Job Duration in the United States: 1973–1993," December 6, 1994, (mimeo).

16. Minimum Wage Study Commission, *Report, Volume 1,* 1981, p. 36.

17. *Statistical Abstract of the United States: 1995,* p. 436.

18. Katharine G. Abraham, James R. Spletzer, Jay C. Stewart, "Divergent Trends in Alternative Real Wage Series," paper presented at a conference sponsored by the National Bureau of Economic Research on Income and Wealth, December 1994.

19. All of the series were adjusted for inflation using the BLS's CPI-U-X1.

20. This is BLS's ES-202 program, or the program by which employer's report to the U.S. Department of Labor on the employment and earnings of their workers covered by state unemployment insurance laws.

21. David M. Gordon, *Fat and Mean: The Corporate Squeeze of Working Americans and the Myth of Managerial "Downsizing"* (New York: Free Press, 1996), pp. 17–20.

22. It is possible in the March CPS (as well as the monthly CPS), of course, to restrict the analysis to workers who receive only wages and salaries, as well as to other specialized universes. This is because of the micro-orientation of the CPS.

23. See footnote 12, Chapter 1, for how the Census Bureau deflates nominal dollar amounts.

24. This is an assumption that has been made frequently in the research on earnings inequality even though it is well known that some persons who report they usually work full-time have several weeks of part-time employment, while others work many more hours than forty in the course of a week. This, of course, biases the implied hourly earnings.

25. Marvin H. Kosters (Director, Economic Policy Studies, American Enterprise Institute), "Major Factors Influencing Long-Term Family Income and Poverty Trends," statement before the Subcommittee on Ways and Means, U.S. House of Representatives, October 26, 1993.

26. Frank Levy and Richard J. Murnane, "U.S. Earnings Levels and Earnings Inequality: A Review of Recent Trends and Proposed Explanations," *Journal of Economic Literature.*

27. Peter Henle and Paul Ryscavage, "The Distribution of Earned Income Among Men and Women, 1958–77," *Monthly Labor Review* (April 1980): 3–10.

28. Robert Plotnick, "Trends in Male Earnings Inequality," *Southern Economic*

Journal (January 1982): 724–732, and Martin Dooley and Peter Gottschalk, "Does a Younger Male Labor Force Mean Greater Earnings Inequality?" *Monthly Labor Review* (November 1982): 42–45.

29. This was the beginning of the popularity of "supply side" economics in which tax reductions, especially for the rich, were considered essential for economic growth because the tax cuts would encourage savings and investment. This was the general philosophy behind the 1981 Economic Recovery and Taxation Act.

30. Barry Bluestone and Bennett Harrison, *The Deindustrialization of America.*

31. Robert Kuttner, "The Declining Middle," *The Atlantic* (July 1983): 60–72.

32. Lynn A. Karoly, "The Trend in Inequality Among Families, Individuals, and Workers in the United States," in *Uneven Tides: Rising Inequality in the 1980s,* Sheldon Danziger and Peter Gottschalk, eds. (New York: Russell Sage Foundation, 1993).

33. Organization for Economic Co-operation and Development, *OECD Employment Outlook,* July 1993, Paris, France, pp. 157–184.

34. Another reason she chose to measure inequality for all workers rather than just full-time, year-round workers was the potential bias that is introduced by focusing solely on full-time, year-round workers since they are a selected sample of all workers. She acknowledged, however, that even her universe of all workers is a selected sample to a certain extent. This is because the composition of the work force is changing from one year to the next and it is not known whether the people who work one year and not the next are a random sample. If they are not a random sample, a problem of selection bias exists which should be corrected for. She felt that this correction was beyond the scope of her analysis.

35. Gary Burtless, "Earnings Inequality Over the Business and Demographic Cycles," in *A Future of Lousy Jobs: The Changing Structure of U.S. Wages* (Washington, DC: Brookings Institution, 1990), Table A-1, p. 116, and Barry Bluestone, "The Changing Nature of Employment and Earnings in the U.S. Economy," a paper presented at the conference on "Job Creation in America," at the University of North Carolina at Chapel Hill, April 10, 1989. (Burtless's estimates were for the period 1947 to 1986.)

36. Frank Levy and Richard Murnane, "U.S. Earnings Levels and Earnings Inequality: A Review of Trends and Proposed Explanations," *Journal of Economic Literature,* Table 5, part 2, p. 1355.

37. Paul Ryscavage, "Gender-Related Shifts in the Distribution of Wages," *Monthly Labor Review* (July 1994): 3–15.

38. The characterization of "hollowing out" was first used by Frank Levy and Richard Murnane.

39. Organization for Economic Development and Co-operation, *The OECD Employment Outlook,* July 1996, Paris, France, pp. 59–108.

40. The precise nature of the earnings inequality trend in the late 1980s and 1990s has become a matter of dispute among some economists, as might be expected. For example, Robert I. Lerman of the Urban Institute believes that earnings inequality in the 1987 to 1994 period either stayed about the same or even declined. See Robert I. Lerman, "Is Earnings Inequality Really Increasing?" Number 1 in Series, "Economic Restructuring and the Job Market" (Washington, DC: The Urban Institute, March 1997), and Robert I. Lerman, "More Difficulties with CPS Measures of Trends in Earnings Inequality," addendum to "Is Earnings Inequality Really Increasing?" (Washington, DC: The Urban Institute, July 1997). On the other hand, Jared Bernstein and Larry Mishel of the Economic Policy Institute believe that earnings inequality did indeed level off in the second half of the 1980s, but then "reaccelerated" in the 1990s. See Jared Bernstein and Larry Mishel, "Has Wage Inequality Stopped Growing?" (Washington, DC: Economic Policy Institute, 1998).

41. John McNeil, "The Earnings Ladder: Who's at the Bottom? Who's at the Top?" *Statistical Profile*, U.S. Bureau of the Census, SB/94–3RV, June 1994, and unpublished Census Bureau data for 1994.

Chapter 5. Suggested Causes of Growing Inequality

1. *Washington Post*, October 15, 1996, section A, pp. A1, A6, and A7. The results of this survey were also analyzed in the academic literature. See Robert J. Blendon, John M. Benson, Mollyann Brodie, Richard Morin, Drew E. Altman, Daniel Gitterman, Mario Brossard, and Matt James, "Bridging the Gap Between the Public's and Economists' Views of the Economy," *Journal of Economic Perspectives* (Summer 1997): 105–118.

2. Other interesting examples of the difference between the public's and the economists' perceptions were: 54 percent of the economists felt downsizings of large corporations were good for the health of the economy, while only 21 percent of the public felt they were good; 32 percent of the economists felt that the jobs being created in the economy in recent years were low-paying, but 79 percent of the public felt that was the case; and while only 5 percent of the economists felt that trade agreements between the United States and other countries had cost the United States jobs, 54 percent of the public felt they had cost jobs.

3. In the *Washington Post* account that reported the results of the survey, one economist explained that the disconnect resulted from the fact that economists, on a whole, are fairly affluent and view the economy in a somewhat more detached fashion than the average working person.

4. *Employment and Earnings*, U.S. Department of Labor, Bureau of Labor Statistics, January 1992, Table B-1, p. 86.

5. Ibid., Table C-1, p. 122. The nominal average weekly earnings for production workers in manufacturing were $374.03, and in retail trade the nominal average weekly earnings for nonsupervisory workers were $174.33.

6. Barry Bluestone and Bennett Harrison, *The Deindustrialization of America* (New York: Basic Books, 1982).

7. Peter Henle and Paul Ryscavage, "The Distribution of Earned Income Among Men and Women, 1958–77," *Monthly Labor Review* (April 1980): Table 2, p. 5.

8. These explanations were discussed by a group of economists in the mid-1980s. See Bennett Harrison, Chris Tilly, and Barry Bluestone, "Wage Inequality Takes a Great U-Turn," *Challenge* (March–April 1986): 26–32.

9. Chris Tilly, Barry Bluestone, and Bennett Harrison, "The Reasons for Increasing Wage and Salary Inequality, 1978–1984," The John W. McCormack Institute of Public Affairs, Boston: University of Massachusetts, 1987.

10. McKinley L. Blackburn and David E. Bloom, "What Is Happening to the Middle Class?" *American Demographics* (January 1985): 18–25.

11. Actually, between March 1991 and March 1992, the educational attainment questions used in the March CPS were changed. Previous to March 1992, the educational information was collected through two questions, the first concerning the highest grade the person attended and the second whether or not that grade was completed. Beginning in March 1992 (income year 1991), a single question was asked concerning the highest level of school completed or the highest degree received. For more information on this change, see *Money Income of Households, Families, and Persons in the United States: 1991* (P60-180), U.S. Bureau of the Census, HHES Division (Washington, DC: USGPO, August 1992), pp. xx-xxvi.

12. For a comprehensive series of essays by economists examining these differentials in the 1980s, see Marvin H. Kosters, ed., *Workers and Their Wages: Changing Patterns in the United States* (Washington, DC: AEI Press, 1991).

13. These data were developed from the CPS by the author. Figures of this type are usually shown in terms of the differences between the logarithms of real earnings at various percentiles of the distribution.

14. Kevin M. Murphy and Finis Welch, "The Structure of Wages," *Quarterly Journal of Economics* (February 1992): 215–326. This article was a revision and update of an earlier unpublished paper.

15. Lawrence F. Katz and Kevin M. Murphy, "Changes in Relative Wages, 1963–1987: Supply and Demand Factors," *Quarterly Journal of Economics* (February 1992): 35–78.

16. For example, see John Bound and George Johnson, "Changes in the Structure of Wages in the 1980s: An Evaluation of Alternative Explanations," *The American Economic Review* (June 1992): 371–392.

17. Their paper appeared in 1989 and was published later. See Chinhui Juhn, Kevin M. Murphy, and Brooks Pierce,"Wage Inequality and the Rise in the Returns to Skill," *Journal of Political Economy* (June 1993): 410–442. Actually, Martin Dooley and Peter Gottschalk, in a much earlier article, had observed that rising between group inequality could explain only a constant proportion of the modest increase in overall inequality in the 1967–1978 period. See Martin Dooley and Peter Gottschalk, "Does a Younger Male Labor Force Mean Greater Earnings Inequality?" *Monthly Labor Review* (November 1982): 42–45.

18. McKinley L. Blackburn, David E. Bloom, and Richard B. Freeman, "The Declining Economic Position of Less Skilled American Men," in *A Future of Lousy Jobs: The Changing Structure of U.S. Wages,* Gary Burtless, ed. (Washington, DC: Brookings Institution, 1990), pp. 31–67.

19. Ibid., p. 54.

20. Lawrence F. Katz and Kevin M. Murphy, "Changes in Relative Wages, 1963–1987: Supply and Demand Factors," p. 46.

21. These estimates were made by the author using annual wage and salary earnings data from the CPS. See Paul Ryscavage, "Trends in Wage Inequality: the Public Sector vs. The Private Sector," a paper presented at the 70th Annual Conference of the Western Economic Association, July 7, 1995, in San Diego, CA.

22. Frank Levy and Richard J. Murnane, "U.S. Earnings Levels and Earnings Inequality: A Review of Recent Trends and Explanations," *Journal of Economic Literature* (September 1992): 1364–1371.

23. Peter Gottschalk and Robert Moffitt, "The Growth of Earnings Instability in the U.S. Labor Market," *Brookings Papers on Economic Activity* (1994, 2): 217–272.

24. For example, see Adrian Wood, *North-South Trade, Employment and Inequality: Changing Fortunes in a Skill-Driven World* (New York: Oxford University Press, 1994).

25. See George J. Borjas and Valerie A. Ramey, "The Relationship Between Wage Inequality and International Trade," and Lynn A. Karoly and Jacob Alex Klerman, "Using Regional Data to Re-examine the Contribution of Demographic and Sectoral Changes to Increasing U.S. Wage Inequality," in *The Changing Distribution of Income in an Open Economy,* J.H. Bergstrand, T.F. Cosimano, J.W. Houk, and R.G. Sheehan, eds. (Amsterdam: North Holland, 1994).

26. Gary Burtless, "International Trade and the Rise in Earnings Inequality," *Journal of Economic Literature* (June 1995): 800–816. For a more recent and extensive discussion, see William R. Cline, *Trade and Income Distribution* (Washington, DC: Institute for International Economics, 1997).

27. George E. Johnson, "Changes in Earnings Inequality: The Role of Demand Shifts," *The Journal of Economic Perspectives* (Spring 1997): 46–47.

28. Alan Krueger, "How Computers Have Changed the Wage Structure: Evidence from Microdata, 1984–1989," *Quarterly Journal of Economics* (February 1993): 33–60.

29. Paul R. Krugman and Robert Z. Lawrence, "Trade, Jobs and Wages," *Scientific American* (April 1994): 44–49.

30. These data were developed by the author from the March CPS.

31. Robert H. Topel, "Factor Proportions and Relative Wages: The Supply-Side Determinants of Wage Inequality," *Journal of Economic Perspectives* (Spring 1997): 63.

32. Frank Levy, *Dollars and Dreams: The Changing American Income Distribution* (New York: Russell Sage Foundation, 1987), pp. 159–166.

33. Ibid., p. 197. Levy reached this conclusion after correcting CPS income distributions for tax payments, noncash benefits, and family-size differences. His corrected distributions showed that income inequality in 1984 was less than in 1949 but greater than in the 1970s.

34. Paul Ryscavage, Gordon Green, and Edward Welniak, "The Impact of Demographic, Social, and Economic Change on the Distribution of Income," in *Studies in the Distribution of Income* (P60–183), U.S. Bureau of the Census, HHES Division (Washington, DC: USGPO, 1992), pp. 11–26.

35. Jacob Mincer, *Schooling, Experience and Earnings* (New York: National Bureau of Economic Research, 1974), and Sheldon Danziger, "Do Working Wives Increase Family Income Inequality," *Journal of Human Resources* (Summer 1980): 444–451.

36. Maria Cancian, Sheldon Danziger, and Peter Gottschalk, "The Changing Contributions of Men and Women to the Level and Distribution of Family Income, 1968–88," in *Poverty and Prosperity in the USA in the Late Twentieth Century,* Dimitri B. Papadimitriou and Edward N. Wolff, eds. (London: Macmillan Press, 1993), pp. 317–353.

37. Lynn A. Karoly and Gary Burtless, "Demographic Change, Rising Earnings Inequality, and the Distribution of Personal Well-Being, 1959–1989," *Demography* (August 1995): 379–405.

38. Peter Gottschalk, "Inequality, Income Growth, and Mobility: The Basic Facts," *Journal of Economic Perspectives* (Spring 1997): 21, footnote 1.

39. Sheldon Danziger and Peter Gottschalk, *Uneven Tides: Rising Inequality in the 1980s* (New York: Russell Sage Foundation, 1993), p. 5.

Chapter 6. Inequality Before 1950

1. Simon Kuznets, "Economic Growth and Income Inequality," *American Economic Review* (March 1955): 4.

2. The data for this figure were taken from U.S. Bureau of the Census, *Historical Statistics of the United States: Colonial Times to 1970, Part 1* (Washington, DC: USGPO, 1975), Series F 4, p. 224, and the home page of the NBER at http://www.nber.org/cycles.html.

3. Oscar Theodore Barck Jr. and Nelson Manfred Blake, *Since 1900,* 3d ed. (New York: Macmillan, 1959), p. 4. Economists have dated the start of the industrialization process in the United States in the mid-19th century, or roughly from 1843 to 1860. See W.W. Rostow, "The Take-Off into Self-Sustained Growth," *Economic Journal* (March 1956): 31.

4. U.S. Bureau of the Census, *Historical Statistics of the United States: Colonial Times to 1970, Part 1,* Series F 125, 127, p. 232.

5. Andrew Hacker, *Money: Who Has How Much and Why* (New York: Scribner, 1997), p. 92.

6. The gainful-worker concept is different from the labor force concept of today. Basically, a gainful worker was one who normally "followed" a particular occupation or line of work, for example, a coal miner or a clerk in a store. Today's concept, which was actually adopted in the 1940s so as to make the labor force concept more precise, is based on one's activity at a particular point in time, such as working at a paid job, looking for work, or doing something else, such as going to school, retired, or unable to work.

7. The Sherman Antitrust Act was passed by Congress in 1890 and the Clayton Antitrust Act was made law in 1914.

8. U.S. Bureau of the Census, *Historical Statistics of the United States: Colonial Times to 1970, Part 1,* Series D 316, p. 141.

9. Ibid., Series Q 148, p. 716.

10. Oscar Theodore Barck Jr. and Nelson Manfred Blake, *Since 1900,* pp. 399, 412.

11. U.S. Department of Labor, Bureau of Labor Statistics, *Employment and Earnings* (January 1992), Table 1, p. 162.

12. Oscar Theodore Barck Jr. and Nelson Manfred Blake, *Since 1900,* p. 637.

13. U.S. Bureau of the Census, *Historical Statistics of the United States: Colonial Times to 1970, Part 1,* Series D 795, p. 169 (for the index of weekly earnings) and Series E 135, p. 211 (for the Consumer Price Index).

14. Harry Ober, "Occupational Wage Differentials, 1907–1947," *Monthly Labor Review* (August 1948): 127–134.

15. U.S. Department of Labor, Bureau of Labor Statistics, BLS Bulletin No.1188, *Wages and Related Benefits,* 1956, p. 35.

16. Herman P. Miller, *Income Distribution in the United States* (A 1960 Census Monograph), (Washington, DC: USGPO, 1966), p. 79.

17. Lloyd G. Reynolds, *Labor Economics and Labor Relations,* 3d ed. (Englewood Cliffs: Prentice-Hall, 1961), p. 485.

18. U.S. Bureau of the Census, *Historical Statistics of the United States: Colonial Times to 1970, Part 1,* Series D 839 and 842, p. 172.

19. Claudia Goldin and Robert A. Margo, "The Great Compression: The Wage Structure in the United States at Mid-Century," *The Quarterly Journal of Economics* (February 1992): 1–34.

20. Herman P. Miller, *Income Distribution in the United States* (A 1960 Census Monograph), Table III-1, p. 76, and Table III-2, p. 77.

21. For example, see Robert M. Solow, "The Measurement of Inequality," in *Inequality and Poverty,* ed. Edward C. Budd (New York: W.W. Norton, 1967), Table 1, p. 51.

22. U.S. Bureau of the Census, *Historical Statistics of the United States: Colonial Times to 1970, Part 1,* Series E 135, p. 210.

23. For background on the development of this series see U.S. Bureau of the Census, *Historical Statistics of the United States: Colonial Times to 1970, Part 1,* pp. 284–285, 287.

24. The income estimate for 1901 was obtained from the U.S. Bureau of the Census, *Historical Statistics of the United States: Colonial Times to 1970, Part 1,* Series G 556, p. 321. It represents the average income of city wage- and clerical-worker families of two or more persons and the average was $651 in 1901. The estimate was converted into 1962 dollars by the use of the Consumer Price Index from *Historical Statistics of the United States,* Series E 135, p. 211, and amounted to $2,359 in 1962 dollars.

25. Simon Kuznets, *Shares of Upper Income Groups in Income and Savings* (New York: National Bureau of Economic Research, 1953).

26. Arthur F. Burns, *Looking Forward,* 31st Annual Report of the National Bureau of Economic Research, p. 4.

27. Jeffrey G. Williamson and Peter H. Lindert, *American Inequality: A Macroeconomic History* (New York: Academic Press, 1980).

28. Ibid., pp. 75–84.

29. Selma F. Goldsmith, "Changes in the Size Distribution of Income," in *Inequality and Poverty,* ed. Edward C. Budd (New York: W.W. Norton, 1967), pp. 65–79.

30. Jeffrey G. Williamson and Peter H. Lindert, *American Inequality: A Macroeconomic History,* p. 77.

31. Eugene Smolensky and Robert Plotnick, "Inequality and Poverty in the United States: 1900 to 1990," Graduate School of Public Policy, University of California, Berkeley, July 1992 (unpublished paper). Smolensky and Plotnick revised their paper (with the help of Eirik Evenhouse and Siabohan Reilly) in 1997, but reached a similar conclusion about the high-water mark of inequality in this century.

32. These estimates were derived through regression analysis. The dependent variable was the Gini index which was based on income distributions from the CPS; the independent variables were the nation's civilian unemployment rate from the BLS, and the income share going to the richest 5 percent of families over the 1947–89 period from the CPS. The adjusted R^2 (a measure of the goodness of fit) for this regression was 0.83 (on a scale of zero to one).

Chapter 7. International Comparisons

1. *Economic Report of the President,* 1996 (Washington, DC: USGPO, 1997), pp. 236–248.

2. Ibid., p. 243.

3. Louis Uchitelle, "Like Oil and Water: A Tale of Two Economists," *New York Times,* Section 3, February 16, 1997, pp. 1, 10, and 11.

4. Ibid.

5. Adrian Wood, *North-South Trade, Employment and Inequality: Changing Fortunes in a Skill-Driven World* (New York: Oxford University Press, 1994).

6. Anthony B. Atkinson, Lee Rainwater, and Timothy M. Smeeding, *Income Distribution in OECD Countries: Evidence from the Luxembourg Income Study,* Social Policy Studies No. 18, (Paris: Organization for Economic Co-operation and Development, 1995), p. 25.

7. Ibid. The OECD published Social Policy Studies No. 18 on income distributions in OECD countries based on the LIS data in 1995. See footnote 6.

8. Organization for Economic Co-operation and Development, *The OECD Employment Outlook,* July 1996, Table 3.1, p. 61.

9. Organization for Economic Co-operation and Development, *The OECD Employment Outlook,* July 1993, Table 5.2, p. 159.

10. For a brief description of the ISSP, see David G. Blanchflower and Richard B. Freeman, "Unionism in the United States and Other Advanced OECD Countries," *Industrial Relations* (Winter 1992): 56–79. The ISSP data, according to Blanchflower and Freeman, are archived with the Zentral Archiv at the University of Köln in Germany.

11. Klaus Deininger and Lyn Squire, "A New Data Set Measuring Income Inequality," *The World Bank Economic Review* (September 1996).

12. Organization for Economic Co-operation and Development, *The OECD Employment Outlook,* July 1996, p.101.

13. Ibid., p. 101.

14. Peter Gottschalk and Timothy M. Smeeding, "Cross-National Comparisons of Earnings and Income Inequality," *Journal of Economic Literature* (June 1997): 637.

15. Ibid., p. 638.

16. Anthony B. Atkinson, Lee Rainwater, and Timothy M. Smeeding, *Income Distribution in OECD Countries: Evidence from the Luxembourg Income Study,* Social Policy Studies No. 18, p. 26.

17. Ibid., pp. 34–37.

18. Peter Gottschalk and Timothy M. Smeeding, "Cross-National Comparisons of Earnings and Income Inequality," *Journal of Economic Literature* (June 1997): 633–687.

19. Organization for Economic Co-operation and Development, *The OECD Employment Outlook,* July 1996, pp. 59 67.

20. Peter Gottschalk and Timothy M. Smeeding, "Cross-National Comparisons of Earnings and Income Inequality," *Journal of Economic Literature,* Table 1, p. 643.

21. Organization for Economic Co-operation and Development, *The OECD Employment Outlook,* July 1996, pp. 68–76.

22. Peter Gottschalk and Mary Joyce, "Is Earnings Inequality Also Rising in Other Industrialized Countries?" Boston College (mimeo), March 1992.

23. Lawrence F. Katz, Gary W. Loveman, and David G. Blanchflower, "A Comparison of Changes in the Structure of Wages in Four OECD Countries," National Bureau of Economic Research, Inc., Working Paper No. 4297, March 1993.

24. Ibid. The primary data for the United Kingdom were gross hourly earnings from the New Earnings Survey and referred to full-time employees; the primary data for Japan was from the Basic Survey on Wage Structure and related to monthly scheduled earnings; the data for France were from the Declarations Annuelles de Salaries and related to gross annual earnings and related to full-time, full-year workers; and the primary U.S. data were from the Annual Demographic Survey, CPS, and related to hourly wages of full-time workers (annual earnings divided by reported hours worked).

25. Richard B. Freeman and Lawrence Katz, "Rising Wage Inequality: The United States vs. Other Advanced Countries," in *Working Under Different Rules,* ed. Richard B. Freeman (New York: Russell B. Sage Foundation, 1994), pp. 29–62.

26. Lawrence F. Katz, Gary W. Loveman, and David G. Blanchflower, "A Comparison of Changes in the Structure of Wages in Four OECD Countries," National Bureau of Economic Research, Inc., p. 27.

27. Peter Gottschalk and Timothy M. Smeeding, "Cross-National Comparisons of Earnings and Income Inequality," *Journal of Economic Literature,* Table 1, p. 643, and Figure 1, p. 644.

28. Purchasing power parities (PPP) are rates of currency conversion between countries that equalize the purchasing power of different currencies. In other words, a given sum of currency from one country when converted by the relevant PPP will be able to buy the same basket of goods and services using a sum of currency from another country. PPPs attempt to eliminate price-level differences between countries.

29. Anthony B. Atkinson, Lee Rainwater, and Timothy M. Smeeding, *Income Distribution in OECD Countries: Evidence from the Luxembourg Income Study,* Social Policy Studies No. 18.

30. Peter Gottschalk and Timothy M. Smeeding, "Cross-National Comparisons of Earnings and Income Inequality," *Journal of Economic Literature,* Table 4, p. 666.

31. Ibid., Figure 3, p. 663.

32. McKinley L. Blackburn and David E. Bloom, "Changes in the Structure of Family Income Inequality in the United States and Other Industrial Nations During the 1980s," National Bureau of Economic Research, Inc., Working Paper No. 4754, May 1994.

33. Peter Gottschalk and Timothy M. Smeeding, "Cross-National Comparisons of Earnings and Income Inequality," *Journal of Economic Literature,* p. 671.

34. Ibid., pp. 672–675.

Chapter 8. The Future

1. Claudia Goldin and Robert A. Margo used this characterization to depict long-run changes in the wage structure since 1940. See Claudia Goldin and Robert A. Margo, "The Great Compression: The Wage Structure in the United States at Mid-Century," *The Quarterly Journal of Economics* (February 1992): 3.

2. Daniel H. Weinberg, "Press Briefing on 1996 Income, Poverty, and Health Insurance Estimates," U.S. Census Bureau, September 29, 1997.

3. *New York Times,* "The Tide Is Not Lifting Everyone," October 2, 1997, p. A14.

4. The economists Lester Thurow, George Johnson, and Richard Freeman, for instance, have been particularly pessimistic regarding the future course of inequality. See, respectively, Lester C. Thurow, *The Future of Capitalism* (New York: William Morrow, 1996), p. 184; George E. Johnson, "Changes in Earnings Inequality: The Role of Demand Shifts," *The Journal of Economic Perspectives* (Spring 1997): 52; and Richard B. Freeman, "Solving the New Inequality," *Boston Review* (January 1997).

5. Paul Ryscavage, "A Surge in Growing Income Inequality," *Monthly Labor Review* (August 1995): 51–61.

6. Jennifer M. Gardner, "The 1990–91 Recession: How Bad Was the Labor Market?" *Monthly Labor Review* (July 1994): 3–11.

7. Actually, at a conference on earnings inequality held by the Federal Reserve Bank of New York in the mid-1990s, eighteen economists were asked to give their views as to the cause or causes of growing earnings inequality. According to this "select" survey, the average respondent assigned 45 percent of the responsibility for rising wage inequality to skill-biased technological changes and only 11 percent to changes in foreign trade practices. The remainder of the responsibility was distributed among other factors, such as the decline in unionization and the real value of the minimum wage and the growth in immigration. See Gary Burtless, "International Trade and the Rise in Earnings Inequality," *Journal of Economic Literature* (June 1995): 815, footnote 11.

8. Robert J. Samuelson, "The Typical Household Isn't," *Washington Post,* October 8, p. A21.

Appendix B. Changes in the Current Population Survey

1. *Money Income in the United States: 1996* (P60-197), U.S. Bureau of the Census, HHES Division (Washington, DC: USGPO, September 1997), Table C-1, p. C-2.

2. Ibid., see footnotes to Table B-3, p. B-6.

3. See Paul Ryscavage, "A Surge in Growing Income Inequality?" *Monthly Labor Review* (August 1995): 51–61, and Daniel H. Weinberg, "A Brief Look at Postwar U.S. Income Inequality," *Current Population Reports* (P60-191), U.S. Bureau of the Census, HHES Division (Washington, DC: June 1996), p. 1, footnote 3.

Index

About the Author

Paul Ryscavage was employed thirty-four years by the federal government as a labor economist with the U.S. Bureau of Labor Statistics and the U.S. Bureau of the Census in Washington, D.C. His fields of expertise are labor force and income distribution analysis. He received a B.S. degree from the University of Connecticut and an M.A. degree from The American University. In 1996 he retired from the Census Bureau as a Senior Labor Economist. He and his wife now live in Santa Fe, New Mexico.